ALSO BY JACQUES ELLUL

The Technological Society (1964)

Propaganda (1965)

The Political Illusion (1967)

These are Borzoi Books, published in New York by
ALFRED A. KNOPF

A CRITIQUE OF THE
NEW COMMONPLACES

A CRITIQUE OF THE NEW COMMONPLACES

BY
JACQUES ELLUL

TRANSLATED FROM THE FRENCH
BY HELEN WEAVER

New York: Alfred A. Knopf 1968

THIS IS A BORZOI BOOK
PUBLISHED BY ALFRED A. KNOPF, INC.

FIRST AMERICAN EDITION

Library of Congress Catalog Card Number: 68–12681

Originally published in French as *Exégèse des nouveaux lieux
communs*, © 1966 by Calmann-Lévy

[v]

Contents

―――――――――――――――

Contents

A CRITIQUE OF THE
NEW COMMONPLACES

THE COMMONPLACES

───────────────────────────

───────────────────────────

The French intellectual treats himself to commonplaces with the air of an epicure, aware as he picks at them that he does not belong to the vulgar herd that mistakes these formulas for solid nourishment. The intellectual savors his superiority, meanwhile passing the cruelest judgment on those who base their mental universe upon these established truths. The intellectual is an iconoclast and, all too conscious of his value, earnestly tries to destroy these popular idols, which conceal contemporary problems and true values. Committed, he wages this battle, knowing that only he represents true values amid the corruption of political activity and economic materialism.

But when one examines the object of these denunciations, these "revelations" as Lenin would call them, one cannot help marveling at a certain absurdity in relation to the facts. We have all read Léon Bloy's *L'Exégèse,* and apparently repetition, after its prominent use by phenomenologists and existentialists, is becoming the sole activity of intellectuals in this domain. The commonplaces? Why, they are the ones exposed by Léon Bloy, the ones he held up to public ridicule. We quite agree! Once and for all, the commonplaces have been put in the pillory. We need only remember some formula from time to time to prove how far we are from those who make these proverbs the code of their belief and the imperative of their action. And we can put out minds at rest on the subject of the commonplaces: the matter is settled.

But perhaps we are being premature! Is it not obvious that these slogans express a triumphant bourgeois society, the bourgeois sure of the permanence of his fortune as well as of his morality, the overthrow of reality by the anonymous wisdom of self-righteousness, the construction of a world whose values are beyond question? And is it not obvious that these values, this *Weltanschauung*, this good will are no longer ours? That this world conceived of as eternal by the bourgeois underwent profound alteration between 1929 and 1950 and that these commonplaces are no longer ours?

How easy it is to stand in Léon Bloy's shoes today, easier than it was for him. We are trampling on the truths of yesterday and even of the day before yesterday. We revile, reject, and vituperate the slogans of the world of 1880. But what importance and what merit is there in this? In doing so we are demonstrating that we are no longer men of 1880 (which one might easily have suspected), that we no longer believe in the bourgeois ideology (but who does any more?), and that we have nothing in common with those dreadful bourgeois. It is easy for us to show the courage that Léon Bloy had in his day. But what courage is there in denouncing what nobody any longer believes?

When Léon Bloy isolated the commonplaces, he proceeded to make a vivisection—these were living beliefs, formulas that were repeated and used by everybody as criteria for judgment, the expression of a hierarchy of values. He was attacking the living man, and as a matter of fact, every living man, for these commonplaces, which expressed the wisdom of the bourgeoisie, had been adopted as the wisdom of nations by all classes of society. We can understand that this raised an uproar, for it caused pain. We can understand the hatred stirred up against this man who came to insult Values and overthrow beliefs. We can understand that it took some courage to oppose unanimous opinion and even more to question one's own values, for after all, everyone lives by these commonplaces. "By the everyday truths, as by the everyday chores, everyone grinds his flour and bakes his bread!" said a disciple of Léon Bloy's. Everyone, including Léon Bloy himself. He had to uproot the commonplaces from his own body before he could talk about them as he did.

But today when we attack the *same* truths, we are merely dissecting a body that is already dead and has been dead for twenty, thirty, or forty years. Dead and embalmed, useful to historians and still a fertile source of false ideas, but certainly in no danger of screaming or reacting. And we are free to study calmly the little pieces we cut off with a scalpel that no longer needs to be very sharp! How easy it is to chuckle over a Dictionary of Folly that talks about the folly of yesterday! You can say to yourself, "How superior we are today!"

Consider the works that are now regarded as "audacious," as defying the taboos. What do they do? They glorify pornography (or eroticism, if you're an intellectual). This is presented as an act of revolutionary courage; but it is happening in a world in which people have stopped believing in the sexual taboos, as today's teddy boys clearly attest. When there is no more morality, when people have ceased to defend this obviously senile old lady, what strength is there in attacking her? (Genet.)

What else do these works do? They attack the family, they scorn the authority of parents—but here again, truth is way ahead of fiction. Recently people went into ecstasies over the courage of a play (*Boulevard Durand*) by Salacrou, who is usually better inspired, that exposes the wickedness of the rich bourgeois class and gives a sympathetic picture of the dockers. But all this courage is being shown half a century too late, when the battle is virtually over and the bourgeoisie is as full of wounds as an old bull missed by a bad matador but no longer strong enough to shake its banderillas. So the dogs and servants come to finish the job when there is no more danger.

Anyone who still dares to write this way shows the vanity of literature, shows that it is only the pale reflection of the workingman's struggles, that its only purpose is to make excuses to the world. What would have had force and meaning half a century ago is only the rumination of an old man who thinks his false teeth are fangs. Must we be reminded that paternal authority is no more and that the family is dispersing like clouds in a high gale? Our heroic literary lights (Sagan, Bazin, Beauvoir) seem to me to be hastily bringing up the rear after the masses have done the work and cleared the path.

What do these works do? Repudiate the primacy of money, the spirit of economy, the pettiness of household budgeting? But here again, the economic realities have moved much faster. It is because of the devaluations, the crises of all kinds, the raising of prices, and the lowering of dividends that the money mentality has been called into doubt—and the intellectual frog swells with pride as he attacks the dollar! What else do they do? Denounce the hypocrisy of men of another age who preached morality and behaved shamefully behind this façade? Virtuous fathers of families who had mistresses, pious employers who exploited the workers? But who pretends to virtue or piety today? The few isolated persons who talk about it seem like old fogies who are behind the times, and in fact they are! What we have gained is that the same behavior goes on openly and that hypocrisy has been replaced by cynicism. But have we really gained? It might be suggested that cynicism simply reinforces the behavior of the person who adopts it and dares to do openly what everyone used to condemn. By eliminating moral hyprocrisy we have permitted the founding of the regime of the concentration camp. In attacking those good old days, our daring intellectuals find themselves in full agreement with their society and with the public (and this is necessary, is it not, if you are to earn your living by creating a deathless work!).

But this is not enough for them, because they must also have the halo of persecution if they are to follow in the footsteps of the immortal Baudelaire, Rimbaud, and Lautréamont. Nobody can be a serious intellectual today unless he is an outcast. This is easier said than done, and it presents certain disadvantages. But if you pretend to believe that the values of today are the same as those of 1860, that morality and manners have remained fixed, that the "right" is still in the majority, that the bourgeoisie is unchanged, sure of itself, full of good will—how convenient! All you have to do is attack the same things that in the time of your ancestors provoked their malediction. You can take advantage in 1960 of the malediction of 1860. (We are fighting the same battle, therefore we are guaranteed the same malediction!)

Thus you win on both counts, spiritual audacity and material success: fame and money. In other words, you reproduce exactly what the bourgeois claimed to be in 1830. The hypocrites of today are the very persons who denounce the values and commonplaces of yesterday, and who make a show of false courage (for it costs them nothing) and false lucidity (for the work has already been done; all they do is take it over and tailor it to the tastes of the day).

But curiously, these lucid individuals do not see the commonplaces of today; what is more, they outdo each other in repeating them as if they were eternal verities. These brave souls discreetly fail to mention the values to which our society attaches importance, and they even fly to their rescue when they are threatened. Always cautious and concerned for their interests, the intellectual heroes of our time engage in politics to avoid defending the validity of their own stereotypes, and sign manifestos to keep from thinking.

Every age has its commonplaces. Yesterday's matter little; they are only fossils that, according to our temperament, we gaze at nostalgically or label coldly and arrange in our collection. But the most contemptible attitude toward them is revulsion. Let us consider those of today. Let us pit our strength and lucidity against something that is alive, something that can react and bite, something that it is painful for me to expose because in so doing I expose myself, because these unfounded beliefs are, after all, my own, because I am of my time, my society, my group.

I certainly will not attempt to continue or improve upon the work of Léon Bloy. I have neither the genius nor the occasion to do so. The work in question is not the kind that can be continued or bequeathed to others: it is a work that must be begun again—in which you always start at zero, at the foot of the wall—and cannot be published more than once. Having taken this path, of course, I will not claim exemption from the judgment that in my opening sentence I passed on those intellectuals who are delicate and critical consumers of commonplaces. I am quite aware of my position. I know that the work I am undertaking exposes me, but that it represents the only serious activity, in this place and in this time, for someone whose job is to use his brain. I know that this work shows my limitations and betrays me for what I am: a teacher (abomination!), a bourgeois (who isn't?), uncommitted (i.e., not actively engaged in politics), and I might add, if it were not so difficult to say about oneself, a Christian (what a reference!).

But after all, are the commonplaces worth bothering with? These ready-made ideas which are found in all the newspapers, these slogans and clichés—are they worth thinking about? Every society produces its commonplaces, just as a living body produces wastes. The commonplaces are the excrement of the society. But it is worth noting that the evidence left by those who have disappeared is rarely evidence of their nobility. When the bird has flown, when the nest has been abandoned and scattered, you know it was there only by the little pile of excrement you find. And the first traces left by man, except for his own bones and those of his victims, are weapons—axes, swords, arrows, and flints—as if all man had been able to leave behind him were the traces of his instincts of death and destruction. "When you find a human skeleton in the ground there is always a sword near it. This is a bone of the earth, a sterile bone, a warrior." (Giraudoux.)

We must realize that we too will leave behind us only our sterile bones and as traces of our civilization what is most absurd, most contemptible, most scorned: our excrement and our commonplaces. Except for specialists, what do we know about the Middle Ages or the bourgeoisie of the eighteenth and nineteenth centuries? Nothing but the commonplaces that they have left us and that we regard as

the valid, accurate, and complete evidence of a group and
a society. We have forgotten, for example, the nobility of
the bourgeoisie, its ideals, its enormous effort to recast all
of society, its correct intuitions, and its Promethean endeavor; now that the bourgeois era is over, we remember
only its commonplaces, which provide a glimpse of the
grimacing, selfish, haughty face of the ugly beast that is the
bourgeois—that is to say, a temporary incarnation of man.
This is all we know, and we feel that we know everything.

Perhaps we would also do well to know the face we are
making for posterity, the image we will leave behind, and
to know how we are caught for history in a portrait that
may be just as false as the one we have of the superstitious
and reactionary man of the Middle Ages or of the cigar-
smoking man of the nineteenth century, but just as indeli-
ble and sure of success. And just as it is through their
commonplaces that we see them, it will be through our
commonplaces that we shall be seen.

The excrement of a society! But although the operation
is not very pleasant, we know the importance of the analysis of waste products: it is a way of discovering what food
the living body used to sustain itself. It is in its evacuations
that one finds evidence, after it is dead, of its choices, its
preferences, its necessities, and of what it has used. The
commonplaces are actually the by-product of the values
that a society insists upon in order to live, the ideas and
philosophies in which it is embodied, the education and
instruction that it gives its members. On the level of *uomo
qualunque,* they are the intellectual form of those activities
which it deems essential, to which it compels the citizen
and the worker; one way or another, it has to "come out."
The man who finds himself engaged in the construction of
a world must express himself, and this expression will not
take the form of a philosophy. The commonplace will be

formulated at the point of confluence of the philosophy, the ideologies, the religions that are being prepared in the intellectual crucible, and the average man's concrete activity to earn his living and to survive. Analyze the commonplace and you will find the nourishment of that society: its intellectual or spiritual nourishment as well as its material or economic nourishment, its insubstantial bread and dreams as well as its hard technical and political realities.

As we were saying, though, it is not a pleasant operation; before one can analyze excrement one must be able to stand the smell. The scatology of commonplaces overwhelms us with the same disgust. We must say goodbye to subterfuge and illusion. As long as we remain on the level of the brilliance of philosophies and the majesty of technological success, we can find a hundred pretexts and justifications, like a man who delights in artful delicacies; but as the primitiveness of Scripture reminds us, everything you eat finishes in the secret places. As long as we consider the activities of our century in their living reality or their pretense of truth, all illusions are permitted. But consider the residue! See what is left over when this activity expresses itself on the scale of the wisdom of nations, and you will have the precise measure and meaning of what we are doing. Evasions or pretexts are no longer possible; much more so than a philosophy of the absurd, analysis of the commonplaces reduces us to zero. The art of the cook (which I certainly do not despise!) loses its power when the science of the chemist reveals the final result of so many artful illusions. But between the two, these illusions, like ideologies, have sustained life. The commonplaces tell us only what this life must have been.

Naturally the operation is not pleasant, either for the soul or for the body. One cannot examine these things without disgust, a disgust that turns these reactions into a

commercial allspice for jaded senses. For here we must face
our disgust at what exists and not at what is imagined, our
disgust at what denies us the quality of pure spirit, demiurge, and creator of progress. We would prefer not to
see. But what's the good of smashing the microscope or the
mirror? The truth is there.

This analysis of wastes also shows us the microbes. Excrement is not only the remains of food; it also represents
a defense of the living body which eliminates toxins and
fights off aggressors. By studying it you discover traces of
the challenges, the threats, the secret operation of death
already at work, a work that is as yet unknown. You can
discover which microbe remains by the one that has been
eliminated, which virus is at work by the effect observed on
the products eliminated. The commonplaces transmitted
by the bourgeoisie contain the microbes that would have
brought on the fatal illness of this society. They were in it.
But we must bear in mind that the society also resisted
them. They were not necessarily accepted just because
they were incorporated into her proverbs. This was also a
way of conjuring them away, of eliminating them by objec-
tifying them, by nailing them to the wall both as exhibition
and as punishment. With the help of these commonplaces
we can not only draw up an indictment, but also determine
the nature of the death sentence already threatening this
social body and of the body's search for a defense.

And now it is our own microbes that we must study.
With a sureness of judgment that may strike us as tragic,
we see our own society also trying to isolate its viruses and
releasing its commonplaces. Alas! If we believe that there is
a certain consistency to history, the operation, though significant, is never adequate. The proliferation continues and
the viruses filter through. The toxins are there, and generally it is not until the illness has become sufficiently critical

that we begin to react by producing commonplaces. The corruption must be somewhat advanced before things become fixed in these definitive formulas whose rigidity, banality, and obviousness already foreshadow the rigidity of death. Analysis of the commonplaces affords only the bitter satisfaction of knowing the diseases of which we will die.

Adopting a scholarly and academic tone, let us say that the commonplaces are the expression of an ideology and can be useful in distinguishing its outlines. This is very easy! I believe that here we can simply take over the Marxist interpretation, which is both correct and convenient: commonplaces are produced by the ruling class, of course. It is the ruling class that knows itself best and that expresses itself authoritatively in its searchings and anxieties, its assumptions and its activities, in these formulas that will be spread everywhere by means of modern instruments for the diffusion of thought. But at the same time they are a catalogue of collective illusions, unconsciously distorted representations of others, of adversaries, as well as unconsciously enhanced glorifications of one's alleged ideals. They are an attempt at interpretation of social situations in terms of political, moral, religious, and philosophical evaluations that imply a point of view. They are collective beliefs based on assumptions that are accepted without discussion, beyond all question.

The commonplace is really common because it does not tolerate any fundamental discussion. It serves everyone as a touchstone, an instrument of recognition. It is rarely quoted, but it is constantly present; it is behind thought and speech; it is behind conversation. It is the common standard that enables people to understand one another when they discuss politics or civilization. To expose it, to

subject it to argument, becomes tragic because it is the
instrument of understanding that is then being disputed. It
is as if the player began to dispute the rules of the game
during a match: play becomes impossible. Or as if the
interpreter questioned the correspondences of language:
translation becomes impossible. Thus it always disconcerts
a person you are talking with when you question his sociological assumptions and his unstated beliefs. Naturally, he
is inclined to shrug his shoulders and say, *"Avocat, passons
au déluge,"* [1] but he does not realize that the deluge has
come, that these commonplaces that express his ideologies
are the visible waters of a flood that has already submerged
his thinking, his reason, his capacity for judgment and
inquiry. Poor fellow, arguing about his future when he is
already drowning!

What most readily betrays the commonplace is precisely
this universal agreement. When you discover a formula
that is equally acceptable to rightist and leftist, Christian
and layman, Marxist and liberal, bourgeois and proletarian,
then you can be sure you are near the bone. The Marxist
will say that this is because the ruling class spreads its own
ideology everywhere. This is partly correct, as we implied
above.

But there is certainly more to it than this. Insofar as the
commonplaces express the values indispensable for the
proper functioning of the society and at the same time
reveal the justifications, perhaps illusory, that the group
chooses to make its action acceptable, we are dealing with
values and justifications of everyone and for everyone. This
is why the same commonplace or formula is often used to
support or justify seemingly contradictory positions. Marx-

---

[1] A quotation from Racine's *Les Plaideurs* which has the force of "Let's
get on with it!" —*Trans.*

ism is mistaken in believing that diffusion begins with the
ruling class, for our civilization has become much more
totalitarian than it was a century ago, and all men are
involved in a process of common evolution. They belong to
the development of the technological world before they
belong to a class; they are people who share the atomic or
demographic risk before they are a socialistic or capitalistic
people; they belong to work and to happiness before they
are rich or poor. Our world has become one in its works and
expressions, and this unity far exceeds all divisions, even
those as serious as class or nation. This is why all people
express themselves in the same way, all have need of the
same justifications, all secrete the same values, and all have
their eyes fixed on the same ideal. An admirable unity
emerges that reveals the most ironic destiny. These rightly
named commonplaces give us a curious insight into the
status of the community of the world.

But we must take a closer look at the origin of these
commonplaces. Those of today—and perhaps those of yesterday, too—have been created by intellectuals, all of whom
have come out of the middle class. When certain economic,
social, and political doctrines, certain observations of fact,
even statistical fact, and certain explanations of social phenomena have been formulated by intellectuals, teachers,
and politicians, a double correlative phenomenon occurs.
On the one hand, there is a great effort to spread these
doctrines, observations, or explanations; in our own day, for
example, consider the efforts of Sauvy, Fourastié, and so
many others. But at the same time, to make them penetrate
deeper layers of the population, succeeding generations
will omit the nuances, dispense with the relevant documen-
tation, eliminate the contradictory facts. Thus there arises a

body of doctrine that is simple and reducible to a few
formulas that are capable of being transmitted—I was
about to say from hand to hand.

And although we are talking about ideas, they are in fact
transmitted very materially and crudely. Larger and larger
strata, students and readers of elite journals, begin to dis-
tribute these abstracts of doctrine, reducing them to lower
and lower levels and to more and more elementary expressions. In this way they reach the newspaper that is most
widely read, but not by intellectuals; and by 1960 *France-
Dimanche* is explaining what in 1955 was the prerogative
of *l'Express*. Thus we arrive at the commonplace. But by a
remarkable backlash effect, this massive extension gives the
formula weight, density, visibility. It ceases to be debatable because it is believed by all. And from that point the
intellectuals accept it as an axiom not subject to doubt,
since not only is the doctrine true, but the support of the
people earns it the cachet of democracy.

"But," the Marxist will say, "there is nothing here that
contradicts our interpretation of an ideology created by the
ruling class and disseminated by it to all levels and all
classes." Granted! But this formula remains much too
vague and does not take into account the present reality.
For a new fact, a double new fact must be considered.
Although the intellectuals I alluded to above came out of
the bourgeoisie, they all have "leftist" ideas. They all believe in the Marxist theses. Sometimes they do not realize
they are expressing Marxist ideas, but this is merely the
result of their misunderstanding of Marx's thought.

Let us admit that there is still a small group of intellectuals who violently reject this orientation. It will be observed that among them some have very little influence,
others lack consistency, and still others are convinced that
they are rightist and antisocialist, whereas in reality their

thinking is firmly based on purely Marxist notions of which they are unaware. Important values of Marxism have in fact become *common* to rightists and leftists alike—for instance, History, its role, its meaning, its tendency to become a Value, to take only one example! The first authentic representatives of a non-Marxist thought (for example, Montherlant today or Giraudoux yesterday) have no importance, precisely because their thought is not in agreement with the general current of the time; they evoke only a few secretly condescending smiles—"poetry and noble sentiments, but not serious."

In our day, in fact, seriousness is the prerogative of Marxism, its latterday disciples, and its scholars; a seriousness that is academic, oppressive, dreary, and self-important. Are these leftist intellectuals in the vanguard, well ahead of their (bourgeois) class? Not at all. For with the exception of a few freaks, the bourgeois class as a whole and the petty bourgeoisie in particular have adopted the socialist orientation, the prejudices of the left, and the commonplaces of Marxism.

When presented with this unqualified statement, the aforesaid intellectuals (who are anxious to be original and advanced!), political scientists, and thinking men of the left will immediately voice their indignation and disbelief. Why, 50 per cent of the voters vote rightist! What about Poujade, and the commercial class, and the trusts, and the pressure groups, and the fascists elements, and the army! And the UNR, and our good general! All this proves, among other things, that the left is a poor minority, threatened and outnumbered, that the bourgeoisie is still the exploiting class, that France is a western capitalistic country, etc.

I have no intention of making a detailed analysis of the fact—that would take me a long way from my common-

places—but I would like to point out some obvious things.
If you analyze the political slogans and campaign platforms
of what is now called the right, you will see that they
correspond almost exactly to the platforms and ideas of the
left of 1900. And *nobody* talks about the ideas held by the
right of 1900! Facts like the nationalization of industry,
social security, the spread of labor unions and their entry
into the organs of government: are they leftist or not? And
are they or are they not accepted by 90 per cent of the
population? Could a government that called itself rightist
today adopt a program that was not "social," that did not
provide for the advancement of the working class? Has this
not become the central preoccupation of all governments,
and is it not accepted by the nation as the keystone of the
edifice? Nobody questions it!

I could amass evidence for the existence of this leftist
society that France represents, but these simple facts seem
sufficient, and if you weigh them they are conspicuously
heavier than the opposing facts. Then there is the famous
sense of history. It is quite true that at this point in time
these facts have the future ahead of them, whereas the
opposing facts appear as survivals, isolated phenomena
without any more significance or future than Poujade or
the rebellion of the generals. We must recognize that, with
the exception of details, anomalies, and survivals, our
French society is becoming more socialized, and that the
great majority of the bourgeoisie belongs to the left. This
becomes even more accentuated when we realize that the
ready-made ideas of our day, the sociological assumptions,
the common stereotypes are by-products of Marxism. Even
Marshal Pétain thought (without wanting to or knowing it,
the good man!) in terms of ready-made ideas derived from
Marxism. (The ideas of corporatism, for example, are very
characteristic of a right which, imbued with socialism, at-

tempts to reconcile it with traditional values, which means that in its eyes socialism *can no longer be repudiated!* It is the famous definition of hypocrisy as the homage that vice renders to virtue!)

But in the face of this invasion of the bourgeoisie by the left, we must underscore a parallel fact that is just as striking: the working class has been won over by the bourgeois ideology. Not, of course, by its political ideology, but by its "life ideal," that life ideal accurately expressed in the old commonplaces, in which we saw the bourgeoisie exalt its admiration for progress, science, and humanity, seek above all else happiness, security, and comfort, despise values, justice, purity, and risk, withdraw into the family nucleus, repudiating the "great causes," insure its little personal destiny, etc. But this very ideal has become that of the working class in France. The watering down of communism (which had become a technique for the seizing of power), the rejection of all the great enthusiasms and of revolutionary fervor, the disaffection toward the labor-union movement, are results of an *embourgeoisement* of the working class that has less to do with the improvement of the standard of living (which is also occurring) than with the *ideal* of "washing machine, insurance against all risks, and a family stroll on Sunday."

The bourgeoisie has won a total victory—involuntarily, of course! Although they vote left and even communist, the workers are the proudest supporters of what characterized the petty bourgeois of 1900, including his chauvinism and his passionate interest in European monarchs! Let's face it, when television becomes a source of *Kultur* (a real culture medium, in fact!) and when the possession of a refrigerator becomes the great goal in life, there is little room left for real revolt and serious consideration of human destiny. So the working class is adopting these formulas that have come out of the bourgeoisie but that nevertheless define the present ideal of the working class. They reveal a background of socialism and at the same time they express the old bourgeois life idea; this marriage, which a century ago would have seemed impossible, has taken place. The by-product, surely a bastard, hopefully incapable of reproduction, reaches us in the form of synthetic products that are extraordinarily active and virulent. These products fully satisfy all the "normal" aspirations of the Frenchman of 1960; in them Idealism is happily married to the Seriousness of Life, and the Necessities of History to Personal Happiness. Everything works beautifully in this well-oiled, though very crude and common, machine.

However that may be, this double movement that we have indicated briefly explains how the commonplaces that have come out of the bourgeoisie through the medium and the mouths of its intellectuals are, in short, commonplaces of the left. There can no longer be any others!

This seems to contradict the frequently stated idea that the "left" cannot create myths and therefore cannot create the petty cash that the commonplaces constitute. It *cannot*—and yet today all the great myths are produced by the left! There is only the gap between the theoretical and the real. Theoretically, if the left were what Marx constructed abstractly, it is true that there would be no myths. Theoretically, if the process of evolution culminating in the reconciliation of man with himself and with nature were as it had been described and were, moreover, complete, there would be no myths. But the left is not what Marx said it would be. The process promised not only is not complete, but does not seem to have begun. Today there is no more reason that the left should ever become what Marx promised than that the Christian Church should by a natural movement become Christ's Kingdom of God. If all Chris-

tians were like Christ, we would long since have ceased to
have any problems, myths, or commonplaces. But leftists
—like Christians—being what they are, we must recognize
that it is indeed the left that is today the great transmitter
of myths and commonplaces.

No doubt the "leftist" reader will be seized with anger
and indignation when he reads these analyses, and will feel
that a terrible injustice is being done to the left. He will
accuse me of being prejudiced against the left. But if I
attack the left in its commonplaces, that does not mean I
am against the left. On the contrary, it is because I believe
in values that only the left has stated, elucidated, and
partially adopted (without acting on them), because the
left has sustained the hope of mankind, because the left has
engaged in the struggle for justice, that I cannot tolerate
the absurdity of the present left, that I cannot tolerate the
absurdity of the commonplaces in which the left actually
expresses what it has become. It is because I have believed
in a human destiny ennobled in such revolutionary forces
that I cannot accept its degradation. I have nothing to say
for or about the right because I have no common standard
with it, I am a stranger to it, it has neither meaning nor
content for me. But the left is my business too, and when I
attack it I think of what Pascal said when after judging
man at his best he added, "I am not talking about the fools,
I am talking about the wise men." If my analysis is more
often directed toward the left, that is also because it is the
left, as I have already said, that is the greatest source of
commonplaces.

Finally, it may be unnecessary to point out that these
commonplaces rest firmly on technological progress, that
they also express a technician's wisdom and popular confidence in the constant improvement of work. And no doubt
this relationship has counted heavily in their universal ac-

ceptance, for are not all of us, whatever our class and
education, equally overcome with admiration and respect
for technological progress; do we not all participate in the
advantages of the works of technology? We would have to
be very bad children and very ungrateful ones not to join in
the praises of this great human achievement. As a matter of
fact, the small children of the century are very well prepared to join in these praises, and by the same token they
accept as self-evident truths the commonplaces transmitted
by such an indisputable medium!

Every society has its commonplaces, but this popular
body of wisdom does not always show the same characteristics. After all, what was called the Wisdom of Nations
was nothing else. But this practical, pragmatic wisdom was
the fruit of long experience, of an invisible creation, of
observation repeated a thousand times until the moment
when it could be distilled in proverbs. If those who used to
harp on the Wisdom of Nations often adopted the moral
lessons of La Fontaine, it must be said that this was owing
to a remarkable coincidence between popular experience
and formal expression. And the primary school certainly
helped. This pragmatism was perfectly sound. It became
debatable only when it pretended to Wisdom, when the
observation of what is was set up as morality, as the formulation of what should be. According as you are powerful or
wretched . . . *therefore* be powerful. This is the best ad-
vice the Wisdom of Nations can offer. The fruit of common
sense, it does not go beyond this common sense, but tries
to apply it to life.

After all, common sense is useful, and nobody, especially
in our time, has the right to despise it. Fruit of the observation of behavior, it carries a real weight of wisdom, for the

very slowness of its creation assures the seriousness of the conclusion. And in addition to the mediocrity of its ideal, this Wisdom of Nations provides a pessimistic view of man, a skepticism, and a certain good-natured defiance that are not without force. The mistake is to try to make it into a life code, for the only lesson you can derive from it then is that of a vigorous, conservative, and limited egoism. The transition from observation to theory introduces a new element; the pessimistic view of man is translated into a cynical rule for action.

And this brings us from the Wisdom of Nations to the commonplace of the bourgeoisie. This group has had the courage and the innocence to formulate its rules of action into principles. An eminently dangerous operation! Few groups or classes in history have shown such rigor; that of the bourgeoisie is explained by the contempt for man that infested it. Why worry? Why not express what we are doing in exhaustive, imperative formulas, since nobody can judge us anyway?

So the commonplaces of the bourgeoisie are marked by a disillusioned cynicism, a thoroughgoing egoism, and a contempt for man as total as it is irremediable. It was extremely easy (although dangerous, of course) to reveal the monstrousness of this morality. The bourgeoisie provided all the weapons to be used against it. But that this was so showed neither stupidity nor honesty on its part, but complacency, the certainty of the permanence of its reign—the conviction, in short, that its success vouched for the moral value of its principles. In its system of commonplaces, the bourgeoisie artlessly revealed its own insolence. Indeed, it is curious to observe the distance between the hypocrisy of bourgeois behavior, which pretended to obey Christian morality and constantly prided itself on having the Christian virtues, and its cynicism in stating in the commonplaces the reality of its action. The duality of these bodies of doctrine in the nineteenth century, with their points of reference (the virtue of work, for example) but also with their total contradictions (organized charity, etc.), would be worth investigating, but this is not the proper place for such an analysis. I merely wanted to indicate this double inspiration of the commonplace—common sense and experimental cynicism—in order to bring out the *novelty* of the commonplaces of *our century*.

These are first of all the expression of noble sentiments. Our society brims over with noble sentiments—or more precisely, the specific organ responsible for creating commonplaces in our society brims over with them. We are obsessed by concern for the human, by the primacy of man, his dignity and his individuality; we take everything seriously, with an anxious eye and a troubled brain; we are assailed by the tragedy of life and the absurdity of existence; we bear full responsibility for the evil that occurs in the world, convinced that we are murderers when we overflow with love for a hypothetical fellow creature whom we know very well we can't help anyway, for in their desperate wisdom, the noble sentiments of our time know that nobody can help anybody else! We are constantly revealing an unbounded idealism, in statements that make no sense, and repudiating this idealism in the same breath.

For we must note in passing that consistency is not the attribute of the speaker of commonplaces in our time. At five-minute intervals, with the same gravity and authenticity, he formulates contradictory commonplaces, eternal verities that have no relation to each other. But what do these successive sincerities matter, as long as you always state them with equal ardor, justifying these contradictions that, no doubt, express the reality of life? We are well aware that concern for moral rigor, intellectual coherence, and continuity in life are the mark of a narrow and obviously rigid mind, and one that is outside the current of history.

The producers of commonplaces overflow with good will; they aspire to values that are uncertain but that they confirm merely by expressing them. And the operation turns out to be complex. It is no longer, as in many moralities, a case of justifying what happens by the invocation of values, or of formulating principles without reference to reality; and we have seen that, contrary to the commonplaces of the preceding period, it is no longer practice itself that is fixed in adages. Nor is it a case of a veil of morality covering an immoral situation, which would correspond to the situation of bourgeois hypocrisy. Marxism has intervened, with the result that several traditional paths are now closed. We know that today we must puncture ideologies, demystify values, denounce morals; and yet our noble sentiments (also evoked by socialism!), our idealism, our need for values are irrepressible! Justification has made a reappearance, but it is justification by demystification, it is the mass rehabilitation of all the ideals repudiated by bourgeois cynicism. The commonplaces of today are utterly saturated with justification and rehabilitation, but not on the same level or for the same reason. Thus we find demonstrations of the purity of eroticism, the metaphysical profundity of sodomy, the political and democratic maturity of cannibalism, freedom through fatality, humanism through terror, etc.

To tell the truth, the most obvious and most sadly indisputable fault is that, as in the bourgeois period, you find humanity divided into good and evil, with the authors of commonplaces tirelessly representing good, right, truth, justice. Their noble sentiments consist in demonstrating above all that it is precisely what was regarded as evil in the preceding period that is the ideal. But since they express these noble sentiments in the pure state, the values approved by morality and the people, it is very bad to laugh at them. For these noble sentiments are obvious! And yet these commonplaces, which by their very presence, reinstate reality, which justify necessity as well as action, purely and simply reinforce the totalitarian character of the society in which we live. They do this by incorporating the noble sentiments. It is not enough that technology, political power, the power of money be what they are; it is also necessary that they be stocked with noble sentiments, and the commonplaces are there to make the connection and to spread these mystifications among the good people as if they were obvious truths. The first step toward liberation would be the elimination of the noble sentiments, ideals, and obvious truths ejaculated by this society.

But where does one find these commonplaces? They have not yet passed into the form of proverbs, which makes them more difficult to perceive. For it is precisely in the nascent stage that they are most interesting, and this is when they should be surprised, when it is most useful to expose and demystify them. When the commonplace is still "gaseous" it possesses a power of diffusion and a flexibility that give it access to many people. When it is crystallized it possesses the force of the object, of course, but also its limitation. It then foreshadows its own end. To expose these commonplaces in formation we must address ourselves to those bourgeois intellectuals who formulate the truths of the society of tomorrow, who create the right awareness by a defense of the future and a criticism of the present (although knowing full well that this future is the present and that what they are criticizing is merely a present survival of a past that is quite dead!), who express the common agreement beyond the superficial divisions of groups and professions, who spread the noble sentiments on which the society claims to be founded. And the more these formulas win the support of men of opposite parties and warring classes, the closer we are to the commonplace. When a formula is repeated a hundred times in the most diverse writings, or, better, when it is implicit, underlying, but inspires developments that are commonly approved, when it is accepted without proof as a self-evident truth, then we have a commonplace.

But with what net can we catch it? Not with a net, but with a recipe. Make a cocktail out of a blend of *l'Express, Marie-Claire, Planète,* and *Paris-Match,* flavor it with the formulas made immortal by our most established intellectuals, add three pinches of the daily column of *Le Monde* and a slice of *Canard enchaîné.* Run the whole thing through Père Ubu's debraining machine, and out will come a proliferation of commonplaces.

WE MUST FOLLOW
THE CURRENT
OF HISTORY

———————————————————————

———————————————————————

The discovery of the current of history is the classic panacea of our good intellectuals and thinkers; indeed, it was the
happiest day of their lives. The disappearance of the Eternal Father from our mental horizon had left a large void.
The situation was becoming impossible, the universe and
our lives seemed incomprehensible, we had neither com-
pass nor sextant nor Ariadne's clue nor radar. Everything
was getting out of control. Then, all of a sudden, the thread
of history was discovered. If we take one end of the thread
and pull, the whole ball of world history, past and future,
unrolls in order, very nicely, at our disposal.

What mastery, gentlemen! Much stronger than the sha-
mans! Much stronger than all the theologians! We can see
where we are going, so we know what we have to do. I also
know the meaning of what I am doing now. My destiny

becomes clear, I can see my duty, as well as that of the collectivity to which I belong. All contradictions are resolved, and I find myself in harmony with my time, with goodness and truth (since they are part of this history that I am in the process of making), and therefore with technology and science. How stupid were those unfortunate metaphysicians who racked their brains over this chaos, when the solution was within their reach! All that was necessary was to reduce everything to history and to transform history into a linear vector. Whether the operation corresponds to truth or reality does not matter, as long as it is satisfying and soothing. Everything is suddenly resolved. "Follow the current of history." "Keep in step with the times." "Be on the side of progress." "History will be the judge." Identical statements, which correspond to the same commonplace in different milieux.

"You're going against the stream of history." "You're being reactionary." Decisive judgments that eliminate discussion: "These ideas are not even worth considering; they are useless and illusory because they will not be realized in history!" What does it matter whether an idea is true if it is not great with history? These dogmatic statements tell us that the commonplace carries within it both a judgment of probability and a judgment of value. What is outside the mainstream of history not only is without force, but is neither true nor good. For it is precisely the discovery of this sense of history that enables us, as we were saying, to hold everything in one hand! If we admit a single exception—that is, if we admit that a single truth does not hang by this thread—then everything falls apart, everything is ruined, and the thread of history becomes once again a tangled skein.

To make this imperative of efficiency the criterion of all

value is an unconscious defense reflex: you know that if
you admit one exception, all is lost. It is panic, the same
panic that seized the pseudo-Christians of the twelfth or
sixteenth centuries when confronted by doubt, if only on
one point, as to the existence of God. The whole system of
universal and individual coherence collapses. For rightists
and leftists, Christians and Marxists, history plays the same
role God did for the formal Christians of the Middle Ages.
And I cling desperately to the idea, for without it my
identity, my life, and my action would be left to chance
and to the devil!

So everyone hastens to prove that he is in the swim. The
fascists as well as the communists prove that they are in the
mainstream of history, the former because evolution is the
state, and the latter because it is socialism. For the Ameri-
cans, of course, since the future belongs to freedom and
democracy, they are the ones who are on the right track.
And even the Christians have come up with a few sleight-
of-hand tricks demonstrating that human history culmi-
nates in an omega that happens to be Christ, or proving
that history has its natural conclusion in the Kingdom of
God. To test the fragility of these arguments it is enough
to realize that they have been constructed only to accom-
modate the commonplace that gives the greatest satisfaction to modern man, and that this commonplace is used in
an attempt to justify various ideas.

Nobody doubts that history has a direction. Nobody,
that is, except historians! A serious historian is obliged to
say, "That's the way it happened"—period. But somebody
who knows nothing about history except what he learned
in primary school immediately perceives a thread, a line.
The bothersome part is that this line is not always the same.
Clear as day, Michelet saw the direction of history in the
development of freedom. In our day this is no longer ex-

actly true; and if Hegel is coming back into style, that is no accident!

But how is it that we do not see the incorrigible stupidity of saying that a given event happens because it is in the direction of history? At every instant hundreds of combinations are possible among the thousands of factors that make up a conjuncture. A good intellectual mechanism can give you fifty or hundred possible solutions. The choice of one solution, the only one that will occur, is in no way a single necessary choice. What makes us see a continuity is looking back on the event *once it has happened,* interpreting it according to the philosophy of the moment and relating it to other phenomena of the same kind. The only direction there is to history is the one we ourselves attribute to the past. So as far as the future is concerned, we are caught between two possibilities: either, Marxist-fashion, we hold a thread that is very crude, elementary, and superficial, which by its simplemindedness satisfies everybody and by means of numerous lies and mystifications gives the illusion of foresight, putting us on the level of the magician; or else we actually try to foresee the event, as by means of electronic computers. But the result is invariably false, because in programming the machine we can never allow for *all* factors. And, alas, it seems that it is always the determining factor that we had not anticipated.

But those who believe in the thread of history do not operate on this level; their intellectual process is more all-embracing, although it retains a scientific façade. The first step is to skim over long sections of history with the predetermined but unconscious or at least veiled intention of finding in it an orientation, a value. It is an open question whether at this moment the *philosopher* already has his little ready-made ideas in his head, or is merely conditioned by the spirit of the age, the milieu in which he

marinates, and the new magazine he digests weekly. It
does not make much difference; the result is the same.

In this history, conditioned in this way, you choose a
certain number of highlights and leave everything else in
the shadow. There was a time when an ideology of the
individual decreed that great men were the condition of
history; today it is classes and economic factors. A question
of style. Having retained the facts that fit this interpretation, you relate them and you have no trouble perceiving a
general line. You apply this key, allegedly taken from history (but really the product of modern ideas and preoccupations), to current events. Then, with great excitement,
you "discover" in our time a certain number of facts that
agree with what history has "revealed" to us: marvelous
science, unhoped-for results! And now you understand decolonization, socialization, and nationalization, as well as
freedom, democracy, syndicalism, etc. And you observe
with delight that these facts fit into the line that you had
drawn to begin with, that they are *therefore* significant,
that they are therefore pregnant with the future, a future
that is merely an extension of the diagram of history previously drawn.

And now it becomes possible to extrapolate from these
facts. All you have to do is continue the movement, and the
sequence of history is clearly seen. And how imperiously
the schoolmaster with his dogmatic ruler slaps the fingers
of anyone who does not sign up for this future! But what
you have to go through to get there! Expurgate history of
most of its content (and only orthodox supporters of the
general line are clever at that!), expurgate the present of
all facts contradictory to the general line by invoking the
irrefutable doctrine that these facts do not count because
they are not in the direction of history.

In other words, man's intelligence sees and creates a

thread in history; the events that confirm it are the good ones, the ones worthy of being considered and retained as historical facts; the others do not make history: you can dismiss them without difficulty; they are not even worth a glance. Fundamentally all you need do is decide what history is: I call history everything that corresponds to a given evolution.

Here, of course, we are on the level of fantasy, and why shouldn't we introduce some of that element into this austere discipline? The only trouble is that there can be three or four threads in history, each just as valid as the next. For the moment we are spared this inconvenience, since one of the interpretations meets with the approval of the majority and consequently is believed to be true. So there is only one direction in history, and we are reassured. I am quite aware that, when confronted by these problems, the believer in the thread of history will shrug his shoulders. His is the broad view. He does not operate either on the level of computers or on the level of archives and scholarship, but on the level of irreversible processes, of the transforming praxis, etc.—that is, the level that enables you to explain why the communist revolution occurred in the USSR and China (contrary to Karl Marx's whole philosophy of history), as well as Stalinism (contrary to the course of history seen by Karl Marx), anti-Stalinism, etc. Everything is foreseen.

But that is not important, for the famous thread of history, like God, is not *proved,* either on the level of the event or on the level of the great transformations, but *believed.* The believer can explain everything by the direction of history, and what assures him that he is on the right track as far as the future is concerned is the *consensus omnium,* the fact that he runs with the pack—in short, the commonplace!

. . .

But this commonplace does not cease to astonish me! We are living in an age when people everywhere are proclaiming energy, responsibility, commitment, an age of record-breaking. Man is constantly outdoing himself, thanks to the marvelous development of technology; the greatest prodigies are accomplished by man. People extol the courage of the astronaut, and they are right; they extol the greatness of man, and nobody would question it! On all sides we hear these appeals to the biggest, the farthest, the highest, a more total concentration of energy. We are at the outermost point, where man may in fact cease to be man by exceeding his limit. And as the sound barrier was broken, so it may be that as yet we have known only the prehistory of humanity; this invisible wall that man has always come up against may be about to cave in at last in a double explosion.

To this end man must employ all his forces, all his opportunities. Everyone has become responsible for everyone and everything. The most perceptive groups, the churches and the Communist Party, are always harping on this individual and universal responsibility, and defining for the faithful their duty to be aware, persistent, responsible. And among intellectuals, artists, and writers, it is commitment that corresponds to the same idea. We are committed; we must be committed. Nothing will get done unless we are committed.

The athletic record is on the same level as the technological record, and the technological record parallels political commitment. But at the same time the thought that dominates the whole is precisely the existence of an implacable and necessary course of history that presupposes that every effort is useless if it does not go in this direction, if you don't get into the boat that follows the current.

The commonplace about the direction of history corresponds perfectly to the ideal of the dead dog: a good little dog with a fat stomach (necessary to float) who enters the strongest part of the current and floats downstream, turning gravely with the air of a professor of political science, and swinging right or left according to the wavelets (his carefully considered opinions). Sometimes an eddy causes him to lose his course, he hesitates as he turns (these are the scruples of conscience), he drifts toward a sand bank (this is a demonstration of his personal freedom); he finds himself being sucked by a funnel toward the bottom (this is anxiety); but soon he bravely overcomes these temptations, a wave sets him afloat again, and he triumphantly pursues his course, having finally recovered the right direction, which carries him, of course, to the necessary end. And the farther he goes, the more proudly he swells with horrible certainties about his freedom and the direction of history, which make him more and more turgid until the moment when the impregnation of his soul by this corruption makes him burst into pieces of horrible rotted matter.

Either there is a current in history—real, powerful, determined—in which case it is perfectly absurd to invoke responsibility, commitment, effort, for all I have to do is let myself be carried along; and my chief concern is to protect myself from unseasonable demonstrations, from attempts that would threaten to decrease the speed of the current; all you can ask of me is to be neither too big nor too active, to slip quietly into the deepest, swiftest part, close my eyes and give myself up. Or else it is true that I must commit myself, act, intervene. But what's this? Am *I* going to change the course of history? If that's true, then it doesn't exist, then nothing is inevitable. By what right does anyone tell me that I am going against the course of history, if it is I who create it from one moment to the next? A simpleminded contradiction? In spite of the profusion and confusion of existentialists and communists I have read, I have found nobody who has resolved it except by semantic games and intellectual puzzles.

The thread of history is fatality reinstated, readmitted, and revered under cover of scientific parabolas and political intentions. But it is the very persons who judge everything on the basis of this commonplace who claim to be free men. If Karl Marx's thought, reduced to a formula and based on confused beliefs, has become this imperious and axiomatic proverb, that is because it answered a profound need.

Unconsciously, modern man knows himself to be the victim of forces over which he has no control. The modern state has become the coldest of all monsters. Nobody can do anything against it or to it: it *is*. It develops for reasons of its own, regardless of governments, constitutions, institutions. Modern technology has acquired perfect autonomy from all affirmations and philosophies. There is a very obvious evolution of this force beyond our calculations: there is no more pilot. Every man trapped in the mass of the big city is aware that there is nothing he can do about it and that his personal destiny depends less and less on himself and more and more on these abstract ukases issuing from truly impersonal forces devoid of responsibility, will, or a face. So in this vaguely experienced situation, why would not the idea of history as a synthetic and implacable goddess seem the very language of reality!

And as with all gods, there must be sacrifices. The imposing goddess who advances with confident stride asks only that I give up my own will and follow her, for which price I am saved, and enjoy her favor! But what's this? Is that all? What I am *forced* to do by my condition as man, humble citizen, employee, product of psychological forces, television viewer, hemmed in by a close network of social, administrative, and legal regulations and political imperatives—what I am forced to do turns out to be all I need do to assure myself of the goddess's favor. How could I not be overcome with gratitude? What's more, when I enter into the mystery, when I am initiated into the esoteric (Marxist or existentialist) explanation of the current of history, I discover that it is precisely my support that makes this history! I become the indispensable agent without whom—would you imagine it?—this goddess would become helpless! And because I have become a believer, because this suits me perfectly, because this takes care of everything, I refuse to see the contradiction, to understand the stupidity. This commonplace enables me to believe in all sincerity in what I cannot dismiss, while at the same time permitting me to play soldier and sound the trumpet of the Zouaves. This is what today we call "being a committed man."

YOU CAN'T ACT
WITHOUT GETTING
YOUR HANDS DIRTY

This commonplace, which we may call "existentialist" because it was put into circulation by Sartre, is merely the
literary form of the very vulgarly bourgeois expression
"You can't make an omelette without breaking eggs." For
this reason I would like to begin with what Léon Bloy said
about this last commonplace, which was almost the order
of the day: "It was with these words that that colossal
bourgeois Stalin/Abdul Hamud must have explained to his
good friend and faithful servant Sartre/Hanotaux the
massacre of two or three hundred thousand Christians of
Armenia (here let us say, to be modest, from two to three
million Turcomans, Azerbaijani, Ukrainians, Balts, and
Poles). However, he did not invite him to eat the omelette."

· · ·

It is obvious that Péguy's celebrated remark about workers who have dirty hands and those "who have no hands at all" has become the basis for a shameless exploitation. If Péguy could see the use that is made of it he would be rather surprised, for it provides an excuse, a front, and a bleach job for all those who delight in getting their hands into the political manure and worry very little and sometimes not at all (and for that matter would be quite incapable of worrying even if they wanted to) about having clean hands. But it also serves to justify the impotent intellectuals, the Parisian intelligentsia, who live on a diet of words, *in doing nothing*.

For it is not the least important characteristic of this commonplace that it is invoked by those who do nothing and who claim to have dirty hands in order to give the impression that they have done something. "I signed a manifesto, I am committed, see how dirty my hands are!" "I made a speech, I wrote an article, I demonstrated and shouted in the street—just look how dirty my hands are! I am not like those awful intellectuals who . . . " To claim that you have dirty hands is a badge, a guarantee that you aren't in an ivory tower, that you are in the world, in touch with the workers.

For the very people who have elaborated the doctrine expressed in the commonplace are the mandarins, "the specialists in freedom, justice, and morality," [1] and although their morality may be a morality of ambiguity, their freedom may be the freedom of a renewed creation, their justice may be the justice of a proletarian social order, nevertheless the applications are deceptive and their virtues are always in capital letters; for where there is only

---

[1] On what follows, see Charbonneau: *Le Paradoxe de la culture* (1965), pp. 154 ff.

ambiguity, there is no morality. For them, freedom is either
total or nonexistent; they cannot be satisfied with the odds
and ends of freedoms that can be gathered by the side of
any road. The communist order must result not in a little
more justice, always succumbing to injustice, but in the
classless society, hence the society without exploitation,
hence without evil, hence without a state: a real paradise
on earth. Short of this, nothing makes any sense.

This excess of absolutism radically seals off all possibilities of human endeavor, and because one can neither see
the real nor take part in a doubtful battle, one praises dirty
hands because they are necessary to action. For action in
itself is well worth this sacrifice, and we have learned that
morality has nothing to do with action. But we must be
careful. This is theory, and we will be the first to repudiate
the tortures of the Nazi camps or the tanks of Budapest.
This forces us to see the ridiculous limit to the dirtiness in
question: a manifesto at the most. But as for really getting
your hands dirty by torturing your fellow man—come now!
The intellectual remains what he is.

It goes without saying that these heroes with their dirty
hands have them only figuratively, by mediation or by
proxy. "Darling!" says the lovely Françoise, "look at my
dirty hands!"—holding out her manicured, bejeweled fingers. The worker has dirty hands, and the intellectual who
supports the cause of the worker is ennobled by this dirt.
The politician has dirty hands, and the professor who signs
a manifesto profits by a few dabs of this reeking slime. It is
the guarantee that you are not a useless person, an idle
talker. You support the sacred cause of the worker. Or else
you are using politics (which is the only way) to work for a
better world.

It is true that in our society anyone who makes his living

by thinking, or trying to think, is not very highly regarded. He must find some useful purpose for himself, he must attach himself to someone or something useful, something recognized as "valuable" by the society and by public opinion. Under these circumstances, the claim to have dirty hands serves as a justification for the man who never leaves his office. But it also enables our intellectual to perform his proper and traditional function of classical chorus: he explains and justifies the actions of the others. For it goes without saying that in profiting by the filth of men of action, he renders them a little service. He explains and justifies this filth in the eyes of a world that is dazzled by such great theatrical subtlety, such great philosophical profundity.

Our hero heaves a deep sigh—"Ah! Look at my dirty hands!"—with the faintest suggestion of disgust, of course, his brow anxious, his lips drawn by this heroic sacrifice, and shaking his head; you must understand that this is not usual for him, that it is only by compulsion and duty that he has come to this. It is not so easy to have dirty hands. But his face also hides a slight sense of triumph; it is the false modesty of the victor. For now this do-nothing is recognized, patented, ennobled by the beauty and purity of the dirt of the worker or the political hero. To be a man you have to pay the price, don't you? And according to the teachings of the master, you are not born a man, you become one, you create yourself by choice, by action; and you can't act without getting your hands dirty. See my hands . . . therefore I have become a man. The circle is complete.

In reality all this is a farce, because—among other reasons—nobody ever bothers to ask whether this action has

any point, whether it is constructive for man; the intellectual is so thirsty for action these days that he is ready to
accept the dictum of a very bourgeois poet: "Learn absurd
things in order to learn good will." Do anything at all, as
long as you do something! Still less does anybody ask himself whether this action is worth the price he is ready to
pay, the price of the filth, and if after all it might not be
better to keep one's hands clean rather than do these idiotic
things and undertake these pseudo-commitments, manifestos, announcements, signatures, and declarations.

The fact is, of course, that it is difficult to draw the line
between a political "action" whose own validity, significance, and complexities are almost impossible to discern
and the moral, intellectual, or spiritual corruption to which
the action forces you. But I am forgetting myself and getting sidetracked by these intellectual concerns, which are
precisely what we want to repudiate by immersing ourselves in action. Away with intellectualizing! Politics calls.
We must live for her, and for her we must die.

This intellectualizing is doubly empty, for the person
who plays the game of dirty hands and has thrown himself
into Sartrian pseudo-commitment *has never chosen.* He has
never deliberated or weighed the reasons and the chances.
Dirty hands are not the result of a decision or a commitment. The person who protects himself behind this commonplace is aware that he is none too clean and pretends
that this is by choice, but this is far from the truth. The
man who affects the grime of the worker is in reality immersed in a very different kind of filth. And when someone
tells you that you have to get your hands dirty, it means
that he is up to his eyes in the septic tank. The commonplace about dirty hands does not imply, as people seem to
think, that everything else is quite clean and well scrubbed,
and that after all you've got to get your hands into the

dishwater, but that fortunately in these modern houses the toilet is not far from the shower.

I seem to be contradicting myself. In my first proposition I said that our man did not have dirty hands in *reality*, but only by proxy. In my second proposition I am arguing that he is fundamentally dirty and radically corrupt. The contradiction is only apparent. The man who *talks* about dirty hands, who *admits* the necessity for having them, is as yet only a talker; he is in fact in no way defiled by action, by real participation, by work, for he plays no effective role, he participates in nothing but words. *"Corragio, lavoratori!"* When Sartre writes *Dirty Hands* or *The Manifesto of the 121,* he is not getting his hands dirty at all—at most, his pen.

But this taint that does not come from action (there is no action!) exists in the conscience. It does not *come* from participation in politics or from the transformation of the world; it is there to begin with, planted in the bottom of the heart. It is a function of existence rather than of action. To anyone who accuses me of making an arbitrary judgment I will reply that I have objective proof in the very fact of formulating the commonplace "You can't act without getting your hands dirty." This simple remark implies on the part of the speaker an *a priori* acceptance of *all* compromise and *all* dirt, all betrayals and all acts of contempt toward man, all degradation and all genocide; it is the voice of consenting cowardice parading as the courage of commitment.

For the man who has acted and killed to repent *afterward* and say "I carry the weight of all the evil I have done" is the true human condition. This man is worthy of respect. But for a man to excuse himself *beforehand* for the abomination, to accept everything in advance and justify himself in advance, is the worst of corruptions. This is to surrender in advance, without resistance and without conscience, to what happens, to what will be deemed the necessity of action. And once one has started in this direction, everything will very readily be accepted as the necessity of action; which presupposes, therefore, that there is no limit to the evil to be done in order to succeed. And the worst happens when it is the intellectual who provides this advance justification for the man of action, for then the magical prestige of intelligence frees him of his last scruples, and he loses all restraint. The road is wide open for him now that he has the benediction of the intellectual authorities, who play the same role that the church once played in wars. We can be sure that in the use of torture, the spread of mass murder, and the development of concentration camps, those intellectuals who maintain that "You have to get your hands dirty" have done far more than soldiers and policemen.

Since we are on the subject of dirty hands, we must be willing to look at mud. Why this doctrine? Why this banner? Is it a question of thought, a question of commitment (although, as we have seen, commitment to nothing effective)? Alas, how fine that would be! Certain writers are more naïve, and admit what it really means for a writer, to be committed is "to be rooted in a collective reality, and the larger this reality is, the greater his chance of speaking the language, meeting the expectations, satisfying the needs of the average reader." In other words, to be committed is to assure oneself an audience, to attract customers.

You think I am exaggerating? Sartre said as much in *The Jewish Question*. To make your living as an intellectual "you must seduce, arrest, win people's confidence . . . the most important thing is reputation: you make a reputation and you live by it." And it is quite true that in our society an intellectual cannot sell his novels unless he is committed, unless he claims to have dirty hands. To sign manifestos (and the more revolutionary, excessive, demanding they are, the more they impress) is to do exactly what the public expects of a writer—this public passionately interested in politics, thirsty for action, believing both in facts and in justice. We are rather far from a lofty reason for agreeing to soil our hands. We are interested only in assuring ourselves an income. But perhaps, after all, this is what the intellectual means by having dirty hands? Ssh, don't say it.

The only respectable human decision is to refuse all compromise in advance. It is to know, of course, that in action, in practice, in combat, "evil eventually creeps in," but never to accept it, never to tolerate it, never to justify it; to know that killing is killing, and that there is no way to resign oneself to it. For the moment this attitude of refusing all compromise is taken, there is no impediment to action, no refuge in sterile purity, etc. It is a point of departure that permits me full liberty, since instead of being bound to action, swept along by the tide of circumstances, I find myself forced to decide again on each occasion whether this action is worthwhile, whether this enterprise is sufficiently trustworthy to merit the risk of soiling my hands. When I have decided to keep my hands clean, it means that at every moment I must consider the degree of corruption that the action involves and how far and how long I can tolerate it. When I have decided to keep my hands clean, I can remain an independent man who imposes a certain direction on politics or on the struggle I am waging instead of yielding to the contingencies of the moment, and in the end I can furnish that testimony to man which contemporary humanists are so eager for but which their commonplaces render them unfit to provide.

There is a final consideration. When we examine these heroes committed to dirty hands, we soon observe that there is no conscience more demanding, more lofty, more moral than theirs—*for their adversaries.* Those who agree to get their hands dirty, who make this enormous sacrifice for the sake of the action that must be taken, turn out to be amazingly scrupulous when it comes to their enemies: *they* must have clean hands. It is the adversary who must become a paragon of virtue, and our heroes squawk like guinea hens as soon as they discover the tiniest spot of mud on the hands of the enemy. They invoke natural morality, the dignity of man, the divine virtues, and the international charter of the rights of man. The enemy is forced to represent everything that we (alas!) are obliged not to represent. So we have two sets of weights and measures, all, of course, in praise of the adversary. The FLN murders members of the MNA, plants bombs in cafés, tortures prisoners: ah! it's very awkward, war involves painful necessities, you know. You don't win freedom without getting your hands dirty. The French army tortures its prisoners: it is an inconceivable scandal to moral conscience and Christian civilization; our great ancestors, the virtuous Jacobins, turn over in their graves in indignation. The first duty of the French army is to keep its hands clean. Surely the most remarkable part is that this demand for honor and purity comes from those who despise the army.

These days we are in the habit of permitting everything and excusing everything in our party, our friends, and our allies, and reserving moral criticism for our enemies. There was a time when the dignity of man implied the opposite behavior! China invades Tibet for no reason, either military or economic: a pure war of conquest, pure aggression. She destroys ancient structures and annihilates part of the population. Why not? The Chinese are carrying out a great plan, they are engaged in an exceptional undertaking that they can achieve only at the price of a few mistakes, and even (let's admit it) a few injustices; but after all, we know what politics is, and if Mao decided that it was indispensable, though regrettable, which of us could contradict him? But, mind you, if the United States tries to intervene in Colombia or Cuba, that is an intolerable demonstration of imperialism. The United States does not have the right to play politics: it must use only pure methods and preserve virtue and morality. Of course, there is a large measure of truth in this demand, since the United States is hypocritical enough to proclaim itself the defender of morality, freedom, and virtue! And I do not rule out this judgment! But I am amazed that it is made by the very people who regard dirty hands as a necessity of politics and of action and who use them to justify all political action.

So far I have cited only examples from the left, for they are the most frequent today. But the right has known the same orientation with Maurras, and albums like *Aucune bête au monde* demonstrate that the nobility of dirty hands also belongs to the other side, *idem*, Montherlant or Saint-Exupéry, to begin with. But in these denunciations of dirty hands by the theorists of commitment we again find the delightful candor of our good intellectuals. Read the juicy *Droit à l'insoumission* and the study in *Combat* in which intellectuals explain why they signed *The Manifesto of the 121*, and you will see clearly admitted that the reason they signed, the reason they committed themselves, was so that nobody could reproach them, as they did the Germans

after the war, for remaining silent in the face of Nazism.
Adorable pure consciences, thanks to the theory of dirty
hands! I commit myself so I can be sure not to commit
myself to anything at all. I sign a protest because that is the
best insurance policy for the future—you never know how
things will turn out. Father, look out on the right! Father,
look out on the left! The main thing is that nobody can
reproach us for not protesting, for not making a fuss. So to
have dirty hands is to insure yourself against the dirt of a
possible concentration camp. Everything depends on being
shrewd enough to guess how it will turn out. This is why
commitment flourishes among intellectuals when the die
has virtually been cast. This, then, by an admirable dialec-
tic, is the theory of dirty hands, the noble affirmation of the
necessity of commitment which serves only one purpose: to
disassociate oneself, in the eyes of one's public and of
history, from those whose hands are really dirty.

But, someone is sure to object, if you absolutely rule out
dirty hands, don't you rule out politics? Granted! It has
rarely been tried. But if this is really so, could we then say
that politics is a dirty game? Why should I judge morality
in terms of politics, considering the first legitimate, and the
second, since contradictory to the first, illegitimate? I have
not yet found any proof that politics is the imperative of
man's salvation, although many impassioned declarations
have, of course, been written on the subject. But I have not
seen one that went beyond the level of the campaign poster.

THE MAIN THING IS
TO BE SINCERE
WITH YOURSELF

The intention is admirable: to shun hypocrisy, to have done with that awful game that delighted our fathers, to see things clearly and directly, to face oneself, not to tamper with facts or evidence, to practice the discipline that forces us to be always consistent so that our outside is true to our inside—in short, not to have a divided heart. Who would not be seduced by such a lofty desire, such a pure expression?

The hesitation sets in—for myself, but not, of course, for those admirably exacting souls who obey this common-place—the hesitation sets in when we ask ourselves which self we mean. For after all, between the inside and the outside . . . But the converse is also true, and does not the self I was yesterday or the one I intend or expect to be tomorrow have any part in my decision? The answer is clear. I am bored with the people I am with, I feel like

yawning, I yawn unrestrainedly in the faces of my neighbors. I am being sincere with myself. The woman I married
no longer attracts me, no longer excites me. I tell her so
quite bluntly and I leave her; that is simple honesty. I
desperately need this money that I see on the table, there is
no doubt that my whole being strains toward it; I take it. A
question of total sincerity.

For such is this sincerity: it has nothing to do with the
self I want to become, the ideal that I have set for myself,
to which I would have to rise, and whose reflection would
put my present state to shame. No indeed! For this would
take us into the realm of loathsome duty, of obligation, of a
constraint unacceptable to these free spirits. Besides, this
model of the future presents a fatal weakness to realistic
eyes: it does not exist, it is not a fact. Nor could I consider
being faithful to what I was yesterday. Yesterday is yesterday. There certainly is no continuity between what I felt
yesterday, which made it possible for me to tell a woman I
loved her, and what I am feeling now. Why should I be
constrained by what I said yesterday? If today I feel and
understand something else, I need only express this something else. If my words have changed, if my deeds have
changed, that is only because I have changed; and since I
know no other law than what I am—*hic et nunc*—why
should what I was dictate my behavior in any way?

Impeccable logic, adorable harmony; the logic of the
desert, the harmony of the void. For it presupposes, of
course, that the other person does not exist, that I refuse to
consider the effects of what I say or what I am on the other
person. If I wound him, if I kill him by my sincerity, what
does it matter? It happens that there is a choice that is
quite unconscious (and therefore suspect and contemptible) between love of the other person and love of the self.
For this famous sincerity is nothing more than self-love. I

indulge my desires, I follow my pleasures, I obey my instincts: on the most superficial level, I am a cad; on the most profound level, I am a spiritual assassin.

When Sartre changes his political opinion like a shirt, sincerity to himself demands that he immediately ejaculate what his cerebral bowels have produced, and he passionately proclaims the conviction of the moment. For, then against, then for the USSR, the Communist Party, socialism, etc. What does he care about the effect that this has on the thousands of young people who follow him in his about-faces, his palinodes? What does it matter that he disorients them, that he provokes crises of conscience? What does it matter that by his abrupt turns, which they follow, *he is preparing them to become a flock that is susceptible to propaganda*, that will follow any leader at all after this prestigious philosopher? He is being sincere with himself! After all, the others have only to assume their own responsibilities.

Cain was right when he asked, "Am I my brother's keeper?" And to these merciless realists, of course, the match between Sartre and a young man of seventeen is as equal as the one between the old seducer and the pure young maiden (assuming that such still exist). But I do not understand why these same sincere people raised an uproar when liberalism declared in no uncertain terms that the match is also equal in the labor contract between the worker and the employer; they do the same thing in the intellectual sphere!

This duty of sincerity obliges me to tell my wife I do not love her any more without worrying about what effect it will have on her. To go on living with her, pretending that I do—would that not be a frightful hypocrisy? To force myself to do something—anything—would be hypocrisy! To act according to a value—hypocrisy! To follow a morality that would actually prevent me from doing or being what I feel like doing or being—hypocrisy! Not to express my opinion at once but to think it over, to censor it— hypocrisy!

The important thing is never to pretend, always to be yourself. But since this self is defined neither by its past, nor by its intention, nor by a value, nor by an essence, since I can grasp this self only in the impression of the moment, in the reaction to the present, sincerity consists in merely reflecting the present. In other words, you follow your guts, you follow the easiest, most elementary thing, your desires (we can't even talk about passion in the true sense, for that implies discipline and duration!). You choose the lowest level, for the impulses of the moment are generally situated on the lowest level; you tolerate no constraint, and while following the most glandular of determinisms, you claim to be free.

Similarly, being yourself now consists in following the impulse of the group to which you belong. This social current provides instant identity, imposes tastes, fashions, vocabularies, on us; we want to be what the social current makes us, and in this admirable rush of sincerity, we conform. It is not astonishing to observe that the groups that respect this watchword of sincerity to oneself are as conformist as possible, with the result that the individuals making up these groups are perfectly interchangeable and their selves are identical. Innumerable *nouvelle vague* films bear witness to this fact. And again, this sociological follow-the-leaderism is regarded as freedom!

But, since there is no longer any reason to say one thing rather than another in this meaningless sincerity, such persons will agree with the idiot who wrote in *l'Express* (June 1961) that *"The important thing* is to deny oneself." This is exactly the same thing, for this denial is the very proof of one's sincerity, and since the self has been reduced to a colander, what difference does it make whether the holes are on the right or on the left?

And given this situation, I am beginning to wonder why anything should be important. If nothing exists outside of myself, and if I myself am nothing more than this impression of the moment, what gives me the right to say that something is important? Important in relation to whom and to what? And why, after all, should I be sincere? Why bring a virtue, a value into it? This looks very suspect. Where does this value come from? And why this particular one? I see myself embarked on a very bad path!

Fortunately the young people who advance this formula, ecstatic over such profundity, never ask themselves this question. The situation is simple, very simple. The idea is justification, once again. The idea is to live without constraint or surveillance, following what is most elementary, most animal, or most contemptible in man, following the line of least resistance. But since we are not animals after all, we must prove to ourselves that we are right to live this way, to indulge ourselves, to let ourselves go; we must turn to history and quote great authors because we have been to school; above all, we must have an easy conscience, so we use the ploy of sincerity. And this justifies everything, this purifies everything; sincerity is better than Ivory and Oxydol put together. You come out Rinso white, and besides, your glands are satisfied, your friends admire you, you are in step with the times. Good little fair-haired boy, all ready to become the good provincial notary who is also sincere with himself. For his hypocrisy, which you hate, is in the last analysis your own.

PEOPLES HAVE
THE RIGHT OF
SELF-DETERMINATION

With a quaver in the voice, a hand over the heart, and a tear in the eye, this immortal principle was proclaimed in 1919. It was the last word in democracy, destined to destroy the Austro-Hungarian Empire and possibly the Russian Empire, but there it was too late and it could not be done. Anyway, it was understood that this principle was to apply only to the right people.

There are people who misunderstood it. Temesvar, Corfu, the Croatians, later the Sudeten Germans: it was explained to them that their case was quite different. And it was in the name of this immortal principle that some remarkable political units like Czechoslovakia and Yugoslavia were concocted, with peoples who obviously practiced self-determination! We know the special love of the Czechs for the Slovaks, and of the Croatians for the Serbs and the Slovenes.

From the outset, the immortal principle (which was not yet a commonplace, but an invention of jurists: commonplaces come from all sources) raised a slight problem for minds that were so perverse as to be truly negligible. What is a people? This seems like an innocent question, but just try to answer it! Is it a language? Then let us hasten to ask the one hundred and seventy-nine linguistic groups of the USSR if they became independent when the liberating power was directly substituted for the colonizing power of the czars. Then let's ask ourselves what China did in Tibet. And shall we side with Tshombe because Katanga does not have the same language as the province of Léopoldville? And let's break up Cameroun, where ten or twelve languages are spoken. And while we're at it, why stop? We must also correct the errors of history. For after all, in the sixteenth century France still did not have one language! French was the language of the Ile-de-France, but Flemish, Alsatian, Breton, Normand, Basque, Béarnais, Catalonian, Provençal were languages in current use. It seems to me that we should consult these peoples.

But, it will be objected, this is absurd, for what matters is the dominant language, such as French in France, Russian in the USSR, etc. Bravo! That is clear. Then let us immediately restore Cameroon and most of the African territories, including the former Belgian Congo, to France, since French is the language these various Negro peoples use to communicate among themselves. And as for English, it occurs to me that Great Britain would make a rather good haul on the basis of dominant language.

So that isn't it. Is it territorial unity? Then what is the meaning of the boundaries drawn in a purely arbitrary and irrelevant fashion between all African, South American, and Balkan peoples, and most Asiatic peoples?[1] The Belgian Congo is a conglomeration of peoples and kingdoms that had little to do with each other, except waging war, before the Belgian conquest; why intervene when it is on the point of falling apart, of reverting to what it was before? I am sure that Koreans and Indo-Chinese were consulted on either side to establish the boundary of the sixtieth parallel, as were the Germans in the matter of the Oder-Neisse boundary!

Then it is ethnic unity—obviously. Here we are on thin ice, for racism is not far behind. And decidedly this turns out to be unsatisfactory as soon as we try to apply it. The ethnic unity of the USSR? The ethnic unity of the United States? We are forced to conclude either that these are not peoples, that they do not have the right to self-determination, or that they should be broken up into smaller ethnic units (which would be a very good thing).

But turning to current problems, this principle has continually been invoked in the case of the Algerians. What is the ethnic unity of this group, made up of Arabs, Berbers, Jews, and Frenchmen? In what respect are they a people? And if I am told that it is the *majority* that is the people, then I could remind you that it was precisely in order to liberate oppressed minorities from oppressive majorities that the principle was formulated! We are in total confusion.

No, you don't understand at all! *It is history that makes a people.* Here it is clear, the forty kings who made France: St. Louis and the Catharians, Charles VII and Guienne, the Convention and the Chouans . . . Quite so, the iron hand

---

[1] It is true that however absurd they may be, these boundaries become "inviolable" as soon as they are drawn, like the eternal boundaries between India and Pakistan, as we were reminded by a communiqué in October 1965!

kneads the individuals and eventually makes them into a people. The USSR will eventually become one people. Fine. But then, *then,* we must give history time to take its course. Why run the risk of interrupting it in the middle? Let France stay in Algeria for another hundred years, and it will be a French province like Brittany, for there is no more real difference between an Arab and a Frenchman today than there was between a Breton and a Provençal in the fifteenth century. Algeria will be part of the French nation. On the contrary, history does not seem to me to have succeeded at all in making Algeria an independent people to begin with.[2] And before the French colonization, the arguments of pseudo-historians notwithstanding, there was no Algerian nation, only separate tribes colonized by the Turks.

A new trap awaits us when we ask ourselves how history makes a people! Let's forget philosophical discussions about common destiny, etc. What is history? War and force? Certainly not, although the history of France . . . Well, the passage of time, then? Surely, when one group has lived long enough on a piece of land—I couldn't agree more! But how long? A generation? Unthinkable; this would justify all colonization. Two or three generations? Would a century seem reasonable? But in that case the French have a perfect right to be in Algeria. No, a century is not enough. It is obvious that the people who have a right to be in Algeria are the Arabs. Excuse me, but the Arabs are invaders themselves. Oh, but that was so long ago. . . . It takes several centuries. Then the Portuguese in Goa and the Afrikaners in South Africa are really a people,

---

[2] And it is not a dreadful colonialist who makes such a controversial statement, but Ferhat Abbas himself who, in an article that everyone knows about but chooses to ignore, *demonstrated* the non-existence of the Algerian nation before the revolution.

and do not have to be thrown out. Especially since the
Afrikaners have been living there longer than most African
groups *now* living in South Africa. . . .

You *are* irritating—the people means the native population, and Africa is a Negro continent. . . . This is very
tiresome, first of all because it is pure racism and completely justifies Hitler with his Sudeten Germans; then,
because of those confounded Arabs, who are whites; and
finally, because then I am forced to admit that the Semi-
nole Indians who demanded their autonomy from the
United States at the United Nations were right. Everyone
laughed, and today the Jurassiens seem to me fully entitled
to self-determination.

Decidedly, history throws no light on this matter! We
must examine each individual case with a different criterion, and the only definition of a people we can arrive at is:
a flexible entity that may or may not exist, according to the
interests and ideologies of the moment. And even if we did
find a good definition of a people, how would that help to
apply the commonplace? *Who* would tell us which people
had the right to self-determination? Would it be the people
themselves? But they are quite incapable of understanding
themselves as they really are. A third party? But in that
case the people are manipulated by an outside force, which
is exactly what does happen!

And it appears that we are plunged into just as cruel a
confusion when it comes to deciding what is meant by
self-determination, by "fending for oneself." Thus there are
people like the Cherkess and the Tuareg, for example, who,
without ever having heard of the immortal principle,
fended for themselves very well. They decided that, being
noble peoples, they were made for war, and that the only
way they could fend for themselves was to pillage neigh-

bors, caravans, etc. They were very quickly made to understand that this would not do at all.

We are now beginning to see that there are several ways
to fend for oneself and that only one of these is the right
one. We have been cruelly deceived, for in our illusions we
thought innocently that self-determination consisted in
doing what you wanted without anybody interfering. I am
self-determining when I work if I feel like it and rest when
I please. A people is self-determining when it selects its
own government (bravo, especially if it is democratic!),
when it chooses its own activities and objectives (of course,
especially if they are in accord with progress!), when it
decides the limits of its own territory and makes war to
achieve them— Oh, no, that's something else again.

And anyway, in the previous statements, our agreement
was merely conditional and relative. If the people are won
over by a monster like Hitler, they do not have the right to
self-determination. If the people give way to laziness and
reject progress, they are not worthy of self-determination.
The same is true if the people give in to reactionary ideas.
Thus in July 1961 the Soviet authorities showed that it was
unacceptable for the people of Azerbaidzhan and Kazakhs-
tan to indulge more and more in religion and magic: the
people do not have the right to choose this, we are told. In
other words, the right of the people to self-determination
implies that they choose what the government approves.
But in that case to be self-determining is not to do as one
likes; it is to respect certain principles, imperatives, or
norms.

Is a people self-determining when nobody intervenes in
its affairs? But experience shows in the first place that to
put a people in a situation where they can fend for themselves, it is necessary that several other peoples intervene in
their affairs. Experience also shows that there is only one

good way to be independent, and that, left to themselves, the people are not qualified to say whether the way they decide to act is the right one or not. This question is settled outside the country. Who, then, is to judge?

In the beginning it was the civilized democrats. A people was not qualified for self-determination until it had reached a certain degree of civilization (when it was out of short pants). It was the duty of the civilized nations gradually to lead these peoples to this level, and then to let them try their own wings, provided they opted for democracy and Western civilization. The yellow and black races, for instance, were absolutely unqualified to apply the immortal principle; the Japanese might do so, for they had opted for technology, but they were still immersed in the barbarism of a theocentric monarchy. Inversely, the Bantu had democratic customs (although certainly not parliamentary ones), but had understood nothing about progress. Truly, it was an operation that raised a great many problems. For these barely civilized peoples were capable of choosing anything at all. It was evident that they could not be allowed to do this, just as a good father cannot allow the fantasies of unreasonable children to endanger their health or their future.

Today things have changed considerably. It is no longer the "civilized Western democrat" who decides on the one and only legitimate manner in which the people can run their country: it is the "progressive who believes in following the current of history." And this is quite another thing. Now that the obstacle is Western democracy and capitalism, all peoples, even the most backward, have the right to self-determination provided their decision is against the West and for a socialist regime, until a better one comes along. We know Lenin's doctrine on colonial wars and untapped proletarian resources in colonized peoples.

Tribes of cannibals in the heart of Africa (we have seen only recently that they still exist) or headhunters in Borneo are invested with this immortal right, provided they hunt the French and the Dutch. This is not very difficult to achieve.

On the other hand, it goes without saying that those who are opposed to the movement toward socialism have no right to self-determination. Since for fifteen years the East Germans have demonstrated their obvious and permanent hostility to Communism by constantly emigrating to the West, they obviously cannot invoke the principle, because they are moving against the stream of history. For this reason their will has no importance; they are quite simply mistaken. And a good government that thinks the way it should cannot allow its people to err in this way. It is obliged to bring them back to the right path, like a good father, etc. The case is exactly the same with the Hungarians and the Poles. It would be absolutely useless and dangerous to let them freely express their will by elections; they might make a mistake about the direction of history. If, on the other hand, they are properly held in check by a government that is in possession of this inside information, these peoples, without knowing it or wishing it, *actually do practice self-determination.* They are being guided with a firm hand toward the moment when at last their well-trained will coincides *ipso facto* with the direction of history; at this moment, they will be completely free. It is simply a matter of letting a little time elapse (see above). On the other hand, it is just as evident that the Western democracies, not being in the mainstream of history, have no right to exercise this authority. And those peoples who wish to free themselves of this tutelage have the immortal, inalienable, and sacred right to fight for their freedom.

·　·　·

But it is sometimes necessary to forsake the splendid heights of principles, thus brilliantly illuminated, and return to contingent realities. We must, in fact, ask ourselves *how* this principle has actually been applied. If we consider the peoples who have been historically recognized as possessing this right and who have exercised it, what do we find? First of all, let us note that in the peace negotiations of 1919, there were certain statesmen, like Pilsudski and Masaryk, who were highly regarded by and well known to the representatives of the powers and who set forth their ideas about the future of their peoples, and that the powers who had won the war sanctioned these ideas. Constitutions were imposed on the peoples in question; they were given the rules of the game and they were told to play within fixed limits. Those peoples who were not represented by eminent personalities or at least by politicians who were in favor with the victors had no right to anything at all. It is obvious that they were not capable of self-determination because they did not have good representatives.

There is no need to cry shame. How would you really go about letting a people make its own decisions? Decisions about what? In what direction? Is it the people themselves, from the ground up, who are going to invent their own form of government, draw their boundaries, establish their economic regime? Is the Croatian at the corner going to decide where the national boundary will run? Obviously, eminent men are going to take care of all that. You decide that a certain human group constitutes a people. You decide that a given constitution is best for this people, then you consult the people about this constitution, and the people say yes, because the people always say yes to all constitutions that are presented to them. You set up an economic regime (this time, however, you do not consult the people, because since the problem is much more con-

crete, there is a chance that the people might not say yes).
You draw the boundaries, and you set up a government,
and the people always approve. This is what is meant by
self-determination.

In our time the situation is identical, though those who
define the eternal principle have changed. Now the work is
done by a handful of agitators, revolutionaries, and propa-
gandists who claim to represent the people as a whole.
They act important, move around, alert the neighbors,
drum up support, stir up scandals, and promise happiness
and freedom, and for quite a while the people who must be
led to self-determination watch them with astonishment,
mistrust, and incomprehension. But they are the elite, and
besides, they are in step with history. Therefore, they are
the people. Eventually they succeed in getting together a
few groups and in provoking dissatisfaction. If in addition
they manage to get thrown into prison, victory is theirs.
This is what happened in Algeria. Naturally, I am not
saying that the injustice, misery, and exploitations de-
nounced by the agitators did not exist, but only that it is
not the *people* who rise up, it is not the people who want
this or that—it is party leaders claiming to represent the
people and passing off their ideas as those of the people.

And it may take the people a very long time to decide to
cooperate. Algeria is a case in point. For years the people
were not in favor of the FLN, nor were they hostile to the
French. But in the long run, of course, as a result of being
exploited and plundered by the FLN, harassed and subjected to searches by the French, slaughtered by the FLN
and tortured by the French, the people finally had had
enough: the time came when the people did want something; they were not quite sure what, except that they
wanted this to stop. Well, it is better to put your money on
the side that seems to be winning, which was the FLN; at

this point, the latter could announce, "You see, I represented the Algerian people!" God help the Algerian
people. . . .

In 1961 the provisional government of Algeria announced that the people have the right "to select the government they want, to freely choose their regime, their
economic and social system, and their way of life." And to
protest against the fixed elections to which the Moslems
were called, and to declare that the "best ones" were in
prison. But what was the result of this enormous effort?
Self-determination? Naturally! Summer 1962 showed us
how true it was that the leaders of the FLN were politicians like any others: personal ambition, venality, conflicts
of interest, the will to get ahead—all this at the expense of
the people. The ringleaders have fought for themselves,
and they do not want to be cheated out of their effort. This
is the reality. And the will of the Algerian people? They are
forced to accept a one-party system; they are forced to
accept fixed elections (September 20, 1962); they are
forced to accept deputies; they are forced to accept an
economic structure; and the world is prepared to make
them a nation at last by all means, including the classic
coup d'état—except the will of the people!

Moreover, as Mao Tse-tung put it clearly (April 1965),
"a people struggling for the right to self-determination
must not be frightened by the loss of human life." What are
a few million men more or less, when honor, dignity, etc.
are at stake? In other words, all sacrifices are good for this
people because the inspired leader has proclaimed their
necessity. Anyway, as soon as the inspired leader takes
charge of them, it is the people who are acting freely. This
is a well-established principle. When a people has determined its fate in this way through the intermediary of
agitators, obviously there can still be two conclusions. If

the agitators are not strong enough or well enough organized, or are divided among themselves, we find ourselves in the interesting situation in which the people actually are in a position to decide their own fate. Experience has repeatedly shown that what happens is quite simply anarchy (the former Belgian Congo or Cameroon, for example).

But generally the agitators have a gang, a party that succeeds in enlisting the people in order to hold them, manipulate them, and convince them to choose correctly—thus we have Sékou Touré. So everything goes off very well without the slightest difficulty! The unanimous will of the people, who are content to cheer, merges with the will of the leader who expresses it, and it is this unanimity that reveals to what an extent these people are self-determining! In this case, to tell the truth, there is always a slight hitch over which political science, in agreement with morality and progress, prefers delicately to lower a curtain. When a people has exercised the right to self-determination in this way only to place itself again in the hands of a magnificent leader, it cannot turn back. The old theologians expressed this perfectly: it is the people who are sovereign and who choose the king, but when they have done so, they have transmitted this sovereignty to him; they no longer have it, therefore they can no longer take issue with the king.

Of course, the high intelligence of our political scientists has far exceeded the primitive stupidity of the old theologians, and they are content to ignore the problem. But after all, whether we admit it or not, the skeleton is still in the closet; for the past thirty years we have seen the same thing happen all around us. The people, inflamed by promises, impressed by propaganda, disgusted with the present reality, rush into the fray, "choosing" a regime, a leader, an independence, a political or economic organization. Six months later the good people, less enthusiastic, begin to think it over; a year later, they are biting their nails to the knuckle, wish they could start over, say time out, stop the game. But at this point they learn that it is not a game, that they cannot go back, that there will be neither time out nor intermission. The power is established. It's all over. The people have sealed their fate once and for all, like a man who commits suicide. The decision he made was not an experiment but a final decision.

This was the experience of the Italians with Mussolini and the Germans with Hitler; and also of the French people with Pétain, for we must not forget that in June 1940, 80 per cent of the French people, including the communists, were pro-Pétain! Of course, international circumstances permitted the French, the Italians, and the Germans to get rid of the regime, but this could hardly be described as self-determination. This is the experience of the Romanians and Hungarians with respect to the communist regime, but here, since there is little likelihood that freedom will come from the outside, popular choice has a chance of being definitive. It is the experience of the Cuban people with their bearded friend. Too late, always too late! By the time you realize the blunder, it has been made and you can't unmake it. The sovereign will of the people who enjoy the right to self-determination now resides in the police, and when the ordinary citizen expresses his dissatisfaction and his desire for independence, he learns that he is a dreadful counterrevolutionary, an abominable scorner of the unanimous will, and a renegade.

The beauty of it is that the very people who proclaim this commonplace the loudest accept the police state of Hungary or Cuba, and even desire it. Undeniably there is a logic here . . .

THE PEOPLE HAVE
COME OF AGE

Actually, it is not the people themselves who pretend to this majority. Therefore this is not a real commonplace, since it is not yet circulated explicitly. But it does exist on an implicit level, for fundamentally, though unconsciously, the people are firmly convinced of their maturity. But the idea is expressed as a basic truth only by a few members of the elite. Periodically, in fact, under certain circumstances, some of our most brilliant politicologists offer this piece of nonsense as the final explanation.

I said under certain circumstances, but the same one keeps recurring. The government is trying to get something and the people refuse; the government is trying to convince the people of something and the people do not believe it; the government is trying an experiment and the people are not cooperating, etc. The people have grown up: that is, they are no longer in tutelage, they are thinking for themselves, they are capable of making informed decisions, you can't deceive them politically any more or pass them a

constitution as if it were a football. It is true that this
assurance is contradicted by the very writers who proclaim
it. And the writer who makes the strongest case for the
people's wisdom, majority, and independence will explain a
few months later that we are facing a possible fascist dictatorship that would inevitably be followed by a communist
dictatorship.

It seems to me that it is shortselling the wisdom of the
people to say that they could not resist fascism and could
throw it off only to accept another dictatorship! But after
all, what's the difference? This does not prevent us from
delighting in the maturity of the people when they express
the same opinions as ourselves. It is probable that on these
occasions the government must find the people absurd, and
led by a clique of dissenters. And since the position taken
by the people has certainly been supported and defended
by an impassioned press, it is difficult to discern whether
this wisdom originates with the people and expresses their
adult character or with the opinions of the few journalists
whom the people intermittently follow. However that may
be, when the government decides on Operation Cairo and
the people are opposed, they are of age! When the government decides on the Siegfried Line and the people reply
brilliantly, "We won't die for Danzig," they are—no, here
there is a mistake, the people were wrong. When the government explains the failure of the conference at Melun,
the people remain quite skeptical because they are of age.
When the military authority wants to take over the power
in Algeria, the soldiers sit on the ground listening to their
transistor radios, and boycott the *Putsch:* these sons of the
people are adults.

In these and in many other circumstances, the people
have demonstrated a profound political wisdom, quite passive, to be sure, quite negative, which expresses itself

rather succinctly: "Leave us the hell alone." I can only concur with the accuracy of this declaration according to which private interests take precedence over what is alleged to be the public interest. The peace and quiet of the average man are unfortunately troubled by the poisonous decisions of the government; politics as a whole is a farce (another commonplace); and nothing beats fishing.

But I don't think this is what our brilliant politicologists mean by the people's coming of age. For the same writers will energetically reject this same formula when it is used by a dictator like General Gursel (July 17, 1961): "The result of the referendum [which gave him the power] conclusively proves the maturity of the Turkish people." No, no, no!

If, as I really believe, the expression refers to the people's capacity to oppose the government for just motives on very concrete issues, the first point that irritates me is the tense of the verb—"*have come* of age." And my irritation increases when it is maintained that the people must be *brought* to maturity. There are some strange contradictions here, because some say that it has happened while others of similar propensities say that it is going to happen. For instance, in September 1965 Mitterrand declared: "If I contribute to the people's coming of age, I will have succeeded." Is it possible? A man of the left who dares to say that the people are not of age? It is true that all it takes is one month's electoral campaign to achieve it!

In any case, this kind of majority consists in opposition to Big Charles. But it would seem that the people have possessed this kind of maturity for a very long time. In 1870 in the face of the Prussians, or in 1830 against the outrageous laws, or in 1674 against the new taxes, and perhaps in the fourteenth century in some of the peasant revolts, we encounter the same order of reactions, the same popular judgments. If it is a question of not believing what authority tells you, not obeying when a decision violates your obvious personal interests, refusing to go to war or to pay more taxes, if this is what is meant by the majority or maturity of the people, then these are not recent acquisitions: the people have possessed them for a very long time!

Before we can announce this maturity it seems to me that we must turn to other criteria, examine other facts. But when I see the people vote enthusiastically in referendum for all the constitutions that are proposed to them, and vote 80 per cent in favor of the government's Algerian policy on a question that is ambiguous, difficult, and largely incomprehensible, I conclude that today the populace is responding as it always has on all referendums: by casting 80 per cent of its votes in favor of the *abstraction* proposed by the government. This does not strike me as a very reassuring index of majority and thoughtfulness. When the people mob De Gaulle and try to touch him, and a man of the people can say ecstatically, "I touched his hand," this seems to me to smack more of primitive magic than of political maturity. It is the good people coming to have their scrofula healed by the king's touch, and we are very close to a charismatic monarchy established by the people themselves! This is not on a very high political level, at least in the politicologist's sense!

But the truth is that evidence of the maturity of the French people abounds. One need only consider the circulation and content of the newspapers: this adult people reads first and foremost the comics, any comics—*Chéri Bibi, Little Orphan Annie, Guy l'Éclair*. The average man doesn't care what happens as long as he gets his little dose of fantasy and escape. We are supposed to believe that this is a manifestation of the democratic mentality, since the fad came to us from the United States. This leading center of interest demonstrates aesthetic sense and high culture, as well as instincts and tendencies that are altogether reassuring. There can be no doubt that comics are the leading reason why newspapers are bought and read; all the polls attest to this fact. When you think about it, the phenomenon has considerable political consequence, for all the children from the age of ten or eleven up, reading the same comics and passionately fond of them, exhibit a maturity much more advanced than that of their elders. We might lower the voting age to ten; we would then have an even more representative electoral body, whose political wisdom would be insured against any preconceived idea.

The second great interest in the newspaper is sports. Never mind, although there would seem to be a relative incompatibility between a passion for the results of the last game, the private lives of football players, and arguments about the validity of boxing championships on the one hand and political analysis on the other. Still, I see no reason why the president of the Assembly should not be a roller skater or a bowling champion. But the other irresistible center of interest is the Royal Family: Grace and Rainier, Margaret and Townsend, the misfortunes of Farah and of Soraya, the miscarriages of Fabiola, and the pranks of the Consort. Here we are in the realm of pure emotion. The subject has everything: human interest, royalty, drama, a sense of self-importance from intimate acquaintance with crowned heads, the vanity of finding oneself in the genealogies, and the democratic sentiment, "See these kings, I have the same feelings, the same troubles as they do—I am a bit of a king myself."

Don't tell me that we are on the level of amusement, that everyone has a right to have a little fun, but that when it

comes to serious matters these same citizens are capable of
demonstrating their maturity. Serious matters? The newspaper that they have chosen covers the whole political or
economic scene in two lines of large type, and it's all the
reader can do to put up with twenty lines of text on these
questions.

I hear all the protestations: these aren't the only ones,
there are all those people who are passionately interested
in politics, the ones who commit themselves, sign petitions
. . . Fine, let's look at them. How are the petitions signed?
Two friends comb the neighborhood, and outside of the
handful of people who have a firm opinion (5 to 6 per
cent), we find two categories. There are those who sign
because it is their friends who come around, or more often
because they see the column of previous signatures—they
would be the only ones not to sign, the whole street is
signing, they don't want to be different. The whole weight
of public opinion is upon them; this is conformism, going
with the crowd. . . . Then there are those who sign because
they let themselves be taken in by high-sounding words
like patriotism, justice, democracy, truth, etc., language
which generally has nothing to do with the immediate
purpose of the petition. In either case, 90 per cent of the
signatories do not know what they are signing. This statement may seem shocking; it is the exact truth.[1]

The well-known maturity of our people is also expressed
by their political changeability or their political constancy.

---

[1] A little incident confirmed this for me. A few years ago a strong political statement had been signed by a number of priests of the Reformed
Church of France, who should have had a certain awareness of what they
are doing and who possess a certain culture enabling them to understand.
When the authorities of the Reformed Church became upset and asked for
an explanation, two thirds of the priests replied that they had not even read
the text! And we remember that in 1960 the same thing happened to
Gabriel Marcel with a statement on Algeria opposing the statement of the
121. This is typical of all petitions!

That the clientele of the Communist Party can make the
sharpest about-faces without faltering—against Hitler in
1937, for Hitler in 1939, against Hitler in 1941, for Tito in
1945, against Tito in 1948, for Tito in 1954, etc.—shows
marvelous skill and critical spirit! Such loyalty is obviously
the mark of a high comprehension of the profoundest political wisdom. It is true that the rest of the people are just as
constant in their inconstancy. Polls indicate a certain trend
of opinion on a certain question, the government takes
steps, and immediately there is a change of opinion, the
people become hostile to the very measures they wanted
three months before. For example, the Suez affair. It is true
that in this very opposition to the government we find
proof of the soundness of popular judgment. And we are
back where we started.

When some brilliant politicologist says that the people
are of age, this is based on two simple notions. One is
superficial: the people are of age when they oppose the
government, provided this opposition coincides with the
general position advocated by the author in question. It is
obvious that the peasants who demonstrated in 1961 were
not of age, but that the people who demonstrated for the
independence of Algeria were of age. It is purely a matter
of opinion: the authors never even consider the problem of
whether at this moment the people may not also be taken
in by propaganda and slogans and be simply adopting a
conformism different from that of the government! Nor do
they ask themselves what, after all, is meant by this notion
of majority or maturity in an age when the individual is
increasingly identified with a class or a mass.

For according to the modern point of view, the individual is considered to be of age only if he shares the common-

places of his society, if he enters into its active groups, if he takes part in collective action, if he runs with the pack, if he works to increase productivity, if, in short, he adopts the "modern" views of the group. The distinguishing characteristic of this maturity is that it is collective rather than individual. It is not by the personal growth of each member that the class or nation comes of age. It is by the majority of the class or nation that the individual arrives at his maturity, which is exactly measured by his degree of integration, and the maturity of the group reflects back on the individual. Perhaps a distinguished politicologist might consider the relation between this notion of maturity and the coming of authoritarian regimes, dictatorships of the right or the left, massive and authoritarian democracies, etc. But this gives rise to one or two other commonplaces that we will have occasion to examine later.

The other motive that tends to advance our commonplace is completely unconscious: the people must be adult if the whole theoretical foundation of modern democracy is to endure. If by some misfortune the people were not adult, this would mean that they were not capable of choosing their representatives or of deciding on great political problems by themselves. The whole political structure of our eminent specialists rests on this presupposition. If by some evil chance the people were still that child who is led by the nose, who obeys its instincts, its impulses, its emotions; if they were not capable of judging economic and political problems, avoiding the pitfalls of propaganda, and having a will of their own; then the noble edifice would collapse. Therefore, the people must be adult. They must be, and so we say that they are, and in this way we all justify certain subtle theories of our own that we are then free to advance!

MODERN MAN HAS COME OF AGE

No, I was wrong when I examined the preceding common-place. I made the mistake of indulging in sociological analysis and of concluding that majority is reached on the level of the group, the association, the class. Not at all! It is man himself, man as in his solitude we can consider him, who is adult, and who is therefore the foundation of the adult character of the people. Our authority for this is the theologian. As usual, the theologian flies to the aid of the politician. It is time to close ranks: man is coming of age. Until 1900 man walked on all fours, now he walks upright. What am I saying, upright? Since 1945 he even has little wings, he walks three inches off the ground.

What has happened, then, that the theologian discovers and proclaims man to be of age? Quite simply that modern man, at last, no longer believes in God. What, the theologian can be happy about this? Certainly. He has discovered what has always been the pagan belief, namely, the greatness of man; but it is only today that man is truly great. Up to now man has been overwhelmed by the weight of divinity. He had to answer to a father. This is the acid test! It is quite obvious that the child who answers to his father, who looks to him for everything, who relies on him and depends on him, is not of age. The child's majority can be recognized fully and clearly only when he turns his back on his father, secures his own food, makes his decisions without worrying about his progenitor, and follows his own desires and his own judgments—a perfectly clear and satisfactory criterion. It is simply a matter of transposition. This transposition may be the operation of an infantile mind, but what does that matter!

Down through the ages God had been regarded as the father, and men as his children. It is true that men expected a great deal of God, and that the attitude of faith and prayer was altogether immature; to kneel and join one's hands is certainly a mark of the shameful servility of the human species. The faith that was expressed in this way was immature, and the height of infantilism was Jesus. Now, at last, humanity has rid itself of its taboos. It no longer believes it has a father, there is no more God in heaven to turn to, man is turning his back on all this childishness, and *by this very act,* he is coming of age. Man has taken his destiny in hand, as it were, he knows what he is doing, like an adult, he knows that there is no more mystery, that he no longer needs someone greater than himself, he knows how to conduct himself in the world, he knows how to organize his society without reference to spiritual categories, he knows that he is his own master and that he makes his own history.

You will tell me that this is not very new, that for several hundred years this has been the attitude of atheists of all stripes, and without making any philosophical assumptions, this was the concrete and realistic attitude of the Romans as early as the second century B.C. But actually you don't understand at all: the new fact is that today the theologian maintains that it is right and proper that man come of age this way. As Father Gauthier de Nazareth says, "Atheism may be the necessary transition from the false religions to the true one." This is a commonplace very popular with theologians of all persuasions. This belief transforms everything, for now it is no longer a partisan matter (the atheist against the Christian); everyone being in agreement, the fact becomes the truth. Moreover, the theologian contributes the admirable rigor of his thought: modern man is adult because he has freed himself of divine tutelage; he has been able to do it through science. Therefore modern man is a man who lives according to science, a man "whose image of the world is determined by science." "He knows that he is responsible for himself." "He regards death as a perfectly natural phenomenon." "He no longer obeys those primitive conceptions of wrongdoing and justice." "He dismisses everything that is beyond the grasp of reason." "He no longer obeys a primitive idea of God." This is what the theologian writes approvingly. But he immediately interrupts, "You don't understand. We are simply noting the fact that man has become rational and scientific. And we are simply saying that Christians must grow up too, and must not *judge* the rational and scientific attitude in terms of their infantile faith. The fact is that man is this way; if as a Christian you want to speak to man, you must accept him as he is."

Very well. I had not understood, and I observe this adult man, and I see him on All Saints' Day taking part in a bizarre rite, a funereal orgy (whether he is a rationalist or a Christian, and maybe if he is a rationalist he enjoys it even more), and on the 11th of November, piously— "Oh, come now, don't split hairs; a few survivals from the past don't

change matters any." Very well. I agree. Let's look at the
present, the real present. Those passages I quoted were
written in Germany between 1942 and 1944. It is evident
that the German people, for the most part following the
inspired leader, torturing, screaming at the Munich Conference, were behaving like sentient and rational adults. And
it is quite accurate to say that they were free of the tutelage
of God, completely purged of outmoded beliefs. . . .

"But see here, don't talk about an accident, for that's all
it was." Even so, that the theologian could have written
that man was coming of age in the midst of the Nazi
madness causes me to doubt his statement. But I know
what you mean. Let's take the average Frenchman, who is
an adult with sober good sense, a rational attitude. The
popularity of the sweepstakes demonstrates abundantly, as
does the growing number of fortunetellers, magicians, and
mediums—four or five thousand in Paris—that he is quite
free of God, so that at last he can entrust his decisions to
Tarot cards, coffee grounds, and the astrological columns
constantly increasing in the newspapers. We are committed
to the scientific vision of the world.

"But don't you understand that you are bringing the
problem down to a ridiculous level? This absurd behavior
in no way changes the general truth that man has come of
age and that he has a scientific image of the world!" Oh, so
we are talking about Man with a capital M, in all his
dignity? You should have said before that you were talking
about an image, a generality, a symbol. Weren't you just
saying that the *fact* was there, that *men* had become this
way, and that it was in order not to cut himself off from
men that the Christian must accept their majority? But if
these ordinary men I was talking about do not interest you,
but only the ideal, the prototype of modern man, I am very
much afraid that this ideal exists only in your head, and

that what you are mistaking for reality is the invention of your brain, frightened at no longer being in touch with the times; unless you would consider yourself Man, you are confusing man in general with the theologian, and are expressing in these statements on adult man your current difficulty in believing in the Gospel.

Of course, the theologian is not so easily intimidated. He holds a radical argument in reserve: "Modern man is adult because he has the hydrogen bomb, and he can put an end to the history of mankind." What did I tell you? The theologians will never cease to surprise us. Not only does man freely make his history, but he can unmake it; the amplitude of his means promotes him to the highest responsibility.

Now that he can exterminate humanity, his responsibility is unprecedented, and responsibility is the outward sign of adulthood. The responsible person is adult; and the person who has such powerful means at his disposal must be responsible.

Extraordinary logic, in the name of which we should increase the means in order to increase the responsibility, and according to which the capacity to commit suicide or murder would be the mark of the adult. If wishing were enough, the thing would be self-evident! Because we have the H-bomb we must behave wisely! This is clear, but the theologian is more daring: because we have the H-bomb, man *has* become adult. All you have to do is place a live grenade in the hands of a six-year-old child and, lo and behold, he suddenly comes of age, grown up and reasonable, able to master his desire to make a big boom or to show that he is stronger than the others. According to the same view, all you have to do is give a girl a diaphragm in

order to render her adult and responsible and mistress of
her destiny.

To generalize, the more man increases his power over
himself and others, the more adult he is. An infantile attitude of irrepressible and irrational confidence in man, and
it must be so, for since the adult man who reasons as a
theologian no longer places his confidence in God, he has to
place it somewhere! Then they will tell you, "Look at the
positive side: the girl who has a diaphragm can choose to
be a mother when she wants to be; responsibility, choice,
transcendent beauty of planned, freely chosen mother-
hood!" Yes, let's look at the positive side! That is, above all
forget about the fact that now the girl will have no qualms
about sleeping with the first man who comes along, and
will change partners whenever she likes—freedom, sweet
freedom—for it goes without saying that it is in this dreary
round that the girl demonstrates her adult responsibility.

But this commonplace, which the theologian formulates
to save his function in a world that is desperately indifferent to theology, shows us how tight, how closely woven the
web of commonplaces is, how interrelated they are. That
the people are of age implies that man is of age; and if man
is of age, then we are all individuals. But the man who has
discovered that history has a thread and the people who
have full freedom to determine their own destiny must be
adult. As the whole edifice rises, the more we watch it
grow, the surer we must be of the plans of the architect and
the calculations of the engineer. If by chance the architect
were off by a hair or the engineer by a milligram . . . No,
let's not think about it; it can't be. Let us sing out our
confidence in chorus, let us shore up the structure with our
commonplaces. Faith is so strong, is it not? It prevents

accidents, and it even moves mountains . . . (Wait a minute; what have I said? Those are the words of a man who has not grown up yet!) What must reassure me in the face of so many uncertainties is precisely this systematic quality of the commonplaces. Proving one another reciprocally, they form a coherent whole that is perfectly satisfactory, provided the first one (but which is it?) is true.

YOU CAN'T MAKE
A PEOPLE REVOLT
AGAINST ITS WILL

This aphorism was revived recently at the time of the war
between India and Pakistan over Kashmir, when this incontestable truth made it possible to know who had started
it. But belief in such a great truth is not a purely modern
phenomenon; it is one of the unshakable foundations of the
thinking of Western politicologists. As a matter of fact, this
commonplace is directly engendered by the marriage of
the immortal right of peoples to self-determination and the
singular observation that modern man has come of age. It
follows from these apothegms with the merciless rigor of
stupidity.

But there is some question as to its true status as a
commonplace, for this idea remains typically liberal, and
only liberals can advance it in all circumstances (albeit
more or less forcefully according to the circumstances!).
But a Marxist-Leninist can only half believe or use it. For

him it is self-evident that the uprising of colonized peoples
is indeed the expression of the will of the people; but it is
just as self-evident that when the people of East Berlin in
1954, the Hungarian people, or the Tibetan people were
stirred to revolution, it was owing to the activities of traitors, saboteurs, spies, and others, and that if the good people of the United States have made war in Korea or on the
Vietcong, it was because they have been horribly deceived
and misled by a clique and because they do not know what
they are doing. For the Marxist-Leninists know very well
that a people is a delicate, extraordinarily complex entity,
and that it can be itself and express its will only under the
guidance of communist leaders. It is a liberal commonplace, then, and consequently not altogether common to
everyone; we will keep it, however, because of its aesthetic
value.

It has a very ancient foundation and might even be
called a myth, the myth of Revolution.

We all know, we have all read in school, that revolution
is the free act of a whole people which rises up and breaks
its chains. In the United States the revolution that liberated the colonists from the English oppressor shows clearly
that it was the American people who were expressing their
will. Let us not go into the nature of this people in 1775 or
the influence of the international situation. It is clear that
the principle of freedom was identified with the absence of
the right to levy taxes and that every last farmer in Massa-
chusetts was expressing his personal will by enlisting in the
militia. But this is a historic dogma, and it was in the
combined interests of many to pretend to believe in it.

Shortly afterward, the same phenomenon was repeated
in France with our great Revolution. Obviously this was

the act of the people in their totality, their spontaneity, and their ingenuousness, and nobody could be convinced to the contrary. The fact that sixty departments rose up against the revolutionary government, that traveling representatives were often put to death by the peasants, that the recalcitrant clergy was protected by the people, that the elections, when they could be held, had antigovernmental and sometimes monarchist results, that the celebrated volunteers of the mass uprising had to be led forcibly—all this, mind you, has no importance or significance. It was still the people in their freedom who made this revolution, and those who were hostile to it are henceforth categorized: either they were animals like the peasants, traitors like the bourgeois, or ideological slaves manipulated by the clergy. Everything that is left over (whatever that might be) is the people. At last the truth is established. The people, on their own authority and expressing their own will, made the French Revolution. We have been living on this truth for a hundred and fifty years.

But precisely because it is an unshakable certainty for the American people as well as for the French people, because nothing has ever contradicted this conviction that you can't lead the people around by the nose, it was not necessary to express it in a commonplace. The formula becomes indispensable and widespread only when the truth seems less certain and a few doubts begin to filter in. There had already been a black cloud: the Commune. It seemed to have been an expression of the people, but it was hard to swallow. The matter became more serious in 1917, and the liberal intellectual was greatly tempted to lose faith in the universality of this truth that you can't make a people revolt against its will. He began to make distinctions, and the Bolshevik with the knife between his teeth or the great mystery of the strategic organization of communism was just as useful as the Nazi sealed cattle car.

A difficult ideological equilibrium was established in the conscience of Western man; on the one hand, Nazism would resolve the crisis, for here it was obvious that a monstrous little clique had deceived the German people and held them in terror, and anyway the great excuse was that all this represented a *coup d'état* rather than a revolution. Revolutionary dignity was acknowledged neither in Germany nor in Italy, and the intellectual was confirmed, comforted, calmed, and justified by the Spanish Civil War. Here the matter was simple: there were the army and the people; the army was not the people, and the people were not the army. What happened in Spain was the defeat of the people by the army. What bliss! The doctrine became clear again, the spontaneity of the revolutionary people became obvious again, with the republicans, and henceforth it was possible to apply the pattern effectively to all situations.

This did not fail to occur, but everything began to get confused again with the African and Asian revolutions. What was clear, of course, was colonialist oppression, supported by the army and the fruit of conquest. The role of the army against the people was encountered again, but it did not appear altogether certain that it was the Cameroonian people or the Korean people who rose up with conscious revolutionary unanimity to shake off the oppressor's yoke. It was awkward to see these peoples become divided as soon as the oppressor was no longer there and slaughter each other; it was difficult to accept the validity of elections offered via eponymous symbols.

But the Western liberal intellectual made an effort. It was necessary to restore meaning in confusion and the famous classical light of the mind. A first principle was laid down: one was a democrat, everything for the people and by the people, nothing could dissuade us, it was axiomatic. If it were not so, then the West would collapse. Moreover, the noblest victory of man could not remain the prerogative of the West: the whole world must be able to profit by it, and in all the African and Asian revolutions, democracy had to prevail. For after all, it is obvious that when the oppressor has been driven out (*mea culpa,* we admit that we are this oppressor), the reign of the people begins. From 1948 to 1962 we heard the endless litany of this credo, borrowed from the revolutionary credo of 1793–4: after the king has been executed, freedom reigns.

And this brings us to the second principle: the intellectual in question is a liberal. It is inconceivable that a movement of national liberation not be the expression of the freedom of the people. Naturally these peoples are not all completely evolved, but nevertheless they are perfectly capable of understanding freedom and expressing their spontaneous wills. If you doubt the authenticity of this spontaneity, you bring on a crisis of conscience comparable to that of the believer when you prove to him the nonexistence of God. It is quite simply *not possible* for a people to be stirred to revolution artificially, and if Lenin spoke of an artificial uprising in connection with the very subject of colonized peoples, he must have made a slip of the tongue.

However—and the whole mechanism depends on this—you must be consistent. You can't say that when white peoples revolt they know what they are doing, while the others . . . Impossible! This is racism. Besides, an immortal principle must be universal, so you assume an offhand manner, as if the question did not even arise, and when confronted with any kind of popular uprising, you announce in a loud, clear voice, "Of course, you can't make a people revolt against its will." The obviousness of the commonplace allows you to pour contempt on anyone who is trying to understand and also causes the hearer to suspect anyone who does not share such a lofty certainty of latent fascism. For let's not forget that the more doubt-ridden the speaker, the more loudly the commonplace is proclaimed. Let's not forget that it is the fruit of a series of assumptions that are never challenged, that it implies on our part the attitude of two of the three monkeys who express Oriental wisdom: see no evil and hear no evil. Happily, though, the commonplace leaves us quite free to talk to our heart's content, so that we can maintain it more loudly than ever.

Thus we arrive at a credo: "We believe that the people, any people, are a single person; we believe that the people are always aware and never subject to influence; we believe that the people are possessed of a will that their understanding of the problems illuminates perfectly; we believe that the spokesmen of the people who revolt are merely their priests and not their dictators. In a revolution (a real one), each Lenin, Mao, Lumumba, Ho, or Castro is simply a Moses on a political Sinai listening piously and attentively to the great voice of the people rising from the earth, and what he writes and does is always at the dictation of this transcendentally immanent sovereign." Strong in this belief, we can read some surprising statements, that of King Sihanouk, for example: "Friendship and cooperation with a foreign power are possible only if they entail no diminution of the independence and sovereignty with which the Khmer people will not compromise." We are used to the sovereign who confuses himself with the people; it is no more ridiculous for the Khmer people than for the French people, but it is ridiculous just the same. The wonder is that we can read statements of this kind without laughing. And yet it is easily explained, for we are in the realm of faith, and this is the subject of a credo. The credo expresses a dogmatic position, which in turn implies the rejection of facts.

Since it is the people who decide, since every revolution is the act of the people, it is possible to declare that the authoritarian government is the most ineffective form of government, and to show that Hitler (who was defeated anyway) made many more errors than Stalin. A despotism *cannot* endure. It is a dogma. A despotism can only lead to errors, and the people necessarily rise up against it. Let us note parenthetically that this explanation is essential to our age of efficiency. To say that despotism is bad is to say nothing in an age that is totally indifferent to values and reverses them. If our opinion is to carry any weight we must speak only of efficiency. Despotism *must be* inefficient. As soon as the despot (who is obviously a freak) falls, things immediately improve: production increases, the standard of living rises, the citizen cooperates, and freedom coincides with efficiency. Since this still raises some little technical problems, we then see the great juggling of symbols expressed in other commonplaces (cf., "Freedom means obeying necessity").

You can't make a people revolt against its will; ergo, the domination of the people by a centralized party or their mobilization by private organizations like labor unions can be explained only if the party is the people themselves, as is claimed by both the Nazi Party and the Communist Party; or else if even in its minority the party expresses the fundamental reality, the authentic truth of the people, like the FLN or the Vietcong. Sieyès had already explained this to justify the difference between active citizens and passive citizens. Lenin had also demonstrated the necessity of distinguishing between the unorganized proletariat and the active proletariat. There is a will of the people that is *latent,* a will of which the people are not yet aware, which they cannot express, but which is nevertheless the will of the people. In this case the people have need of an interpreter, someone who understands their will better than they do themselves, someone who knows what the people unconsciously want, what they yearn for in perfect ignorance: this is the role of the party.

Of course, part of the duty of this party will be to convince the people that this really is their will. Obviously a child of six has no desire to learn to read, but even though he does not know it, it is his fundamental desire to learn. At first it is necessary to teach him what his true desire is beyond his incoherence, his inattention, his impulsiveness. A few smart taps of the ruler across his hands will make him understand. It is for your own good, my child. It is for your own good, my people; your real desire is to rise up, to make war, to commit yourselves. And if I force you to do it at sword's point, I am merely expressing your own true desire, of which you are unaware. Thus the Middle Ages baptized *en masse* Christians who did not know themselves, and the Führer, because he enjoyed a great ancestral communion with the people, expressed the underlying and unconscious will, the visceral impulse of the whole German people. Each of his decisions was the decision of the people, and in fact the German people did a pretty good job of marching in the indicated direction, thanks to the leadership of the party.

You can't make a people revolt against its will; ergo, psychological methods and propaganda are ineffective: if this were not so, all would be lost. The liberal democrat cannot bring himself to accept one of the most obvious and incontestable facts of our age, and he cannot accept it because of his credo. For if you could stir up the people by mere artifice and make them act independently of their own will, then the revolutions that have liberated oppressed peoples might begin to look like mere palace revolutions and the power struggles of clans. And what is far worse, elections would no longer mean anything, and consequently democracy would be very diseased. But this is not possible. Like the scholar Cosinus on his bicycle losing his balance and announcing, "According to my calculations, I should not fall," propaganda should not be effective.

But since we are serious intellectuals, we demonstrate. We cut the phenomenon into fine strips, which we study under the microscope. "Hey, you told me it was a mammoth, but all I can see are a few harmless-looking cells, and yet my microscope is certainly scientific." You catch the phenomenon and you put it away in the refrigerator. "Hey, you told me these were very active microbes, but I find them all frozen, immobile." You set the phenomenon in motion under conditions of perfect isolation, and at the starting signal, "Hey, you told me the subject was extremely restless, but it's hardly moving at all. . . . Come now, you were exaggerating. I have observed none of these alleged effects of propaganda."

"Whew! That's all over, no point prolonging the experiment. The will of the people is quite steady and not so easily influenced. Democracy can endure, and the future belongs to freedom."

Be careful, good liberal democrats, if it is really true that the German people as a whole were responsible for the Nazi revolution and what followed, that the Russian people wanted the massacres in the Ukraine, that the Algerian people were truly represented by the FLN in the tortures

and attacks, as were the French people in the tortures by
the right and the left from 1940 to 1944, that the anti-
communist uprising in Indonesia and the regime of terror
that was established were acts of the people; if it is really
true that the massacres in India and Pakistan were the
expression of the free will of those peoples, that the uprisings of the whites against the blacks, and vice versa, in the
United States are the act of all the people, then I have the
impression that only a few effective genocides would make
such voluntary uprisings worthwhile.

How lucky that this is only a commonplace, that when
the people revolt or make war, it is because their heads have
been filled with the idea for the necessary length of time.
How lucky that only a small minority of the people aspires
to enter the stage of history, and that the vast majority—
alas! always fair game for war and taxes—bend their backs,
wait for it to pass, take refuge in the intimacy of their
families or of their souls, and choose the lesser of two evils,
and take one step forward in the direction of the strongest
master.

POLITICS FIRST!

This idea is a commonplace among all the serious people of our society, although actually many of those who believe in it and carry it in their hearts repudiate it verbally and would deny their belief. Indeed, that belief is not always expressed by the crude statement of the commonplace in this form. But when faced with a given event, a given set of circumstances, or a given choice, we suddenly find to our great astonishment that perfectly normal men with whom the best relations were possible become silent and intransigeant and put obstacles in the way of further relations.

You do not understand this sudden rigidity. To you the discussion seemed unimportant, the disagreement minor; but the man you're talking to seems to regard it as a matter of life and death! Look no farther: a transformation of this kind may be explained by our commonplace. It was lying dormant in the back of his mind. It was not expressed, for an insurmountable obstacle confronts anyone who would be tempted to adopt it: *it was the slogan of* L'Action Française. This congenital taint prevents any sensible man from pronouncing these two words. And although the communists say exactly the same thing, they do not say it this way, they cannot say it this way! This does not prevent the truth expressed by the phrase from being the same.

As I said, this commonplace lies dormant at the bottom of the heart until suddenly a certain turn of events arouses it. But it will not be expressed in its synthetic and general form. It will be embodied in a second formula that is dependent upon previous belief in "Politics first." So don't be surprised that this commonplace is so infrequently heard in this form, and that you find it on so few lips. But I invite you to try a very simple little game, excellent in society, which consists in perceiving the inevitable reflex conditioned by the concealed commonplace behind the considered opinions of your guests.

A commonplace of serious people, this slogan makes it possible to distinguish accurately the people who think from the intellectual dilettantes, the people who have civic consciences from the irresponsibles, the people who have a sense of national solidarity from the contemptible individualists. We have taken enough from these people who refuse to vote in elections, these readers of Pascal, bowlers, anglers, and other admirers of Rimbaud! If politics goes badly, everything goes badly, and if everything goes badly, who is at fault? Obviously, those who are not interested in it and do not participate in it; those who do not devote their strength and intelligence to it, those who do not stand up and defy the parachutists of Algiers with their bare chests, those who do not dedicate themselves to the public welfare, those who give a free rein to the politicians, those who have renounced their sovereignty; in short, those who prefer their own selfish peace and quiet to the noise of the great political arena where the destiny of men is decided.

Much good it will do them to come and complain afterward! Taxes are increasing? The war goes on? Prices are rising but wages are not? Production is disorganized? The police reign everywhere? What are you complaining about? You only have what you deserve. This is the inevitable result of the absence of civic virtue. If you had carefully read the newspapers, participated in all the elections, signed all the manifestos, followed all the speeches and demonstrations, talked with all your neighbors, spread the right ideas on the bus and combatted the evil adversaries of these ideas, then *everything* would have been different. Of course, if you had devoted yourself to all this vital political activity, your children might not have been brought up; your wife, tired of waiting for you, would probably have deceived you; your work would have suffered; your health, taxed by such lofty concerns and a nervous tension that kept you running back and forth between the radio and the telephone, would have been delicate. But civic virtue would have triumphed and popular sovereignty would finally have achieved its full and definitive expression.

And does not man's fate depend on politics? But what does politics depend on? This is the crux of the matter! On the unanimous will of men? (It is certainly on this idea that the commonplace "Politics first" is based.) But then why bother with politics? The will of men guides men: an absurd truism.

On the power with which the leader is invested? But then why should I worry? What can I do about it?

On the state of economic development? But the person who sees economics as the basis of everything is arguing

backward when he states that the only revolution is political and in subscribing to the idea "Politics first."

On the social structure, on the inexorable forces of technology? But here again, what can I do about it? Alas, as
soon as you begin to think about politics at all, your mind
stops dead, wanders over paths more tangled than the cord
of Samivel, and never succeeds either in justifying the
primacy of politics or even in finding a reason for its existence. I strongly suspect this commonplace, so profoundly
entrenched and so skillfully camouflaged, of being no more
than incantatory magic, rune, sibylline oracle to assure the
speaker of the control of forces and to attribute a meaning
to them. We must find some way to compensate for our
obvious helplessness! We must eliminate our inability to
understand by pretending to understand! We must shake
off our sense of dependence on some mysterious game by
entering into the game itself! It's a magic that exploits
man's capacity for emotion as the myths of war and love
once did. Now the searchlight has shifted. The great myths
are political, but still rest on the profound drives of name-
less forces. And like all magic, it is ambivalent; but does not
he who practices it realize that by the very fact that he
believes in the commonplace, publishes his faith in politics,
and assigns it the place of honor, he is reinforcing the
implacability of his destiny, increasing the strength of politics with his own strength and nourishing it with his own
blood?

Madame does not want to take part in politics!

But come now, after all, politics is the principal activity
of the nation. Everyone must take part in politics. The
highest interests . . . justice . . . peace . . . Besides, de-

mocracy requires that women take part in politics. Democracy means the will of the people. The will of women is part of this will, therefore they must take part in politics, whether they want to or not. And if 90 per cent of women are not interested in politics, we will simply force them to be. They don't realize it, but we are doing it for their own good. Their hidden will must be formed, educated.

"So it is just when you men are ceasing to believe in it, when the disastrous experiences of democracy and the horrifying experiences of the Russian and German dictatorships show the absurdity of the political game, that you want to throw us into it and ask us to believe in it."

You have no right to talk this way about democracy (the republican will say) or about the proletariat (the communist will say). You must be interested in politics: politics is the flower of our whole civilization. Besides, what prevents you from being interested in it is a stupid tradition, a tissue of insignificance: taking care of children and all those other feminine pursuits. We are going to free you from all that!

Down with homes; up with the hotel, the furnished apartment, the drugstore! Down with traditions; down with differences between the sexes; down with history; down with biology; down with love! Make way for the giant leveler! You have to have it to make a democracy or a dictatorship. At last the land is clear, the trees uprooted, the stumps and boulders that you mistook for the foundation of the world removed; all you need is a bulldozer. Everything is flat; on to the mangler! The good woman and the good man have already been through it. Reduced to the thickness of a sheet of paper, well pumped, drained, and hung out to dry, at last Madame will take part in politics, at last she will be interested in important things, at last she will vote; and why shouldn't she? There is nothing left of her life; her life has become a state of abstraction.

Thin as a sheet of paper—a ballot—on which she can write anything at all.

At last the Africans have entered history: they are taking part in politics.

The meaning of the revolt of the Negroes in Africa and of the Arabs in Algeria is the conquest of their dignity. Of course nothing could be easier to understand, provided you start by believing in "Politics first." Consider this Berber whom I meet, with his calm bearing, his royal manner, his confident gaze that takes my measure and puts me in my place, and, under the jellaba, which may be torn, the dagger attesting to his status of free man, who walks at the head of his flock over paths which only he knows. Of course, he has no dignity, has he? He is obviously deprived of this quality, is he not, by the fact that somewhere far away there exists a foreign administration that rules over offices and makes statistics? This Fezzani whom I pass in these secret alleys whose doors cut the universe into two halves, the public one of no importance dedicated to the dazzling sun, a dusty and mortal façade, and the private one where all life is closed in, where human dignity finds its last resort, where authenticity is discovered; this Fezzani has no dignity, has he? [1] When I myself feel completely at a loss before him and when in a second he has been able to establish the distance that separates us, and indicate both by his politeness and by his remoteness that I remain on the outside, in the street, that I belong to that public domain of no importance?

Strange idea, to consider that the dignity of man de-

---

[1] Naturally, I am not saying here that every Barber or Fezzan has this dignity, but only that dignity is independent of the political or economic situation, that it operates on another level.

pends on some political manifestation, on some political power like the power to vote, or even on driving out the foreigner or the invader. Dignity depends on life itself, on who I am. It is a quality of being; nothing can take it away from me if I have it, and nothing can give it to me if I do not. The presence of the enemy, the white man, the colonizer does not take away the dignity of the free man any more than prison or poverty does, when the man is a man. This dignity is not given to him by some political privilege but by a spiritual gift, by the slow and difficult formation of the character in the course of a given life, by a discipline that is also experienced in the family, by the heritage of a long, slow culture. Granted, the free and dignified colonized man will feel the weight of the insult inflicted by a stupid or drunken Frenchman who forces him to step off the sidewalk or to wait on him. Granted, the free and dignified man will be filled with hatred for the conqueror and the denier of the values in which he believes. But this is in no way a political matter; to drive out the colonizer or conqueror becomes a visceral matter, and does not involve any intrinsic virtue or benefit. This is not an act of justice: it is the expression of wounded dignity.

But today, from the outset, and precisely because the whites are mixed up in it, and because, alas, the colonized peoples have been perverted, the matter *is* political, it can no longer be otherwise. So dignity becomes an excuse; and the man without dignity, the man who has allowed himself to be corrupted, who has been corrupted, whether by the white man's ideology, his technology, or his morals, corrupted because he was already vile to begin with, ready to be degraded, without dignity, without nobility—this man thinks that by entering into the political game he will recover his virginity and become a man of dignity! Because the French will no longer be here, because we have won a

victory, because we will govern ourselves, because we will
be invested with sovereignty, therefore we will recover our
dignity! [2]

A strange conception of dignity, a strange place to locate
it! A dignity that does not depend on the person but is
received from the outside, like a garment that you put on or
take off; a dignity for show, a dignity shown in the street
but left at the door, a parody of dignity. And from us the
colonized peoples have learned to mouth empty words and
to play with political illusions; they are just as corrupt and
just as corrupting without us as they were with us. National
honor replaces personal dignity, according to the best
Western jargon, and at the time of the war between India
and China we heard this admirable statement: "And it has
only been eighteen years that we have enjoyed independence! Why couldn't we just once be allowed to fight to
defend the national honor?" Honor and dignity depend on
war. Politics first!

I only hope that the intangible personal dignity of that
Berber and that Fezzani will resist the tide of illusory
political dignity that is going to wash over him as well as it
resisted our contempt.

The Arab fights against us for his freedom. This commonplace, whose subject could be any people at all, is
similar to the preceding one and is also based on the commonplace "Politics first." Everything hinges on the confu-

---

[2] A man who is in no way suspect, Mr. Bechir Zahra, who fought for
the independence of Tunisia and has an important position there, stated in
October 1965 that since the independence there had occurred "a deteri-
oration of morals that is proceeding with a rapidity that makes us fear for
the future of the individual, the family, and the whole society." He observes a dissolution of morals in Tunisia the like of which had never been
seen before. Blessed independence!

sion between freedom and independence. Let us say that the Arab fights for the political independence of his collectivity. I have no comment to make, I am simply recording a fact: the mischief begins when you start slipping the word freedom in here and there. Then the matter becomes serious, for this is a flagrant misuse of language that is not terribly important in itself, but that expresses a hypocrisy and contempt for man, which are intolerable. To tell a man that he is not free because his land belongs to a foreigner, to tell a man that he is not free because he does not have the right to vote, to tell a man that he is not free because his nation does not enjoy international sovereignty and because he does not have a national army, is to have a conception of freedom so empty, so insolently childish, so unreal and artificial that one is at a loss to understand how he could be taken in by it.

What's this? I can come and go as I like, carry on the customs of my fathers, live off my flocks, have the space to lead a life that is undoubtedly hard but that has no other rules than those of my traditions and of nature, and I am not free because there are military posts here and there? On the other hand, now that my country is becoming independent and the tyrants have been driven out, what does this mean for me? First of all, compulsory military service for all, which will weigh more heavily now that it is my country and my government that must be defended. Freedom means military service! Next, taxes a hundred times higher than before. When there was no government, there were no expenses. When the administration came from the outside, we did not pay much for it; now we must pay for everything ourselves! Freedom means taxes! And since now we must produce *everything* by and for ourselves, like any independent nation, we must modernize, that is, put all our forces to work: no more siestas, no more wandering in the mountains, no more wasted time. Time is money and a national resource: to work! Now that we no longer work for an employer, but for that nation, freedom means work! And since we will have to show that we are a nation worthy of independence, we must have order, we must have scrupulous obedience, we must have an organization (for nothing must be lost!) the like of which the tyrant never achieved: above all else, we must have a police force. Freedom means police!

As for the form of government, the progress of democracy in the independent countries of Africa and Asia may be observed every day. Let us not speak of the dictatorships established from the beginning. But in 1964 one could observe with delight that Mr. Maga had concentrated all the power in his own hands in Dahomey and that Mr. Houphouët-Boigny had finally eliminated the remaining opponents to his government. In 1965 the good parliamentary democracy of Nigeria was transformed into a presidency (to use a nice word) by sentencing the leader of the opposition in the parliament to hard labor. And the last opposition press in all of black Africa was thereby silenced. As for the others, the people of Cuba and elsewhere, they have known the joys of freedom through political independence for a long time. The fact is that, through the miracle of politics, dictatorship means freedom!

As a matter of fact, you can establish a theorem that *in the world today,* national independence means the suppression of personal freedom! (However, the converse is not necessarily true! I am certainly not saying that national alienation assures personal freedom: I am only saying that there is no necessary connection.) But we are so dominated by the commonplace "Politics first" that we attach no value to a freedom that is not political. We cannot conceive that a real and not merely a mystical freedom could have existed under an authoritarian regime (the average Frenchman was much freer in 1685 than in 1950!), and we regard the meaningless formulas of popular sovereignty and national independence as substantial realities. So totally have we lost the sense of human freedom that we experience it secondhand. We hide our loss from ourselves by announcing with our eyes popping, "Politics first," hoping in the apocalypse of the political future to recover a freedom that we would not be expected to experience or to win because it would be handed out by a providential administration that placed automatic dispensers of chewing gum and freedom at every street corner.

After dignity and freedom, there are many other examples of these untruths based on "Politics first." Thus "The greatness of the nation means the greatness of its citizens" or "Every man is dishonored when dishonor strikes his country," or "The wealth of the nation is the wealth of everyone." None of these statements is verified by reality, none of them corresponds to actual reality, but we believe them simply because we live by this good commonplace of the primacy of politics. The movement can be accelerated. M. Jean Vilar, the great authority on culture, announced in January 1965, "Culture is politics." Anything goes: making love is politics; swimming is politics; driving a car is politics; "Politics takes precedence over science." But this is not a joke: it appeared in *Le Drapeau rouge* as a New Year's greeting for 1966. And at just about the same time it was announced in Peking, "The best weapon is not the atom bomb, but the political thought of Mao Tse-tung." Madness is upon us.

What presumption to assume that before the invasion by politics there was nothing but oppression, contempt for

man, and exploitation! I say that when in Rome a condemned man received the weapons of his death and was
left alone to kill himself, it showed greater respect for man
than our juries, our codes, our lawyers, and our guillotines.
I say that when in Japan hara-kiri constituted evidence of
the injustice suffered and an appeal for vengeance upon the
designated culprit, there was a greater sense of honor, a
greater belief in values, than are found in all the pro-
nouncements of our moralists. What, in comparison with
these things, are the formulas of our professors of political-
ized virtue and our parliamentary journalists? I am not
saying that I *approve* of these actions, I am saying that
they attest to a human nobility that no political reiteration
will ever produce.

And Christians, too, although they seemed unlikely to
fall into this way of thinking, have not, in fact, resisted it.
One need only consider the great preoccupation of the
churches today. Are they interested in better understanding and formulating the truth? In converting men to Jesus
Christ? In discovering ways in which a Christian can live
by his faith? These are merely minor preoccupations. The
great thing is to know what political position to support, for
the church to prove it is a political force, to formulate a
message to the world on its political problems. Until the
church has stated its position on decolonization or Berlin, it
has said nothing. And the tendency is the same in the
Roman church and the Protestant churches and at the
Ecumenical Council. We know that the church must live in
the world, but the Christian (not the average Christian,
alas, but the aware, thinking, and responsible Christian)
knows only one world, politics, and sees only one way of
living in it, to engage passionately in politics. Everything

else, everything that really constitutes the life of man and
of which politics is the mere reflection, superstructure,
epiphenomenon—everything else is regarded as worthless
by the Christians themselves.

We know that faith without works is dead, that faith
must be incarnated. But for Christians this incarnation has
only one form and one face: political commitment. And it
does no good to say that Christ never chose to enter this
realm any more than his apostles did; this does not matter
(any more than any reasonable argument matters in the
presence of the commonplace). The *rabies politica* has
infected the best among the Christians so gravely that for
them the incarnation has become identical with political
commitment, and all judgments passed are now political
judgments. The cat-o'-nine-tails with which these Christians constantly flay the church is "The church did nothing,
the church is doing nothing." For this read: The moment
the church ceases to influence politics directly, the moment
it ceases to be in permanent relation to the state, it does
nothing. All judgments passed on the church in the nineteenth or twentieth century are political judgments—and in
the preceding centuries too, for that matter! The church
did not establish democracy. The church did not prevent
war. The church did not oppose colonial conquest. The
church did not denounce fascism, etc. Thus the value of the
church is measured by its capacity for political judgment.
For non-Christians to think this way is understandable—
but Christians! The mind boggles. And the Protestants are
forever glorifying themselves: once the church was the
church, at the Synod of Barmen that condemned Nazism
and anti-Semitism; *there,* the Truth was spoken. I wish that
this had been the work of the Holy Ghost.

But I believe that if the church were not under the spell
of this commonplace, it would recognize it elsewhere too.

It is not only the church that is measured in terms of its political commitment; judgments passed on people are also of a political order. I heard a typical Christian say, "You can't be a Christian if you don't have a certain position on the Algerian problem." I was dumbfounded! Thus one's political opinion on such a difficult question, characterized by such fluctuating information and criteria for judgment (one must also take into account individual capacities and knowledge), becomes the criterion for the authenticity of one's faith! This is nothing short of grotesque. Nevertheless it is quite true: personal virtues do not count. A just and upright life, the attempt to live by one's faith in one's milieu, do not count. You are told, "This does not keep you from being a member of the bourgeois, and therefore exploiting, class. Your virtues are nothing, because you are one of the oppressors of the proletariat"—even if you personally have nothing to do with it; or again, "A Christian life conceived in this way, being individualist, has no value. All that counts is to participate in the movement of history and of society: in other words, in politics." And it takes more than a few passages from the Bible on the exploitation of the poor or the history of the nations to give a semblance of truth to what is merely obedience to the most pernicious commonplace of the age.

However that may be, the *rabies politica* is so virulent that it is resulting in a devaluation of theology. Christians previously divided among themselves by theology are coming together, at last theological problems are disappearing, theological opinions are becoming academic, and differences are dwindling. And everybody is singing, "*Alleluia!* See how much smarter we are than our ancestors! They split the church, but we have put it back together again. We understand the truth much better than they do and we live much more in peace. *Alleluia!*"

But we carefully avoid asking ourselves whether, by chance, this might simply be a result of the most benighted indifference to the formulation of the truth. We carefully avoid asking ourselves whether, by chance, it might simply be a result of a tendency peculiar to this age. Theological problems no longer interest anyone, so why should we argue about them any more? And we even more carefully avoid asking ourselves whether, by chance, there might not be other divisions in the church, in preparation or already existing. If you throw the Suez question or the problem of Algeria in 1959 before a congregation of Christians, you will see them tear each other to pieces like dogs over a bone.

Nobody gets excited about the divinity of Jesus Christ, but as for Algeria, now there's a real question. The churches are united over and above their theological divisions, of course, but if you raise the problem of communism or merely the problem of peace, you will get a massive condemnation formulated by the churches of the East (naturally united among themselves on this common foundation!) against those abominable churches that are the servants of capitalism, colonialism, and exploitation (thus the Vienna Conference in 1961), and vice versa.

The question of salvation by grace is no longer important, of course, but the question of the church's position on political peace is essential. Churches are really united by political agreement and are increasingly divided by varying political decisions. You often hear people boast that we have now reached the post-Constantinian age, but, alas, it has brought us not to the age of freedom, but to that of the politicalization of the church. After the period of independence came that of liaison between church and state, but the church remained itself (sometimes under the control of the state but usually claiming that the state should

be under its control). At the present time the risk is greater
still: this third period threatens to be that of the triumphal
entry of the political virus *into* the church. Truth is becoming political. Morality must be political. Faith is expressed
in terms of politics. The man who formulated this illumi-
nating revelation would make a good Christian: "When
you grant priority to politics, actions and people become
good. When you do not, people and their acts become
bad." Unfortunately, it was only Marshal Lin Piao.

Worthy men, racing after the truths of the world; and
you are amazed, O Christians, that men do not listen to
you?

But this solemn judgment "Politics first" is by no means
the expression of a choice, a mature consideration, a conscious will. It is not by applying a sound scale of values that
one arrives at this formula. It is not the free decision of the
man who is aware of his responsibilities that gives rise to
this utterance. It is pure obedience to fact. The phenomenon of the state is constantly growing in our world. This is
obviously not the place to describe the how and why of this
growth. The state is expanding in and by its resources. The
state is expanding its prerogatives and its provinces. The
state is expanding its authority and its powers. The state
dictates the total life of man and judges truth; it is taking
over all functions. It penetrates to the inner recesses of our
hearts by psychological influence even as it defines what is
right. And this has not come about as the result of a deliberate choice on the part of man, but by a blind and
systematic growth, an internal necessity of power and an
external necessity coming from the society as a whole. We
have arrived at the realm of pure fact. And fact being what
it is, we have no choice but to live with it. The common-

place in question is nothing but man's acceptance of the *de facto* invasion of all realms by the state. It is always necessary to occupy the front of the stage. The tank of the state advances, running down everything in its path, and gravely the little ham actor struts about, saying, "I did it on purpose; it was my idea, Politics first."

O miles gloriosus! The state controls the economy: of course! Politics first, the state was right. The state is taking over education and welfare, is developing police methods or methods of psychological influence: "But this is exactly what we wanted: Politics first." And in 1965, after a thousand others, Premier Pflimlin declares that it is the state that combats tyranny and guarantees the rights of man. Everyone can observe this every day. And when the state provides us (at last!) with absolute truth, with doctrine, and demonstrates the total confusion between its decisions and justice, between its intentions and the right, then madness is upon us: Politics first.

This acceptance of the status quo rests on the increasingly obvious impossibility of man's living by himself! Amid the terrifying complexity of the modern world we need a godfather, we need a support, we need a protection and a mold. In the face of the insoluble problems to which the news media are constantly exposing us, we must have a great leader, we must have a strong power. The individual can experience only his own helplessness, he can verify only his own incompetence and weakness. But where can he turn? God is dead. He must be replaced! Only a creature invested with superhuman powers, a multiple will, and an intelligence born of several brains can give us enough confidence: the state! For the state is us; and conversely—at last I can surrender to the mystical delirium—I am the state. At last the problems are solved (and by me!), at last there is power in action in the world (and through me!), at last what was impossible for me has become a reality through the intermediary of politics.

Under the circumstances, how could I fail to say "Politics first," especially since it is possible for me to extend this idea? And because the state solves these difficulties, it will solve others, always more numerous, always vaster and more profound. Miraculously, this points to a hope, a real hope this time, a tangible one. Solve the political problem and *all* human problems will be solved. Unassailable logic, perfect consistency. Since the state is gradually taking over all activities and all organs of society, it is quite true that it has the answer for everything. And suppose I *also* solved my personal problems? Suppose by chance the political solution could succeed in making me just, good, virtuous? Suppose temptations and evil disappeared by the grace of the state? We have just reached the point where this question is answered in the affirmative. The moment has come when man will finally be rid of himself, thanks to the benevolence of the state. How could we fail to sing in chorus the hymn that begins with the words "Politics first"?

FROM PERSONAL DEMOCRACY TO ORGANIZED (OR MASS) DEMOCRACY

"You can say what you like," says God, "This democracy is very badly organized, it works very badly. It is not at all what we had in mind. Everybody says what he thinks, everybody claims he has a right to do whatever he likes, everybody is pulling a different way. The citizen believed, really believed, that everything belonged to him: the power and the idea and the controls and the initiative. What a mistake! But we are going to change all that, and out of all this evil we are going to create a greater good, as we alone know how to do."

It is true that we became involved in inconceivable errors, errors that lasted—think of it!—throughout the Revolution and through almost all of the Third Republic. Of course, we are for the republic, one hundred per cent, and for democracy, two hundred per cent. Everything for the people and by the people: that's our motto. But you have to know what you're talking about. And in the beginning we obviously did not know what we were talking about! Just look at this democracy that was founded on the individual! The solitary One! The idea was that the individual contained the whole national will, that he was capable of thinking everything and knowing everything, and that it was his will that decided everything. You must admit you have to be rather simpleminded to have such an idea of the good man. And the greater his personal solitude, the better the system was supposed to work. He was the "political monad," and from a few million monads a single will was supposed to emerge. How did you expect that to happen? There were no two men who wanted the same thing! And as soon as a minority formed, it was so convinced that it represented the true national will that everything was paralyzed!

And then, say what you will, you must admit that this monad citizen had no competence, no clear will, no comprehension of the problems. Why ask him what he thinks? He did not think anything. But alas! This did not mean that he did not want anything. He wanted—oh how much!—to protect his little private interests and to get as much as he could from the state. This individual saw everything through the wrong end of a telescope. He was incapable of rising above himself, taking the long view, considering the general interest, the national interest, and so forth. Not to mention that the public powers could not get their bearings amid so many tendencies, claims, and interests: nobody agreed with anybody. How to choose? According to the majority? But the majority changed constantly. Imagine, everything depended on opinion, and is there anything

more fragile, more inconstant than opinion? Anything more
deceptive? Quite obviously, it was impossible to govern,
administer, or organize under these conditions. The whole
trouble comes from the individual. That awful egoist, that
incompetent, that corrupter, that bald, mangy character,
the awful donkey who ate the little meadow: that is the
individual. It is primarily his fault if democracy has still
never really worked!

Fortunately we are going to change everything, and
quickly. That is, we . . . Well, *things* are going to change.
But for the better, as they should. The individual is stran-
gled, cut up, rolled flat, smoked, packed like a sardine,
sealed and forwarded collectively to a Dachau, a *sovkhoze,*
a dynamic group, a paratroop squadron, a professional
group. He must learn, *volens nolens* (especially *nolens,* but
what does it matter? it's his own fault), what is meant by
solidarity and the community. He must lose the bad habits
of the stubborn, backward bourgeois. And events help considerably to further this moral and instructive work. The
increasing density of the population; "human relations";
the collectivization of the environment, working methods,
leisure, and transportation; social security and the necessity
of forming groups to protect one's interests; technical education and educational techniques; military service and the
morality of commitment: yes, everything contributes to the
progress of democracy. For let's not kid ourselves: only
when the individual is suppressed can democracy triumph
at last! Let us admire the way the necessary course of blind
circumstances produces progress, the good, and the right!
Let us admire and give thanks to providence if we are
Christians (with a bad theology, true, but what's the difference!), or to the laws of history if we are Marxists, or to the
greatness of man, who blindly but infallibly chooses the
best, if we are secular humanists (it goes without saying

that Man has nothing to do with that pig the individual).
Thanks to this happy evolution, democracy is arriving at its
highest and most advanced stage. It is becoming organized
democracy for some, mass democracy for others. At last,
and for the first time in history, we are going to show what
is meant by *true* democracy!

   Let's be reasonable. To represent opinions, real, stable,
important opinions, you must have groups. And what a
convenience it is for the state if instead of having to deal
with an anonymous dust, a sand that disintegrates under-
foot, it can address itself to groups. If the nation is made up
of societies, associations, parties, or groups, in which the
individuals are *all* incorporated, *all* represented, then it
becomes possible to construct something. "To shape this
individualist sand into blocks of sandstone or cement: this
is the future"; Napoleon had already said it explicitly. (Oh,
excuse me, I didn't mean to mention an embarrassing an-
cestor; please overlook it.) Then it becomes possible to do
something with the individual. Consider, for example, the
fine discipline, the order, and the clear expression of opinion that prevail in so many of these spontaneous, active
groups that already exist. When a political event occurs, or
an international explosion or a national trial, at once you
see this organized crowd go into action. Four abreast they
march by, in perfect formation. The leader came to see you
the night before, let you know you would lose your job if
you didn't march, and sure enough, virtue has triumphed.
You march! And spontaneously you are going to break the
windows of the Belgian embassy because of some stranger
or demonstrate in front of the Berlin Wall, and spontaneously you cheer and boo—after a well-learned lesson.
   Just look at the wonderful discipline promoted by the

unions—let's say the teacher's union. A teacher doesn't
want to join? Fine, he'll spend the rest of his life in some
little hole in Brittany. What else could you expect from such
an awful individualist? He must pay the price for thinking
only of himself and cutting himself off from his comrades.
Does a teacher fail to accept the union's slogans, its recom-
mendations to vote or strike; does he refuse to take part in
a demonstration? Very good, he is observed. From now on
he will be barred from all advancement, he will never
become a principal, he will not be supported if he gets in
trouble, and if he gets demoted, he will get only what he
deserves! For the secondary-school inspector bows before
the union.

At last we are arriving at something a little coherent, a
little unanimous, a little solid. How else would you have a
democracy function? How fortunate that there are a few
dedicated men—the secretaries of the unions, for example—who make it function this way; otherwise everything
would go to the devil, everything would be disorganized
and above all ineffective! For after all, if teachers have all
the social prestige and the high salaries that we know they
have, who do they have to thank for their privileged position in the nation? The good and dedicated secretaries of
unions! Is it any wonder that such masses of young people
are rushing into this profession? Weren't we just saying
that the *true* interests of the individual are protected only
by the association? At last, thanks to the group, individuals
are *truly* represented!

They are so well represented, in fact, that it is not always
worth the trouble to get their opinions. Here again, the
self-sacrifice and dedication of the group secretaries is
given full play. Say a vital political event occurs, an event
about which a position must be taken at once (and we
know how important speed is in the present political

world). What would happen if we were still at the backward stage of individualist democracy? *Nothing!* The individual would not move. Nobody would take the initiative, and all would be lost. Whereas now, look at the admirable machine! The secretaries of the associations meet at once. Sometimes the Paris secretary meets all by himself and draws up a vigorous motion clearly expressing the obvious and unanimous opinion of his troops, who have not been consulted at all. Then he sends it to the press, which immediately publishes the statement of the X association or the Z group, agreed upon unanimously (except that 49 per cent or even 75 per cent of the members disagree with the text, but no matter, the text is approved, and the meeting to elect new officers is still a long way off, there's still plenty of time to manipulate the representations). And thanks to this ingenious democratic system, opinion is arrived at *by the next day!* In this way you see a good thousand motions crop up that, at every turn of events, express and form opinion. (The opinion of the nation? At any rate, of the four or five hundred individuals who "represent" the most active associations and groups!)

To tell the truth, even with this marvelous edifice the government is still sometimes troubled, for unity is still not achieved. There are still some troublemakers who do not fully realize that in union there is strength. Instead of a purely rational system in which each profession is represented by a single, compulsory group, each body has only one group of representatives, and each activity only one set of officers, splits and divisions still occur. Thus in many fields there are several unions (scandalous!), just as there are several political parties. An aberration of this kind is hard to understand.

How fortunate that we have developed the ingenious idea of the most representative group. We still have the problem of choosing it. Here the criteria are a bit vague. Size? This seems obvious and simple. But alas, in many groups the dead still vote and persons who have resigned are still on the register; the one that distributes the most cards does not always have the most members. It is difficult. Sometimes the issue is clear: of two groups, one is in agreement with the government, the other opposed; it is obvious that the first is the more representative of the two. Otherwise how could democracy function? I ask you! Sometimes circumstances themselves point to the most representative group or party. Thus in Algeria, how was one to choose between the FLN and the MNA? It was absolutely impossible to count the members. Fortunately, everything went off very well: the more representative side was the one that committed the most acts of aggression, victimized the most people, and spread the most propaganda. This is how Tito's party succeeded in winning out over Mikhailovich's party in 1944. Here, however, there were a few difficulties, the second being five or six times larger than the first; but these were settled rather quickly: the execution of Mikhailovich made Tito's party the more representative and democratic.

This good example is a fitting introduction to mass democracy, which is the ultimate and supreme stage, the last word in democratic progress. For example, in an article in *Esprit* in 1946, M. Lacroix invited us to a democracy of unanimous and centripetal conviction. Up to now democracy has depended on a mass of divergent opinions that were expressed in diverse and even contradictory ways. This was its whole weakness and its failure. Now, thanks to organization, we are gradually arriving at a democracy of consent. Everything must be subjected to the same stand

and the expression of the democracy will take univocal forms. It is even necessary to go beyond forms, according to M. Lacroix. It is no longer enough to count voices, to express opinions; a communion must be created. Thus the forms of democracy become rites and liturgies. A single heart, a single voice: such is the truth of progressive democracy.

After all, why should it be necessary for the people to be divided? Why should there be different opinions? Why? No reason at all! And this is also why it is scandalous that there is more than one school. The free-school system *divides* French youth. How do you expect democracy to last if people are divided from the outset because they have received different instruction, different education? We must be logical! Only a single united body of young people receiving unilateral training can lead to a progressive mass democracy. What is more, this body of young people should not be allowed to splinter off into a hundred groups of all tendencies. We must be logical: the single school presupposes and helps to maintain a single association of young people. And since we know very well, alas, all the ominous antidemocratic, anticommunal tendencies that lurk in families, membership in the single association of young people should be compulsory. This training would assure us of having the right kind of citizens tomorrow. For this democracy must be a democracy of participation.

Away with that ridiculous method of constructing the society, the state, the economy in terms of individual activity, everyone adding his little stone to the edifice. We know only too well what that produces: a wobbly and unaesthetic structure, a democracy, in short, in which you never know exactly where you are! Instead of this, we have before us a prefabricated society, a finished and perfect whole, and the citizen has only to step into it; he is spared

all trouble and all exertion. He has only to participate; his
life, his thought, his gestures are merely the expression of
the single democratic phenomenon, and his individuality is
integrated into the social body as harmoniously as possible.
And in 1953 M. Lacroix continues in *Esprit,* carrying the
portrait of the perfect democracy one step further: "The
liberal society ignores the leaders as much as it does the
masses. Parliamentary government does not have leaders,
but deputies, that is, representatives. The leaderless mass is
abandoned to disorderly and anarchic reactions that never
come to anything and make it more and more vulnerable to
the power of the exploiting class. But the leader who is not
content to express the needs of the mass and loses contact
with it isolates himself in his own purely subjective conceptions and infallibly becomes a revolutionary and a renegade."

Thus the future of democracy is clear.

The united mass, welded into a unit without a crack or
divergence; and, to speak for this mass and guide it, what?
A representative? Oh, no! A leader who will maintain contact with the mass and express its inclinations. How will he
know them? By a vote? By a referendum? You're way off!
Those are individualistic, backward methods. The leader
knows the inclinations of the mass because he is in profound communion with it, because his thought is always
oriented by it, because, like a prophet, he receives impulses
and vibrations directly from the mass as a whole. And the
leader depends upon this communion, which is the source
of his authority, and the mass listens to him because he is
its exact reflection.[1] So democracy is reaching its comple-
tion. Through the alchemistic gropings of past ages we

---

[1] A few years ago in another country this doctrine was given a convenient name that it may not be without purpose to recall here: *"Führertum."*

have finally found the philosopher's stone that transforms the ridiculous liberal democracy into the wonderful gold of the powerful, unanimous, mystical democracy transcended in a leader hypostasizing the mass. How can we fail to be impressed by the glorious path that opens before us, along which we will advance onward and upward?

PUBLIC INTEREST
COMES BEFORE
PRIVATE INTEREST

The commonplaces, as we have often said above, are luminous and good. They express the most irrefutable virtue.
This one, for instance, is the most vigorous attack ever
launched against the stupid particularism of groups and
the petty egoism of the petty bourgeoisie. When confronted by that sly defiance with which the French peasant
responds to everything that is general, grand, or generous,
how could one fail to agree with this maxim? Could anyone consider defending the narrow-mindedness of the pen-
sioner who cares about nothing but himself? After me, the
deluge! Let the world go to hell as long as I am saved!
Every man for himself (and if there is no God for all, tough
luck!).

No, no, it is obvious that the general interest is a good
and a fine thing; these sterile private interests must be
overcome. Stop pretending to be busy cultivating your own

garden. Stop pretending that all the trouble in the world is caused by the fact that you weren't smart enough to stay in your own room. Start thinking about, and serving, the general interest. For not only does this principle represent virtue, but it is also *self-evident!* How can anyone fail to understand that *everything* depends on the general interest, that if, for example, there were no more nation because the soldiers refused to die for their country, there would be no citizens either, that individual life would be destroyed? (Well, I say this without thinking, because I've often read it, but it doesn't seem that certain.)

Perhaps we ought to begin by making a few reservations about what is self-evident. The old myth of Genesis about the tree of good and evil that man was forbidden to touch tells us that when Eve looked at it she knew *at a glance* that its fruit was good to eat, pleasant to look at, and useful for obtaining knowledge. All that was self-evident. We know the result of this self-evident truth, this "good, pleasant, useful!" For once the useful and the pleasurable were combined—as in the commonplaces. Let's be on our guard.

On the level of principles, we are invincible. We can invoke generosity, the spirit of the community, the historical survival of the nation. No argument. But let's try to be a little more specific. Let's leave sentiment and passion and go to the dictionary. What is the general interest? What is the private interest? Again, there is an obvious answer: the interest of All and the interest of One. Fine. But this is a very dangerous path. In the opposition between the general and the private thus defined, the general interest becomes the interest of all, *minus* One. Perfect. But this One is rarely One, he has friends, allies, supporters . . . So the general interest is the interest of all, minus how many? Can you still talk about the general interest when 10,000 Frenchmen are against it? Of course. What about a million? Naturally. And twenty million? Since there are forty-five million Frenchmen, the general interest becomes identified with the majority.

Let's suppose that there are only two parties to choose from to solve a problem; then the majority is a matter of arithmetic. Thus, 22,499,999 Frenchmen represent the private interest, and 22,500,001 Frenchmen represent the general interest. But let's suppose that these two voices shift and the general interest shifts along with them. This means that the general interest can be reduced to *one* or *two* persons. This seems pretty private to me! We must be on the wrong track. Politicologists and constitutionalists know this very well, and all their treatises are crammed with high-sounding and complicated definitions of the general interest. No, the general interest is not represented by people or by particular groups. Therefore we will refer to the state, which alone represents the general interest. That's fine with me, but still you can't take it too far, for either the state is democratic, in which case it represents the majority and we are back where we started, or else it is some kind of monarchy, and there is some appearance of truth in the idea that the king, dictator, or secretary general personally embodies the common good. But this presupposes a strong dose of mysticism, religion, and other doubtful tendencies that we have long since repudiated.

Besides, even if the general interest has to do with the state, there could be no question of confusing the two things. Horror, horror, horror! If they were the same, it would mean that what the state does—*everything* the state does and what *every* state does—is for the common good! But then the Nazi state . . . No, no, impossible. So the general interest must be individualized outside of the state, the state being there only to represent it. We are back where we started! And in fact we are getting into some confusing complexities. The general interest is Something that enables everybody to live and prosper, it is Something Else that permits a national community to develop in the direction of history, it is the sum total of the forces of progress, or the symbol of all the resources of the society . . . there is no end to it.

But what appears most strongly indicated is that because this interest is general, it is not encountered in any particular enterprise. If somebody tells you It is here or It is there, don't believe a word of it. By the same token, it is never the interest of one person, for then it would immediately become a private interest. No, no, the greatness of the general interest is first of all to be nowhere, and next to belong to nobody. Only under these conditions is it truly general. For it becomes a pure idea, a perfect abstraction, and it is very satisfying and soothing. It is the strict expression of equality.

But, alas, in practice you can't live on the pure air of these heights of the ideal, for to tell the truth it is extremely rarefied. We are in the presence of a commonplace, that is, a truth of a practical nature. So let us see how this maxim is applied in practice, what situations it is used to justify, in what circumstances it has actually been invoked. Perhaps in this way we'll be able to tell where this famous general interest resides.

Everybody knows that Paris is in a rather dangerous situation with respect to drinking water. All local sources have long since been exhausted; it is necessary to go farther and farther away to get water. So about fifteen years ago the Loire Valley project appeared to be taking shape. Studies were made that appeared to be very serious and that concluded that such a project would be disastrous. First, there was the risk of exhausting profound water levels, which would cause wells and springs to run dry and vast stretches of productive farmland (some spoke of a whole department) to become barren. Moreover, the water level of the Loire would suddenly be lowered, and it is known that even in summer this river is not very high. This lowering of the water level would supposedly also entail a whole group of disadvantages for the people living on the banks of the Loire. Finally, there was danger of land cave-ins. But in the face of these objections the general interest was invoked. It was obvious that the riverside population of the Loire represented mere private interests, whereas the population of Paris represented the public interest. This is not a question of numbers; it is a question of prestige and psychological value. The capital represents the general interest, especially when it bears the name of "Paris"; everything must make way before Paris and the Parisian. It is in the general interest that the French desert be extended, as long as Paris continues and proliferates, like a monstrous and magnificent blossom at the end of a branch that is being exhausted and will soon be dead.

Another example. At the time the natural gas industry was starting in Lacq, reservations were expressed from the outset. There was the problem of the dangers to man, and also that of the sterilization of crops over rather vast areas because of the unavoidable emission of noxious gases. There was the problem of the sociological modification of the environment by the transplanting of working-class populations onto traditionally rural soil, and also by the disappearance of the salubrious quality of the air of Pau. There were the enormous capital expenditures (which were not made) for sanitary and educational equipment. And some expressed doubts as to the economic value of the operation: was the pocket of gas as rich as it was said to be?

There was disagreement among many of the figures, and if you took an average you found yourself well below the official level. Would the massive amount of sulfur produced be salable? The disadvantages proved real. The pessimistic economic calculations proved correct. But those who had advanced them were called reactionaries, traitors to their country, and evil minds, and all the arguments were swept away with one grand gesture: it was in the general interest to go ahead with the exploitation of Lacq and to invest the necessary millions. Here we see clearly another aspect of the general interest: it justifies technological progress, even if this progress has nothing to do with the welfare of man and of men, even if the undertaking is extremely doubtful, even if the results of the enterprise are not known. The moment technological progress is introduced, the project is in the general interest. We must not say, however, that technological progress is made *in* the general interest; this statement is too reasonable and would still permit discussion. No! In the minds of our contemporaries, the identification is complete: technological progress, whatever it may involve, is one with the general interest.

This is exactly the same definition that we find for atomic research! We are quite aware of the immense and unquestionable dangers entailed not only by atomic explosions, but by the so-called "peaceful" utilization of atomic energy, as a result of fumes, the contamination of water, the dumping of wastes, etc.[1] We know perfectly well that *if* an accident occurs, *if* the increase (which is much more rapid than we thought) of the rate of radioactivity reaches the threshold of tolerance (which is much lower than had initially been estimated), the harm done will be irreversible, decisive, and perhaps final for all of humanity! Ra-

---

[1] Cf. the studies of Ch.-N. Martin.

tionally, this consideration would be enough to stop the
movement: even with a probability of 50 per cent, a risk of
irreversible and ultimate harm should outweigh any other
motive for action. Not at all! We continue as if it were
nothing, and at every turn we invoke the general interest:
the general interest of each nation not to let itself be out-
distanced by the others; the general interest of the proletariat, which will cease to be exploited, thanks to the
harnessing of new sources of energy; the general interest of
the human race, whose standard of living will rise fantasti-
cally when we have energy that costs almost nothing.
When you take into account that there will probably be no
more nations, no more proletariat, no more human race to
take advantage of this situation, or that if there is a human
race left 80 per cent of it will be idiots, defectives, and
monsters, you can see that the general interest is well
represented.

But this brings us to another aspect of this commonplace: it is completely irrational and inconsistent. It would
seem on the face of it that if there is a general interest, it is
to keep the human race from becoming involved in a fatal
adventure. But it appears that this view is superficial, inadequate, and absurdly pessimistic. Indeed, it is in the name
of the general interest that we throw ourselves into the
adventure. So we see clearly that nobody tries to define this
general interest: it is merely used to justify enterprises that
are carried out beyond human control, by pressure of circumstances, by technological necessity, by irrational sociological forces. It happens because it happens. But man,
who certainly does not want to give up his starring role as
king of the creation, as a spiritual and highly superior
creature, will insist that this is still the result of his decision.
So he invokes this general interest, which cannot be defined but which nevertheless satisfies everybody.

Let us take one last example of the lofty motivation of the general interest. To assure social harmony and a certain standard of living in France in 1960, it was necessary to keep prices from rising. This is a sound and just policy. And it is known that food plays a major role in the computation of the cost of living. So it was necessary to do something about the price of food, especially when certain industrial costs and rents started to rise; consequently, the general interest was invoked. Agricultural prices had to be cut, thus reducing the peasant to misery. Although the peasant class still represents two fifths of the French population, it is only a private interest. The general interest means other people, that is, people who live in cities. The workers, because strongly protected by unions and because the threat of communism causes all governments to give in. The tradesmen, because they have the money. Civil servants, because they serve the state. These people represent the general interest. The essential fact in all this is that the general interest means the city, whereas anything that has to do with the countryside is only private interest.

Armed with these concrete details about the nature of the general interest, it will be easy for us to apply the idea to modern circumstances. We even find that the principle is neglected. Given the increasing number of automobiles, it is obviously in the general interest that there be more and more roads: lay them out, and pave away, cut down the trees because they get in the way of the speeding cars. Do away with the arable land, which is obviously good for nothing, and cover it with concrete on which at last you can drive safely at 120 miles an hour. Tear down the houses that impede the construction of highways and truck routes. Throw out the people who live in them—private interest!

Anyway, what good are houses? Everyone is on the move,
everyone lives in his car. The ideal is an unbroken ribbon of
houses on wheels moving endlessly over a dense network of
roads crisscrossing a treeless landscape with, at most, a few
patches of land in the interstices.

Since the general interest means culture for all, all personal culture is an abominable privilege, a scandalous aristocratic inequality, a private interest. Open the universities
to idiots and incompetents: they have the same right to a
college degree as everybody else. Bring the level of exami-
nations and instruction down to the dullest student, do
away with everything that threatens to make people different, spread culture by television and *Paris-Match*. Everyone must have *this* particular culture *and no other*,
otherwise there would still be distinctions. Everybody to
the school of stultification, which will also be the school of
social beatification. Those who claim that culture is anything but what is distributed there and what the masses
can get out of it represent private interests, and their scandalous egoism must not impede the triumphant march of
progress.

It goes without saying that the national interest is also
the general interest. And in an age of decadence, degradation, and decline, it must be stated very loudly that the
general interest requires greatness! The greatness of France
has become a national policy. And people rush after all the
signs and symbols of greatness. The trouble is that greatness is expensive, expensive in terms of men and of money.
For the sake of greatness we must raise taxes for everyone.
For the sake of greatness we must decrease everyone's
income and invest it in something that will not serve anyone. This is essential for greatness! If it served *uomo qualunque,* there would be no point to it. Today we are in a
position to satisfy this requirement fully: bombs to explode

in the desert, rockets to send into space . . . Of course, it is a greatness comensurate with our smallness.

But all things being equal, this is the same idea of the general interest as that of the USSR. A couple of years ago I was rather impressed by a letter from a Soviet worker who made this sensible remark: "If they spent the money on housing that they waste on sputniks, the comrades would be better lodged." But it is quite obvious that here we are on the level of the pettiest private interest. It goes without saying that the general interest requires an ever greater production and, what is more, a growing *productivity*, which now means always work harder! Those idealists who talk about a civilization of leisure and who claim that it has already begun have no perception of the economic and social reality. A civilization of leisure? A good hundred years from now, if all goes well! Today everyone must put his shoulder to the wheel. We must produce. Everyone must make fuller use of his nerves, his heart, and his brain: we must, we must produce. There must be no more useless members of society, no more do-nothings, people living off their income: we must produce. Everyone must become a technician, a specialist, devoted to the increase of production. The production of what? What for? It does not matter. What matters is to produce *more*. For the whole general interest depends on this *more*. More gas, which will become more expensive, more corn, which we won't be able to sell, more steel, to make armaments. In America, more refrigerators and cars, which nobody needs. More television sets, the better to stultify more people with more entertainment. In the Soviet Union, more farm equipment, although the good Soviet farmer won't see the color of its paint. And all this, which does people no good, at the price of more human labor. It is not a question of political or economic regime: the same direction is being taken in all of them. Everywhere the sublime general interest takes precedence over petty private interests. As a final image, I offer this excellent expression that was popular in Denmark in 1946: "Keep producing more butter, keep exporting more butter, and we'll all starve together."

NOBODY CAN HELP
ANYBODY ELSE

Or, "When philosophy reaches the level of *Paris-Match.*"
When, at the end of a trying experience and a no less trying
appraisal, man arrives at this intense, desperate awareness,
it is in self-hatred that he concludes, "Every man dies
alone," "Nobody ever really communicates with anybody."
When a hundred times the hand reaching out toward the
other person falls back, useless, without having been
grasped. When a hundred times the truest, most decisive
word has been said and has only caused misunderstanding.
When one after the other you have watched those dearest
to you cross the line that divides subject from object—
whether it be in death, and the uselessness of the hand you
were pressing, or in spiritual petrification, when the eyes
become glazed—and from then on you know that you are
separated by a world of incomprehension; when the one
you loved has entered a universe of prejudices, stereotypes,
dogmatism, and cold certitude, and one death is the same
as another, and you'll never be with him again!

When the profoundest good will has resulted in the
worst errors, when the greatest charity has somehow degraded its object, when you have seen all truth deteriorate
into violence and all love into a lie.

When the writer of Ecclesiastes can say, after the experience that he *describes*, "Vanity of vanities," and know that
ultimately we are all alone.

And before the man overwhelmed by this wisdom I can
only be silent and respect his suffering, which will spread
through our streets.

But soon we see the junk man go by and fish this wisdom
out of the gutter, put it in his cart, and take it to the
intellectual flea market, and we see the merry bands who
come out of the bars to listen to this wisdom passed out to
the sound of an accordion; and we see the slow-witted hack
looking for inspiration for his weekly article, and who will
receive some echo of despair and anxiety from a green neon
sky.

Then the wisdom begins a strange avatar. Because everything is useless, the desperate man made the mistake of
letting it hang around. And now we see the pig rushing to
take pictures of the expiring wisdom, and he will make a
very good movie out of it, and hundreds will rush to take
part in the greatest tragedy of the century, and he will even
get a little St. Mark's lion [1] (poor St. Mark, who would
never have thought of such a thing). And now the ass will
pick up a piece of the lion's skin and put it on and begin to
give courses at the Sorbonne and lecture tours in the Amer-
icas, which are overcome at being admitted to the higher
realms of thought. Fools, clucking with pride at having
attended these lectures, will go and spread anxiety in the
bars. And to give the doctrine a foundation, to support

---

[1] The "Oscar" of the Venice Film Festival. —*Trans.*

such a fine movement, the Paris weekly will repeat week after week how you can't help your fellow man or communicate with him or love him or . . . (Although by a strange inversion reminiscent of Oscar Wilde, we know that it is only the killer who makes contact with the victim, and that it is at the moment of killing him that he loves him! And Sade had already reminded us that inflicting pain is the only way of reaching another person!) At this point the harm is done, the commonplace is here to stay.

It is impossible for me to decide with any finality why this should happen. It is not enough to say that the pseudo-philosophers who spread this commonplace have an ax to grind. For the important factor is the public: why is there a public to welcome this idea? Why has this truth, which has been debased until it has become a lie, spread like radiation poisoning?

I think the phenomenon must be regarded as the expression of a sociological reality. The people of our Western society have accepted these desperate doctrines because they live in a world of confusion, disorder, anonymity, incoherence, and nonvalues. The man in the housing project who meets the same strangers in the elevator morning and night cannot help feeling his anonymity, his inability to say what is important to him to these people whose fighting or lovemaking he hears through walls that are too thin, these frightening anonymous persons whose every secret he knows. The man who knows himself to be subject to the arbitrary control of his employer, the police, the party, and the state, and who has absolutely no way to defend himself because when he joins forces with his friends and finds strength in numbers, aggression attacks him where he is most vulnerable. The man who lives in the obscurity of the cinema and amuses himself alone, who experiences solitary joys and pains by virtue of the flickering image. The man who sees his destiny mapped out day after day at the factory or office, punctuated only by dreary escapes on the weekend in an old jalopy that joins a hundred thousand other jalopies lined up bumper to bumper along the roads. The man who retains more or less vaguely in the back of his mind the image of the atomic mushroom, and who knows in spite of himself that "It" will happen for reasons he will never know, at the decision of a man over whom he can have no influence. The man who sees his love for his wife, which he had believed to be eternal, gradually deteriorate because of the mediocrity of life and daily attrition, and who sees children whom he had believed to be his gradually drifting away from him, adopting a vocabulary he no longer understands and morals he does not recognize, and judging him harshly.

Such a man, conditioned by this whole life routine, which is the same as everyone else's, readily accepts the commonplace as the last word in wisdom. And I could paint a similar portrait of young people who, with other motives but for the same reason, share this acceptance with the older generation. So this formula becomes the expression, dishonestly exploited by contemptible intellectuals, of a sociological despair that is unconscious but real.

Once it has been accepted, the commonplace becomes a justification and a rule of life. Since nobody can help anybody else, what's the use of trying? You know *in advance* that it is useless. So when you see a man suffering, turn away. You can't do anything about it, you might as well let him die alone, for he will die alone no matter what you do. It is not worth the trouble to have an unpleasant experience, to waste your time, to be bored with a sick person, to breathe bad air, and to run the risk of catching something!

It's the same thing with the poor man: you can't do anything for him. It's not worth the trouble to give him money,
so keep it for yourself, and go have a drink to his health. He
won't die any sooner or any later for it. Nobody can help
anybody else! Would it have helped him if you had given
him a quarter? No, of course not. For here again, those who
practice the commonplace are compulsive: it is all or nothing. They must either solve all the problems of this man,
my fellow human, and give him the absolute truth, or do
nothing at all, turn their backs on him and let him go on
living with his stomach cramps. It's not worth getting upset
or feeling sorry or trying to do something: that's the way it
goes!

Nobody ever communicates with anybody else; what's
the use of trying to explain yourself, use language, listen to
what someone else has to say? It does no good, there is no
such thing as real, total, absolute communication. Here
again, it is all or nothing: either you communicate for
eternity, about truth itself and on the profoundest level of
being, or not at all. And since trying the first seems too
difficult, you content yourself with the second, gracefully
flinging back the lock of hair that would have satisfied the
desperate person. Since language no longer serves any purpose, it can be simplified. Onomatopoeia is enough to communicate; sound replaces speech, because it evokes more
direct sensations and has the power to stir your insides;
dialogue is not even attempted, since everyone knows that
in every dialogue both people cheat, and that language is
used only to deceive. It is completely useless to pay any
attention to the signal given by the person opposite; the
sound will cover both his expression and mine, both his
speech and mine, in this objective wave that washes over
us and by which we communicate. Perhaps by means of
this stimulus I may have the same emotion, the same sensa-

tion at the same moment as my neighbor. This may be the most nearly perfect communication possible; what's the use of looking for anything further?

And because nobody communicates with anybody, love does not exist. There can be no real meeting, there can be no union of two creatures, there is always an invisible gulf dividing two people sharing the same bed. What's the use of exhausting myself trying to cross it, to conquer this red desert, to create this unity? If it is not there to begin with, it does not exist. And because it is not there to begin with, it is enough to maintain our own separate egos, to get as much pleasure as I can without worrying about the other person, since she is not I. It is enough to use her for my pleasure, and if I cannot reach her as a person, at least I can use her as an object. So love is only skin-deep. And we have the little tales of Sagan to illustrate the pseudo-wisdom of pseudo-despair. And above all, above all, the great refusal to live, to try to overcome the destiny of absence by a stronger presence in which everyone will find himself by finding his fellow man.

But after all, this statement is still unalterably true: nobody can help anybody else. One has only to consider the subject of the sentence. Nobody. *Nemo.* Where there was a face there is a shadow that fades, and I can see nothing but empty space. There is no doubt that "nobody" can help nobody! Absence, emptiness, and nothingness can neither help nor speak nor love. Do away with man, leaving nobody, and you do away with all possibility of a meeting: a meeting with whom, since the subject is nobody? And who would want to help, speak, or love, since the subject is nobody, and since "nobody" obviously cannot want anything? And since "nobody," being an absence, cannot be a presence to anybody else?

But what unconscious severity the user of this commonplace shows toward himself! For it is about himself that he is speaking, is it not? Since, as we were saying above, it is to justify himself for not helping or loving or communicating that the desperate young man advances this maxim. In speaking of himself he admits that he is "nobody," so empty, so useless, so anonymous, so absent that he can carry only this vague name. In making this statement to justify himself, he is admitting that he does not exist. By adopting the commonplace, this modern man admits that he has already entered the kingdom of the dead. There is nobody left. Let the dead bury their dead.

WE HAVE BEEN
DECEIVED

This commonplace can also be stated, "I understand you;" but in this case the speaker has changed. These two commonplaces represent the truest possible dialogue between the government and the governed. When the government announces that it understands the people, they should be seized with a holy terror, for this is the worst thing that can happen to them. Not because in saying this the government is deceiving them; not at all. It is saying just what it means, and it actually does understand them. But it is at this precise moment that the government becomes dangerous.

As long as the government has not understood, it can make foolish mistakes, it can overlook the problems, it can do nothing at all, but all this is not so dangerous. When the government has really understood, then there is everything to fear. For the role of the government is to govern. It is therefore to suppress opposition, obtain consensus, solve problems (not on the purely material level, as is mistakenly believed, but on the *human* level, by including the passionate, the sentimental, conflicting interests, etc.), to guide the whole country toward a goal that only it sees clearly. Because it represents the general interest, the government cannot consider any private interest (see that commonplace). When it has understood, it is disastrous for the individuals. The government alone draws the political line because the good people are quite incapable of setting their own objectives. When the government has understood, we see the good people catapulted in a direction that they have not chosen, since they are incapable of choosing one for themselves. The measures taken by the government have no importance at all as long as it has not understood. Only when it does do they become dangerous.

Of course, the good people do not interpret this fine phrase in such an unwholesome manner. They believe in it, reading into it something that is not there at all: "Therefore I am going to do what you expect me to do. I understand you because you are right. I approve of you, I am on your side." And they conclude, "The cops are with us" (I am following an association of ideas, but such a method is often good; the French Communist Party [1] should know that when the cops have understood, they become worse, *dixit* (Clemenceau). But all this is not in the statement. The tragic error results from the fact that the good people know nothing about the nature of governments. They still believe that the government must be on their side, that it must do their will, and that when this does not work, the reason is merely lack of mutual understanding.

---

[1] In 1917 the French Communist Party was the "poor bastard in the front line"!

What a mistake! The government necessarily sees things from another point of view. No matter how strong it is, it has no choice but to use force and Machiavellianism. It cannot share the common sense of the people or entertain good and pious sentiments toward the citizens. Between sovereignty and the exercise of power there exists an abyss of difference that no treatise on political science has bridged. And idealistic speeches on political ends to be achieved on the one hand and Marxist speeches on the doomed class system on the other are mere propaganda, equally inadequate. The practice of politics is always the same under all regimes. It implies a mysterious falsification of man and secret procedures that nobody has ever controlled. The government says, "I understand you." The good people conclude, "Then I will do what you ask," and the government concludes in turn, "Then I will be able to possess you."

It is obvious that at this point the good people will quickly become scandalized and will very soon protest: "We have been deceived." Since they are always respectful of power and great men, they express their disappointment or their anger in the impersonal. Is there something that isn't going right? We had expected this, but nothing came of it. A big "They" got in the way. And the good people are always realizing that they have been deceived. (Which is not true for that matter, for it was the people who had imagined something.) But it is never any use. Always credulous, always game, they are always ready to believe again in schemes, promises, enthusiasms, reforms, wars, revolutions, peace movements, international movements, dictatorships, democracies, fascism, communism, speeches, referendums, colonization and anticolonialism, until they

see the handwriting on the wall: we've been had. Alas!
It is always in the past participle that the good people
think.

But just let someone come along and explain to the good
people *who* deceived them, *why* they were deceived, *how*
they were deceived, and immediately, moved by such candor, dazzled by such clarity, delighted by such a profound
political revelation, revived, in short, the good people will
accord their confidence. This explains much of the appeal
of fascism and communism. Lenin was not mistaken when
he insisted on the importance of the "political revelation."
The person who was able to tell me that the other (of
whose falsity I had bitter experience) deceived me—he at
least understands me and does not deceive me! Alas, he is
not deceiving you when he tells you that the other deceived you, lied to you, played with you, ridiculed you,
exploited you, murdered you. But he does it only to set his
trap and to pluck you, bone you, violate you, bleed you,
humiliate you, and debrain you in his turn.

No amount of experience is of any use. The French
Communist Party was able to applaud Bardamu; its children marched as one man in the Resistance in 1943. The
Popular Front performed its three little marionette tricks to
allow Franco to put down the hydra of anarchy with the
valiant support of the Spanish communists. This prevented
neither the good people's approval of Marshal Pétain in
1940 nor the conviction in 1945 that communism was the
key to truth and freedom; the betrayal by the Red Army at
Warsaw did not illuminate anyone. Here again the big
"They" had intervened. The coldest of all cold monsters
knows just how to talk to the people. When the monster
tells them that it loves them, it represents them, it understands them, let the people tremble!

·   ·   ·

Incidentally, this formula reveals another aspect of the formation of commonplaces. Whereas they generally develop gradually, we see here that they can be born overnight! You need only a great man who hits upon an exact formula in an ambiguous situation for this formula to suddenly become invested with a kind of magic power. It establishes some bond, some spiritual union between the magician and the bewitched. The latter immediately adopts the magic formula that seems to him to resolve the ambiguity of the problem, and in his passionate desire for insight, surrenders to the obscurity of the commonplace. The success of the simple phrase depends on the conjunction of the speaker, the hearer, and the occasion. Through this communal quality it acquires the value of the commonplace, for we must not forget that the adage then possesses a force of communion. And not the least ironic aspect of the matter is that the "I understand you" whose only meaning is distance, remoteness, and objectification has been adopted as a commonplace of participation in power.

IF ALL THE GOOD GUYS IN THE WORLD . . .

It would take so little—there are men of good will all over the world. All you have to do is find them. One friend meets another; why not a hundred, a thousand, a thousand million? All friends. It's so easy to add—one plus one— what's to prevent it? The great brotherhood of men exists, doesn't it? First of all, we saw it in a movie. And deep down we are ready to believe it, because we are good. Like the good public we are, we shed good, purifying tears over this good movie full of good heroes that showed us how, thanks to science and good will, all these good sinners can be saved (for naturally the worst of all was converted at the end). There are no more barriers, no more competition, no more conflicts among nations, parties, or coalitions. All that was yesterday, an evil past of divisions and incomprehensible hatreds.

But today we realize that all the good guys in the world

can join together. Today we have progress, and the idealistic promise of the future now guaranteed by scientific excellence, the sciences united in the service of man, men
reconciled by scientific virtue, a beautiful 1900 fresco realized today in this great mystical movement. All the world
is on the same side, which is, of course, the side of man! I
immediately feel a great flutter unleashed in my breast. At
last I am justified! I am on the side of man (and therefore
of myself!), once again I am part of this vast history, this
marvelous solidarity, this delightful warmth of the herd
who are doomed to die, no doubt, but who in the meantime
can take their stand as one man. From such heights I
perceive the vanity and stupidity of what separates us.

So just make the simple gesture of holding out your
hand, and *keep smiling*. Who could resist this overture?
Don't you see all the fine sentiments that emerge, showing
the little pink snouts of well-fed pigs? A torrent of idealism
falls on our heads, like the flurry of snowflakes in a glass
paperweight. And I find myself in love with all these good
people—Yellow, Black, Red, White, Blue, and Shit Green;
what do I care whether these colors refer to skin, flags,
uniforms, or opinions? Noble sentiments sweep that all
away in floods of Lamartinian emotion and Jaurésian eloquence. With his well-known philosophical profundity,
M. Jeane Duché recalled on the occasion of the film of the
Olympic Games in Tokyo: "It takes so little to bring about
universal communion without distinction of race or nation-
ality; all it takes is enthusiasm for the pole-vaulting champion or for the winner of the hundred-yard dash, and seven
thousand young men and women march around the track
arm in arm singing, dancing, a joyous medley of races." It
takes so little . . .

All political, economic, and social problems melt like

cheap candy. And you can't understand why they
don't . . .

Oops! The cat is out of the bag, for here, at last, is the
rub: all the good guys in the world *do not join hands.* It's
no use, it doesn't happen; so there must be an obstacle.
Now, we know very well that this obstacle is no longer
material, for science has overcome all material obstacles.
There are no more Pyrenees, there is no more Pacific
Ocean; a jet plane spans them in an hour. So there must be
some *other* obstacle. And since people are good, it isn't
they.

There must be a traitor. That's it. Whose fault is it? First
of all, the government. Governments breed false distinctions, false conflicts. But already it is difficult to agree. For
in the democratic countries people are inclined to say, "It is
our government." In the authoritarian countries people will
say without hesitation, "It is our neighbor's government."
In any case, the government has very happily relieved the
churches in this area. But it is still very inadequate. There
is a traitor and this is a real villain who corrupts the pure
hearts of these good people, who works secretly to sow
dissension among those who want to get along. The whole
world is ready for unity of action, there is only one little
microbe that secretes hatred, and . . .

Ah, I have it, it's the communist! No, it isn't, it's the
capitalist! You don't understand at all, it's the Jew. But
you're forgetting, the only real villain is the fascist. But
who breeds hatred? The military! But who confuses the
poor people with a mass of red tape? The civil servant!
Well, whoever it is, even if the face of the villain remains
indistinct, we know very well what must be done. If all the

young men in the world are good guys, ready to get along,
if there are only a few villains who cause all the evil, they
must carry all the evil; all we have to do is eliminate them
as quickly as possible. After this minor purge, it will be so
good to join hands all around the world, purified at last.

So give free rein to your feelings; they will carry us with
the force of gravity to the crime and our subsequent self-
justification. The disgusting flabbiness of noble sentiments
turns out killers by mass production, for make no mistake,
killers are full of idealism and humanity. It is always in the
name of man and humanity that genocides are performed.
And I mean *always,* for even the inquisitions and auto da
fés of the church are organized for the salvation of man
(much more than for God!), as Dostoyevsky well knew.
When noble sentiments and idealism flood the heart of
man, they also stop his ears. It is at this precise moment
that man ceases to be able to hear Cromwell's admirable
apostrophe and plea for peace: "I beseech you, in the
bowels of Christ, think it possible you may be mistaken!"
But where noble sentiments prevail there is no possibility
of error, and since we have such lofty virtues, how could
we be mistaken?

Knife idealism in the belly, strangle the fine sentiments,
lance the noble emotions, explode the lie of humanism,
learn to look the truth in the face and practice a rigorous
skepticism, and then perhaps you will have rendered some
service, for which your only reward will be the insults of
the good guys of the world.

If all the good guys in the world . . . *If!* The conditional
is the mode of the devil. (To every man his due, this idea
was given to me by the priest Maillot.) Everything would
be fine if . . . ! This is the exact form of every diabolical

proposition. For the *diabolos* is the principle of separation, and there is no surer way to separate than to introduce the *if*. Between the bone and the marrow, the *if* introduces the destructive bad conscience; between the husband and the wife, the *if* introduces the condition that dissolves the marriage; between the state and the citizen, the *if* introduces the mutual abnegation that divides the nation; between the Christian and his God, the *if* introduces temptation. An admirable lever with which you can overcome all inertia, but only to set a man against his neighbor: just think, if the workers stopped being communists, how quickly the world would achieve happiness. And if management stopped exploiting labor . . . But the devil is also the man who diverts human energy toward false hopes and false problems.

The *if* is of such evocative power that it catalyzes all of human hope and directs it toward the condition that, if fulfilled, would assure us happiness. But the *if* is the way to avoid facing reality, the way to escape into the dream, the ideal, while *claiming* that we are still on the level of reasonable things. The process is always the same: you formulate the desirable, then you impose the condition, which gives an appearance of realism, but in the conditional it is underplayed—"All you have to do . . . We need only . . ."—and our good man is embarked upon an adventure that means the end of the possibilities of his life, which he will overlook, and of the shred of reason to which he could lay claim. And the more the conditional involves noble sentiments, the more it shunts man toward the denial of his life, toward false problems, false solutions to true questions, and illusions that can be fatal.

The devil is also the denier. And the *if* will play its negative role even though it has the best positive appearance. The moment man is impressed by the truth of the conditional mood, he finds himself justified in doing nothing as long as this condition is not satisfied. The *if* has an admirable capacity to excuse me from responsibility. It's not I . . . it's *if;* when the condition has been fulfilled, of course, then how good, how noble, how active, how truthful I will be! But in the meantime I can sit back and watch things happen. I am not responsible for anything. And if all the good guys in the world . . . but what's this? "Come on, fellows, join hands, form the circle of good will! Hurry up, now!" I am waiting for all the good guys in the world to get together; then, of course, I'll join them myself. But where are they? What do I see? All the world has approved and I have spoken in the desert.

WORK IS FREEDOM

This can still be said in bourgeois circles: laziness is the mother of all the vices (therefore work is the father of all the virtues).

The Christian believes that he who works prays, the socialist that work is the condition for the liberation of the proletariat.

According to the spirit of the time, in fact, you could make all values dependent upon work. You could just as well say, work is truth or justice or brotherhood or health. That would be neither more nor less true. No more true, because in reality it is hard to see what work has to do with any of these things. No less true, because in reality this is the universal, profound, ineradicable belief of people today.

And yet it is a difficult commonplace to swallow, for after all, with rare exceptions, it cannot be said that man spontaneously likes to work. That he may work to become rich or important or famous—that is, to satisfy his pride, his love of pleasure, or his egotism—can be understood. That he may work to deaden his feelings, to distract himself—

that is, to run away from himself, to avoid the ultimate
questions or despair—this can also be understood. That
very exceptionally, like an artist or an old-fashioned arti-
san, obsessed with kerosene or an enthusiast of zinc, he
may work out of passion for an idea or an object or a
sensation, can also be understood, but contrary to popular
belief, this is rather rare.

In any case these are secondary motives that drive one
to work, to accept or endure work. There is absolutely no
question of love of work as such. No, the normal man finds
work fatiguing, painful, and tedious, and does everything
he can to avoid it, and he is right. "Work" is originally the
yoke imposed on the animal to geld him or shoe him.

The first meaning of the French word *"travail"* is "constraint, pain, suffering"; it is no accident that this word has
accurately been used to translate the English word "labor."
The peoples of antiquity, the Arabs, and the Hindus have
all regarded work as the business of inferior beings. In
Judaism and Christianity work is regarded as a punishment. There is no foundation for the claim that Christianity has ennobled and dignified work. Except for one or two
passages from the church fathers, always the same ones,
the vast majority of early Christian and medieval writers
state that work is the consequence of the fall, that it is
associated with sin, and that it is in no way a virtue. In the
"Christian" Roman civilization, or in the "Christian" centuries of the Middle Ages, work was always regarded as
menial, a sign of inferiority and disgrace, a blemish, and in
the division of orders, the order that works is the lowest. If
the religious rules, as at Cluny or Cîteaux, make work an
obligation, it is not because work is good or ennobling or
because it has a value—but for exactly the opposite reason:
it is in the name of humility and mortification that you
subject yourself to work as to the hairshirt, fasting, vigils,

etc. In a society obsessed by the beyond, by the conviction that the face of the world passes away, by the sense of the spiritual, it is absolutely impossible to see what work could have signified. People worked because they had to live, but work could not be either a means of redemption or a means of salvation, therefore it was not important. If some good writers today, historians and philosophers, claim that Christianity is responsible for raising the value of work, this is only because they are infected by the commonplaces of our age, because they themselves believe in work and it is always necessary to find predecessors.

Work did not start to become noble until the eighteenth century, the bourgeois century. Even in the seventeenth century the church, ahead of time for once, had become the echo of the bourgeoisie, and the most bourgeois of the theologians had proclaimed that through work you "beguiled boredom, saved time, and cured the languor of laziness and the pernicious reveries of idleness." Obviously we are on the right track! Fénelon had only to follow suit to guide us straight to the glorification of work by the *"philosophes"* who expressed bourgeois thinking, especially Voltaire, that father of commonplaces of all kinds: "Force men to work, and you will make them honest people." How could that champion of liberty fail to see that he was foreshadowing the concentration camps? "Work banishes three great evils: boredom, vice, and poverty." Diderot followed close on Voltaire's heels, as did Raynal and Mirabeau.

Next we find nobles waxing enthusiastic about this activity and increasingly obtaining permission to work without losing caste. Then a receptive and understanding Christian church makes heroes of the workers, whom sermons en-

courage in this virtue. It is true that at this time the
"worker" was the bourgeois. But already work *per se* was
becoming the keystone of all morality. Such a wonderful
find had to be put into operation. It was the Revolution
that completed the edifice by entering the realm of action.
Bourgeois in its inspiration, its men, and its achievements,
the Revolution could not overlook such a splendid opportunity! The committee on begging of the Constituent Assembly proclaimed the obligation of universal labor, and
able-bodied poor who refused to work became criminals.
The Convention established workhouses where loafers
were forced to work, and if after their release they became
idle again, they were deported to Guiana. In this way work
really demonstrated its virtuous quality and its capacity to
liberate man.

But after these excesses, we come to the wisdom of the
beginning of "the stupidest century." The bourgeois began
by raising the value of work in regard to himself. It was to
himself that he first applied a strict and rigorous morality
of work. He created an educational system oriented around
work, he gave meaning to life through work, and the greatest reproach he could address to his children was that of
laziness. Conversely, for the man who works everything is
permitted, everything becomes a minor sin. He can deceive
his wife, exploit his fellow man, be cruel, selfish, proud—it
makes no difference as long as he is a good worker! Work
washes away all sins.

And let's face it, this transformation of work into a value
is the most popular system of justification. Because the
bourgeois is in fact committed to work, it is clearly necessary that work be more than a condition of life: it must be
a virtue. But soon—and why not?—the bourgeois began to
apply this code to others, that is, to the working class. After
1780 the worker found himself reduced more and more

tragically to the situation of destitution and excessive labor with which we are familiar. This was a result of the industrial explosion and bourgeois exploitation. But how could he endure this excessive labor, which did not even provide him with a living wage? Out of necessity, of course; because he could not escape his condition. But because he was a man, it was also necessary to give him a justification, a meaning for his condition. And now the bourgeoisie offered him its own morality: redemption through work. Work purifies; work is virtue. And then the church came along to add its two cents' worth of blessing: "He who works prays"; "Good worker, if you miss Sunday mass because the boss keeps you at the factory, have no qualms, your Father in Heaven has said that work is prayer."

Obviously the propagation of this admirable morality coincided almost miraculously with the interests of the bourgeoisie. And the worst of it was that the worker eventually came to believe in this virtue. In the nineteenth century it was working-class and socialist circles that were to produce the most impassioned speeches on work. Both Proudhon and Louis Blanc were taken in by the idea. The great sleight-of-hand trick succeeded. Bourgeois morality became the morality of the working class. This was almost inevitable. Here again, the worker of 1848 obeyed the same motives as the bourgeois of 1780. When your whole life is monopolized by an activity and dedicated to it, when life has no other meaning or value, what heroism it would take to admit, "After all, this activity is absurd, and therefore my life is worthless, it is a waste!" This is an intolerable situation. What heroism it would take to refuse to give one's life significance and value through what one does! When, having lost the dimension of eternity, and circumscribed by his time on earth, man sees himself surrounded by nothingness on all sides, where is he to find his consola-

tion or his certitude? But just at this moment work offers
him the miracles of technology, lights a way for him
through the blackness of time. How could he fail to transfer all his fervor to this solace?

And of course Karl Marx put the final touches on the
edifice by providing the theoretical justification for what
was as yet only emotion, impulse, need. Marx is truly a
bourgeois thinker when he explains all of history by work,
when he formulates man's whole relation to the world in
terms of work, when he evaluates all thought in terms of its
relation to work, and when he gives work as the creative
source of value. Although he did not believe in values, he
implies that work is a virtue when he condemns the classes
that do not work. He was one of the most articulate inter-
preters of the bourgeois myth of work, and because he was
a socialist and a defender of the working class, he was one
of the most active agents in spreading the myth to this
class. Besides, it was through work that this class would
one day win power and freedom.

For the post-Marxian working class, therefore, work
meant both the explanation of its condition and the certainty of seeing it end. Once the motive of doctrine had
been added to the motive of necessity, how could the
workers fail to be imbued with this ideology? It was the
bourgeois who invented the dogma of the eminent dignity
of the worker, but it was Karl Marx who led the proletariat
to this thenceforth ineradicable conviction. From then on,
the myth of work became a myth of the left, and the
bourgeois and the worker were united in the same commonplace: work is the be-all and end-all of life. The only
difference is that for the bourgeois, work tends more and
more to be the work of other people, while for the worker
only he himself can bear the noble title of worker. Anyone

who does not belong to the proletariat, being a nonworker, is a parasite.

Arbeit macht frei was the great motto inscribed on the gates of the concentration camps by the Nazis. For they too shared the fraternal communion in the value of work. And having clearly understood and expressed the fundamental commonplace, they are not so stupid as to write over their doors *voi ch'entrate, lasciate* . . . Not at all, for on the contrary, there is *one* hope. This is the trick and the greatest lie, but a lie that is provided by bourgeois society *and* communist society alike. You are imprisoned, undernourished, mistreated, and cold; you live under threat of death, but there is one hope: work. Although you are behind barbed wire, work liberates you, work brings you dignity, virtue, and justice, you are still a man because you work. You are a *free* man, because work is the guarantee and fulfillment of your inner freedom. And this admirable find, which only evil minds can regard as a mockery, can be applied everywhere. Workers under the boss's thumb, work makes you free; same demonstration. Russians subject to the dictatorship of Stalin, work makes you free; same demonstration. And you, the ordinary man, who live in an absurd society, who have lost faith in Jesus Christ, who are the victim of unlimited forces, who do not know if there will be a tomorrow, who are struck by the anguish of your condition and feel that your life has no meaning, you are in luck, great good luck: work, work hard, work harder and harder, and in this way, you will see, everything makes sense, you are a free man. Same demonstration.

. . .

In close intellectual communion with Nazism, communism in the USSR and in the popular republics has adopted the myth and the commonplaces of work in accentuated form. Following the Convention, work became strictly obligatory for all. The loafer is the arch-enemy, the person who threatens to undermine the whole socialist society, for he consumes but does not produce. It is known that in the popular republics, especiallly Bulgaria and Romania, those who cannot claim a specific employment have no ration cards. And Yugoslavia has also followed this excellent example; there they have even gone farther, and have decreed the deportation and imprisonment of the unemployed. But this deportation, which has long been practiced in the USSR, is to concentration camps. And what are these camps called? "Camps of correction through work"!

Didn't I say there was a resemblance? According to bourgeois morality, work reforms the corrupt, improves the moral standard of the delinquent, makes man virtuous. According to Nazi morality, work combats undesirable tendencies and individualism.[1] And in these camps of correction through work (what's the difference if since 1958 they have been called colonies—the phenomenon is the same), severe methods are used to deal with recalcitrants, that is, monsters who do not want to work or to comply with the rules: sentencing to more arduous tasks, extension of the working day (which is normally ten hours long), decrease in remuneration.

In spite of all these measures, the loafer has not completely disappeared. As recently as 1960 Mr. Ilitchev (head of Agitprop) announced that it was necessary to step up the struggle, to wage all-out war against do-nothings and

---

[1] Cf. the first issue of the *RDA Review* for 1961, which adopted a typically Nazi theme: the elimination of individualism by work.

parasites. Consequently, in a decree of May 4, 1961, Mr. Khrushchev's liberal regime legalized what under Stalin was merely a rather disgraceful practice: deportation, forced labor, internment, and confiscation of all possessions for loafers, do-nothings, and all those who refuse to do "social labor." And these crimes may be only supjective! And a little later the RDA published a Draconian work code. It was no longer simply a question of stamping out idleness. Obviously, since work is freedom, the more you work, the freer you are. Since work is virtue, the more you work, the more virtuous you are. Since work is the construction of socialism, the more you work, the better a socialist you are. Now, in the miserable bourgeois society, people worked under coercion and to earn their daily bread, and *in addition* they achieved virtue and freedom. In the socialist society the progress is obvious: the authorities must see to it that all the comrades are free and virtuous. If the people work, it is not under coercion, but joyously and out of conviction. Consequently it is completely legitimate, for example, to outlaw all strikes (as in the USSR). In striking, by ceasing to work, the worker destroys his very being. This is obvious.

But output and discipline must also be determined by the state. The job can no longer be left to the choice of the worker. (The wage earner may be forced to accept a different job from the one specified in his contract, or sent to another place: salutary exercises in virtue.) Salaries will be paid only if standard output is reached; and the Saturday holiday is abolished. Thus the worker gains an additional 16 per cent of freedom and virtue. All this progress has made it possible to outstrip the Western states by a wide margin, and these measures have just been imitated fervently in the worker-peasant state of Castro. August 1962 saw the introduction of the work booklet (of Napoleonic

origin, and so dear to the worker's heart!), which controls
the whole life of the worker. At the same time, vacations
were reduced, the length of the working day was in-
creased, and all interruption of work was penalized. Virtue
reigns in Cuba. One cannot help admiring the universality
and effectiveness of commonplaces, since this one, at least,
is embodied in institutions!

Work is freedom. This is certainly the ideal form of this
commonplace. Even so, how much the average man must
prize freedom to formulate such obvious untruths, to swallow such perfect absurdities, and for there to be profound
pseudo-philosophers to explain it "phenomenologically,"
and powerful politicians to apply it legally! But of course it
is precisely because the average man is quartered in giant
monoliths, tied to the machine, hemmed in by administrative regulations, snowed under by red tape, kept under the
vigilant eye of the police, stripped naked by the perspicacity
of psychologists, manipulated by the invisible tentacles of
mass media, transfixed in the beam of social and political
microscopes, dispossessed of himself by a whole life that is
prepared for him for his greater happiness, comfort, hygiene, health, and longevity; it is precisely because work is
his inexorable destiny that he must, if he is to avoid intolerable suffering that would immediately lead to suicide,
believe in this commonplace, espouse it passionately, bury
it in the bottom of his heart and, *credo quia absurdum*,
transform it into a reason for living. Which is precisely
what the vigilant guardians had in mind.

WOMEN FIND THEIR FREEDOM (DIGNITY) IN WORK

This commonplace follows the preceding one as closely as the smell follows the skunk. Even in the commonplaces, women must come after men! And those ladies who wish to win their dignity and independence from men express the idea in a commonplace that depends on a very masculine one.

Long live freedom, Madame!

Day breaks. It's nice in bed. But I haven't time to enjoy it. My husband is about to leave. I must start the fire, make coffee . . . there, a little light . . . . and so another day begins, a day like ten thousand others: the soup, the kids, the wash, the cleaning. And tomorrow it will start all over again: the fire, the coffee, the cleaning and the soup, the kids and the husband. A restricted universe, punctuated by a few intervals of joy or anger. But how would you change or expand it? There is no time. There is no change. Change comes from the outside, like an eagle. Unfortunate comparison; today it is like a rocket. Change is unemployment or war, which have graciously replaced plague and famine. Maybe on Sunday, mass. But we don't go much any more. And yet it gave a certain meaning, a certain color, a certain direction to the whole week.

Come, Madame, you must be liberated. You must shake off this apathy, emerge from this meaningless everyday limbo. After all, preparing food for your husband and children has no value, even if this simple cuisine reflects a very high civilization. Waiting on someone is drudgery, your back bent over the hearth is a slave's back, and we want you to be a Person. Stand up straight. Stop blowing on the fire. Suppose the clear flame is not there every morning, a symbol of life and resurrection; who cares about symbols? Perhaps the house will be dusty and lifeless, will cease to have a living heart, but you will enter into the great world outside. You will be in contact with political change and high culture, with Events and History. At last you are becoming a character in the drama. For thousands of years you have been tied to inferior tasks, imprisoned within the self-centered, narrow, limited family milieu, you have missed out on Life. Now at last we are letting down the barriers, taking off the chains. Now at last you are immersed in that mainstream of freedom which is Action.

Not being stupid idealists, we are quite aware that there is no freedom without money. So where will your first step lead you, woman liberated at last? To work, of course. However, mark it well, keep it in your heart, tell it to yourself every day of your life: it is a *free* work, a work that gives you money, money of your own! "What a relief! For years we have had to take our miserable money from a husband who grumbled and scowled. What horrible dependence! But now we have this money all to ourselves!" But from *whom* do you receive it?

Don't misunderstand me, it is not the woman who works that I am attacking, but the commonplace. The wife of the laborer or employee who is forced to work because the single salary is not enough to live on or the Russian woman who is forced to work by a regime that deifies work is a victim, a pawn of fate, a slave to the necessity that forces her to bend her back, and I would not want to add to her troubles. But I resent, I mortally and violently resent the liars who come along and falsify her condition by demonstrating in learned articles—sociological, psychological, psychoanalytical, ethical, metaphysical, and theological— that this is a good thing, that this is not coercion, but freedom, that this is not a hardship, but an achievement!

I resent those who declare that the image of the woman as center of the home, rearer of future men, and creator of the hearth is only a myth, the expression of a localized society and age. Which is more important? Raising children and making a real life for them or punching holes in subway tickets?

I resent those who tell you that black is white, confusing what is with what should be, and proclaim the excellence of female employment, while indicating, of course, that it is necessary to "plan working hours," "give the woman a specific title," etc., things that everybody knows are impossible to apply.

In the USSR the majority of women are manual laborers and roadworkers.

I resent the fools who declare that it is by each working

at a productive job that men and women complete and
help each other, in the name of the commonplace that this
kind of work is ennobling!

I resent the intellectuals who confuse the experience of
the middle-class woman with nothing to do with that of the
woman who is forced to work. That the middle-class
woman with nothing to do may take a job and thus emerge
to some extent from her limbo, I will not deny. But this has
nothing to do with the usual experience, that of the spinster
who must earn her living. Nobody has the right to tell her
that her life is much better, much more fulfilling and
rewarding, than marriage. For in the last analysis, the
charlatans of our commonplace accumulate their scholarly
evidence only to justify society as it is, to adjust the woman
after absorbing the man, to see to it that she is satisfied
with her lot.

Day breaks. It's nice in bed, but I haven't time to enjoy
it. No time to start the fire, no time to warm up the house;
outside it is dreary. No time to stay inside. I must get the
children ready, it's already seven o'clock, I'm going to be
late. No time to swallow the scalding coffee. Off with the
children, off with the husband, I have to leave too, hurry
the two older boys to boarding school, hurry the youngest
to nursery school. Actually it would be simpler just to leave
him at nursery school than it is to take him there at seven in
the morning and pick him up at seven in the evening.
We're locking up the house. There. (Ten after seven,
good.) It will be dead until tonight. And tonight we'll
barely have the energy to go to bed. Faster and faster. The
subway isn't moving this morning. Don't let me be late!

Only last week . . . getting cussed out by the foreman, the head of the department, cussed, cussed . . .

Kissed by the foreman, the head of the department, maybe by the boss or the manager, kissed, kissed . . .

Haggling over my salary, which was cut by the bookkeeper. Defending myself, defending myself, tired, bored with the typewriter, bored with the paper, bored with the words, sick of the smell, sick of the faces, sick of the fatigue and the absurdity.

No government can change this. There will always be a foreman and a department head; what difference does it make whether the regime is capitalist or socialist? Harnessed to tasks that are mechanical or absurd. How much subtler cooking was than typing! How much less absurd mending your boy's trousers was than filing!

My money, *my* money, but I am still receiving it. The boss, the manager, the cashier, they throw it in my face: my money, the purchase price of my strength and my life. The money I received from my husband was the fruit of a human relation, and it is true that human relations are not always pleasant. I did not want to receive it within this profound and unique relationship, and now I receive it from a boss who despises me or a state that is unaware of my existence.

It is true that it is my money now rather than our money. It is true that I no longer depend on anyone, or rather, that I no longer depend on my husband, on someone who is flesh of my flesh, but on that vast sociological hierarchy, anonymous and all-powerful, whose marks are cruelly stamped on face and body. I am the servant of the administration, the boss, the capitalist, the anticapitalist . . . At your orders, sir!

Don't be silly, you have to depend on somebody in so-

ciety. Why not on my husband, then? It seems that with
my own money in my pocket, I am independent. I do what
I like with my money. Or do I? It goes into that bottomless
abyss of home expenses. A home that no longer exists. And
at the end of the day, there is the movies: at the end of
exhaustion, there is the plunge into oblivion. To forget, to
forget that you exist, that your back hurts and your head
aches, to forget for an evening by sinking into the dream
and the lie. You'll come out a little more numb, a little more
drained, and since you go to bed at one o'clock, it will be
even harder to get up at six. Tomorrow you'll be even more
beat, but so what, this evening you had to have a drug, and
you had to spend your money, too. My money, my money,
what will I use it for? To buy furniture for the house? But I
am never in the house. What's the point of fixing it up? I
don't recognize it any more. To buy good things to eat? But
I don't have time to prepare them properly. Sunday? Oh
no, I'm too tired to cook, and anyway I've lost the knack.
But I can buy a refrigerator, a television set, fancy canned
goods. The anonymous furnishings, the hi-fi set, the missing
food for missing people. And nylon stockings. This is freedom, this is the whole substance, the whole reality of my
freedom!

My husband's vile humor; it is true that when he came
home he was always on edge, I used to complain, and I
didn't understand. Now we meet at the door of our house,
both coming from work, both irritated and tense, both in a
bad mood. We could both use a real home, some relaxation,
a smiling and affectionate welcome: we meet with the same
requirement and the same need. But there is nobody to
satisfy it, nobody to calm our nerves, and all we can do is
bicker in front of the closed faces of our children. Faces
that I can no longer read, for I only see them when they are
sleepy in the morning or tired at night, faces that are being

shaped by other hands than mine, that receive other affection than mine, faces that become more unfamiliar every day, faces that do not know me and that I do not know. Long live freedom, Madame!

The freedom of nothingness.

NO FREEDOM
FOR THE ENEMIES
OF FREEDOM

"Freedom is different from licence"; "The freedom of the
individual is limited by the freedom of the group"; "No
freedom without security"; "No freedom without money";
"Freedom is always in danger"; "Freedom is like religion:
you have to have it, but too much is bad." Out of this
medley of nineteenth-century expressions emerges our
twentieth-century commonplace. It goes without saying
that if we want to hold onto freedom, we must not risk it.
We must keep it carefully protected. We must not expose it
to the elements, for, alas, it is a fragile bloom, as we know
only too well. A gust of wind, a flash of sun, and there is no
more freedom. It is obvious that since freedom is our most
precious possession (another commonplace from the inex-
haustible Voltaire), it is important not to waste it. And if
you carry it in your pocket, you always run the risk of
losing it. If you show it to everybody, somebody is bound

to take it away from you. To want to share it with the average man is truly the height of imprudence. How can you fail to see that this poor maiden will be prostituted and defiled, pawed by perfect strangers. No, no, she cannot be abandoned this way! Especially not to people who declare themselves openly to be her murders. It is quite obvious that they must be prevented. Everybody will readily agree that each man has a right to a freedom that is reasonable, moderate, and largely internal, but we must deny all freedom to the man who wants to take away the freedom of others. How calming and reassuring these truths are!

But if we are unfortunate enough to examine them a little too closely, what a shock! First of all, those who openly acknowledge that they are the enemies of freedom are very rare! Take the Nazis, for example; everything they did was in the name of freedom. Have you forgotten so soon? Review their speeches and writings since 1933, *and you will find our current commonplaces clear as day:* "No freedom for the enemies of freedom"; I believe it was Hitler who was the author of this fine statement! For his primary concern was to free his people from those who were reducing them to slavery: the bankers, the Jews, the intellectuals who were infecting them with their lies. He had to free the Germans enslaved in Poland, Czechoslovakia, and France. Then, expanding his mission, he had to free all peoples who were oppressed by this dreadful clique of exploiters and liars. As for the concentration camps, they were for the enemies of freedom.

In 1948 our commonplace was adopted, with lengthy commentary, by Tito; more about this later. In France the staunchest defenders of this commonplace are the communists, who invoke it constantly. But the democrats are necessarily in agreement too, although with reservations and a guilty conscience. Democracy, of course, is possible only if

everyone respects the freedom of all, if people are quite
determined to preserve *this* democratic regime, the guarantee of freedom. This is fundamental, and this is why the
democrats are sometimes tempted to deprive the communists of freedom, for after all, do they not openly admit that
they want to abolish *this* democratic regime, and deprive
the whole bourgeois class of its freedom? Well . . . But
obviously, as soon as democracy begins to take this line, it
contradicts itself, and the communists are the first to insist
on this freedom of which they are ready to deprive others,
for the others are necessarily the enemies of freedom.

And here, in fact, is the whole difficulty! Who are the
enemies of freedom, since nobody actually admits that he
is? The label must be applied from the outside, duly drawn
up, objective. You can't leave this responsibility to the first
person who comes along! In the end, obviously only the
state can be trusted to tell us what freedom is (on that
point we have agreed since 1789 and the immortal principles), and *consequently* also to determine who threatens
this freedom, who is its enemy. It is truly amazing that it
has taken over a century to draw such a logical conclusion.
Especially when since 1789 everybody has known that the
forces of the state are devoted to the service of freedom. It
is written everywhere.

And this is where we concur with the unassailable logic
of Tito. The individual citizen obviously does not have the
strength or the power to defend his freedom himself; it
must be protected. And just as everyone's life is protected
against murders by the police, so is his freedom. This is the
responsibility of the state, and consequently the state must
be strong enough to do this. Everyone knows how difficult
it is to take care of all, to guard the life and liberty of

everyone. Therefore, the more powerful the state is, the better everyone's liberty will be protected. In other words, the greater power of the state is the proof, the guarantee, the very ground for the greater freedom of all. Q.E.D.

Seriously, this is the sum and substance of Tito's major speech on the organization of the state in 1951. Once this is established, all is smooth sailing. Since it is the state that has the responsibility of defending freedom, it follows that it is the state that knows *against whom* it must be defended. Thus, the American state will prove that the enemy of freedom is the communist, the Russian state that is the capitalist, and the French state in 1960 that it was the fellagha, whereas for the provisional Algerian government it was the Frenchman. In other words, *whatever his doctrine,* the enemy of freedom is necessarily the Other: the person who does not favor this form of state, this type of society! This is obvious since freedom invariably becomes identified with a given state or a given social structure.

In other words, the enemy of freedom is the person who uses it (for as we said to begin with, if you use it, it gets used up, and the first requirement for preserving freedom is to put it in a museum and appoint a curator of the Public Freedoms). If logic brings us this far, it also brings us to the idea that freedom is the freedom to agree with the government. Freedom cannot be left to the hazards of the exercise of freedoms by individuals, or worse, a single individual's conquest of his freedom.

But if, by the operation of the necessities of politics and the laws of society, freedom is necessarily reduced to these limitations, let us at least be aware that we are staking the exact opposite of freedom. For what is the meaning of a freedom that does not allow one to challenge norms and definitions? What is the meaning of a freedom that does not *also* allow for the possibility of dissent? What is the meaning of a freedom that does not recognize the other person's freedom, with which you come into conflict and which may oppose you and threaten to destroy your own? What is the meaning of a freedom that is a standardized procedure whose results are known in advance? What is the meaning of a freedom that the free man does not assume full responsibility for and that he himself does not defend? What is the meaning of a freedom that does not involve risk or come into conflict with its opposite? What is the meaning of a freedom that is not a confrontation of necessity, and thus, in the political context, a struggle against its own enemy? It is a parody of freedom.

In the circus ring our political heroes of the right or the left play at freedom, but it is only in a circus, and presently the well-named M. Loyal will fold up the tents, with us inside them. Anyone who expresses this commonplace is simply a totalitarian, and any government that adopts it is no less than a dictatorship, down to the dreary puppetlike quality that characterizes any dictatorship, right or left.

FREEDOM IS
OBEYING NECESSITY

We used to talk about making a virtue of necessity, and the good La Fontaine had already mentioned those sour grapes that are out of reach. His excuse was that he was ridiculing the idea, and could not foresee that an entire civilization, the thinking of all the intellectuals of a society, would come to rest on the premise that the inevitable is a virtue. At a primitive stage of thought, the untutored man feels that when he is in prison, he is not free. We have changed all that, and everything goes to show that, on the contrary, it is *precisely then* that he is free. We know now that history unfolds in an inexorable, inevitable manner, according to a necessary process, and that the sole virtue of man consists in entering into this process. His only freedom is in helping along the inevitable. The only good is to reach the goal that history cannot fail to reach. It is clear, then, that the more fully you submit to historical necessity, the freer and better you are. The man who tries to stand in the way of this necessity is the very man who is not free. In this extraordi-

nary reversal, the man who is not free is the man who tries
to disengage himself from the implacable course of history,
from the laws of sociology and economics. The man who is
free is the man who obeys them. Such an obvious idea has
spread like wildfire.

Even so, eventually we will have to ask ourselves *why*
modern man has accepted it with such alacrity, for little by
little unanimity is growing, not on the form or application,
but on the idea itself. Thus, Alain in his celebrated statement: "The tool, the honest and straightforward instrument of necessity, with which we overcome it even as we
obey it . . . " Once again, then, it is by *obeying* necessity
that one can overcome it, that is, prove oneself victorious
and free. It is true that Alain added the tool as Marx did
the party. Let's not stop while we're on such a good path.
Remember Marshal von Keitel, who declared at the time of
his trial that with Hitlerism they were all caught in a
machine that led them step by step from necessity to necessity, but that it was the only way to ensure the freedom of
the German people. Thus, to obey the necessity of the
government is to demonstrate the freedom of the people.

Finally, the latest and the best, De Gaulle himself declared with his traditional rigor, on April 13, 1961, "Decolonization is in our interest, and consequently it is our
policy." But here, you will say, it is a question of interest,
not of necessity. Read what follows: "Why should we remain involved in a domination that is costly, bloody, and a
dead end . . . " How could it be said better that since the
situation is a dead end, it must be abandoned? And what is
dead end, if not an image of necessity?

In this chorus of free and happy lads who sing the merits
of necessity, only the Nazi ended by raising a problem of
conscience. It is true that he was defeated, and that obeying necessity had led him before a tribunal. Nevertheless,

this Nazi marshal finally put his fingers on the real question. In this same statement he asks, in effect, "At what moment should we have stopped? We were obeying necessity." We realize now that it was not exactly virtue to follow the movement of the mechanism. But when you have put your hand into the works, can you get out of it? Is the next step more evil or less necessary than the one before? Once you have accepted the idea that destiny is freedom (another of Hitler's doctrines!), how and where do you find the freedom to deny destiny at one moment rather than another? The same problem was submitted to us by another Nazi marshal, Von Paulus, over Radio Moscow, after he discovered that it was bad to obey the Nazi necessity, a discovery he had made as a prisoner of the Soviets. Of his own free will, of course.

You receive your induction notice. The police and the military court have the last word, but forget about that. At the sight of the little black letters you are seized with a delirious enthusiasm, a sacred frenzy, the highest expression of your freedom, and of your own accord you rush where you know you must go. That is also indicated on the paper. But for shame! You're certainly not going just to obey an injunction; it is your freedom that you are obeying, I tell you. And through communion with the entire nation, you spontaneously know what must be done! You don't need to receive this little piece of paper. Conscious of your country and the meaning of your life, you would have volunteered, you would have discovered on your own that this is precisely what had to be done!

Do not think I am attacking those who, not being eligible for the draft, actually go and enlist voluntarily. Although they are obeying another compulsion, that of public

opinion and the wave of patriotism, they still have a
semblance of freedom that they are using. But the people I
have in mind have no alternative but to go to war, whatever their opinion; and what I object to is that they use
this as an excuse to offer themselves a patent of authenticity, that they deceive themselves into thinking that it
would be the same in the absence of compulsion and necessity. It is the Christian preachers who, precisely at the
moment of mobilization, discover that it is a Christian duty
to serve the state *perinde ac cadaver,* and that the good
Christian must be a good soldier. Pure coincidence. It was
the labor-union leaders of 1914 who discovered the sanctity
of union. It is the moralists of every stripe, Alain or Montherlant, who turn the necessity of war into the essence of
human virtue. These are the liars.

We find ourselves in a universe proliferating with machines and technology. Buds are popping out all over.
Every day a thousand new things appear. A technologized
world is growing up around us at an increasing rate. An
organization that is steadily becoming more pitiless, more
precise, more compelling, and more complex is closing in
on every man and every instant of man's life. And we can't
do anything about it. Nobody can do anything about it.
Nobody is directing or controlling this proliferation. An
operation set in motion a century and a half ago is contin-
uing under its own power. Nobody is responsible for it any
more. The chemist, the sociologist, the urban expert, the
engineer, the organizer, and the economist find themselves
involved for a thousand reasons of social pressure, education, prestige, and money, in an irreversible process that
forces them to serve technological progress, a process
whose connection with all the other processes occurs out-

side their will or anyone's will. Technology, in its development and its application to man, is the most complete
mechanism of necessity.

But what is unacceptable is when the flatterers, the
pseudo-philosophers of freedom, the technologists, the humanists, and the theologians vie with one another to prove
that this necessity is freedom itself. Through technology,
man frees himself of natural necessities. Look at Titov!
Through technology, man frees himself of the state. Look
at the effect of television on democracy! Through technology, man fulfills his vocation: has he not been *homo faber*
since the beginning? Is he not a demiurge, by the will of
God? And if he carries out the will of God, is that not the
essence of freedom? There you are! Through technology he
acquires culture, which is the freedom of the mind! Overflowing harvest of high-sounding nonsense! Martial music
designed to make man accept the condition in which he
finds himself cruelly immersed. The concrete experience of
man in the technologized world is one of necessity, of a
compulsion that is not solely the compulsion of work, but of
each aspect and every moment. But we must save appearances. We must convince man that he is freer than ever, and
that the necessity in which he finds himself is virtue itself,
the essence of goodness, that never has humanity been so
happy, so peaceful, so balanced, so virtuous, so intelligent,
that the technology in which he is trapped is the very thing
that sets him free! "In all countries of the world, you are
the victim of a police regime that is more and more scientific and hence implacable, but look at the sputnik, there is
your freedom! Pigeon, fly!"

It is obvious that the density of the population, the
complexity of administrative and political life, economic

growth, and the problems raised by the encroachment of technology all imply an organization that is constantly becoming more precise, more meticulous, more rigorous; that is, a planned society—planned economy, planned cities, planned distribution of wealth, planned distribution of work, space, and time, planned administration, planned traffic, planned education, and planned parenthood. There is no alternative, I agree; but the chorus of humanists is there to prove to us that all this planning is the prerequisite for freedom. It is *obvious* that the man who lives in a traditional society is not free, I grant you that. But as for us, the more traffic regulations they pass and one-way streets they create, the more production quotas and work rhythms they set, the more they standardize police files, controls, and methods, the more they bracket public opinion within the framework of the Plan, the more they multiply the indexes of compulsory growth and productivity, the freer we are! You shrug your shoulders and say that we have no choice? I never said we did! But it makes me wonder when, during the debate on the Fifth Plan, Pompidou declares, "The planned economy ensures the freedom of each," mouthing the commonplace of the whole left. Why bring freedom into it? Why must it be that when surrounded by so many admirable achievements, man is still not satisfied and must have that flower in his buttonhole as well?

But is not the crux of the whole matter to succeed in proving that necessity is freedom? And so it is that you will hear presented as a progressive, liberating idea what is nothing more than a lumbering intellectual attempt to catch up with the most compulsory, impersonal, and pecuniary obligation. No point in multiplying examples, they are legion. But if man has invented these commonplaces, if our intellectual carrion beetles swarm around them and proliferate with ideas, it is because this corresponds not to a truth, but to a need. Obviously, we live in a world that is no picnic. Obviously, we are not very proud of taking every morning, as Léo Ferré's song puts it admirably, the "bus of adventure," to return in the evening "after the daily grind, with vague aches and pains." The life that our organized and hygienic universe offers us is less and less inspiring, personalizing, or ennobling. It is hardly conducive to stirring the creative passions. Under these conditions, the nineteenth-century bourgeoisie announced, "It is too sad to look at reality. Let us speak, therefore, of the ideal, let us keep our eyes fixed on heaven, only the dream is worthy of our devotion," and so on. This lasted quite a while. Today we look at reality, no doubt, but we distort it. For man's attitude remains the same! "It is too sad that it is this way. It is too horrible to be chained. It is unacceptable that man's life be conditioned . . . "

And perhaps, after all, this impulse is a permanent tendency in the heart of man; perhaps, after all, man invented the soul because it was too horrible to be only a body, a wretched body subject to all the necessities: fatigue, hunger, suffering, and finally death. He had to find a way out, to make himself a little domain of freedom. But there was still the dichotomy, which is a weakness. Besides, the refuge of the soul no longer works, for psychological methods are perfectly capable of conditioning the soul as well, and the inside is just as well organized as the outside. So we went one better. All we had to do was bring the opposites together. All we had to do was convince man that the more he obeys, the more virtuous he is, and the more he is compelled, the freer he is, and all is saved. Neither despair nor revolt nor suicide is any longer to be feared. On the one hand the inevitable occurs, Ananke has found the way open; on the other, man lifts his head and asserts himself more than ever. It is no accident that today all our pseudo-philosophers have rediscovered Hegel!

I am the first to admit that we are in the hands of necessity: the rope around the neck and the kick in the pants. We have no choice. Granted; this is simply the human condition, and my first real experience is of frustration, of the limits of my strength and resistance, of the invincible sleep, of fear of tomorrow or of the law. I am bound by the state, by work; I am conditioned by my body and by the social body: such is my weakness, such is my cowardice. There's no point in making scenes or having complexes about it: these things are common to us all. But what does become inadmissible in this situation is to crow triumphantly, "Just see how I have won, and how free I am!" or to wink at the assembled company and say, "See what a clever fellow I am, and how I have outsmarted necessity!" For this heralds the reign of the Liar.

THE SPIRITUAL SIDE
OF LIFE CANNOT
DEVELOP UNTIL THE
STANDARD OF
LIVING IS RAISED

This is not the doctrine of a conscious Marxist materialist, but a commonplace familiar to all circles, especially intellectual ones. A curious phenomenon, but one for which we shall see the explanation, is that the more "spiritual" the milieu, the more deeply rooted this idea is. It takes many forms. The Salvation Army declares that you cannot preach the Gospel to a man whose stomach is empty. A more radical example is the progressive Christian for whom all evangelism is a scandal as long as six hundred million

Chinese or Hindus are starving.[1] There is the professor for whom no culture can appear until the physical needs are satisfied. There is the moralist for whom it is often axiomatic that the man who is hungry has no moral problems.

And the philosopher of history today declares that thus far humanity has known only its prehistory. It has reached only a minor stage of development because it has been living in poverty and the torment of hunger. And it is only now that the history of humanity is beginning, only now that a *true* culture, a *true* spiritual life will be possible. This is a matter of great scope, since people have almost reached the point of thinking that everything humanity has achieved in these domains is negligible. Before one undertakes the analysis of this commonplace, certain things should be understood. In the first place, it goes without saying that I do not regard starvation and a state of underdevelopment as virtues. It goes without saying that I do not look upon material possessions with contempt. What I object to is confusing *pâté de foie gras* with dog food. Secondly, we are going to be forced to adopt a dull and laborious procedure. Since this commonplace is presented not as an opinion or a value judgment, but as the observation of a fact, the expression of a tangible reality, we are obliged to use a rigorous method for examining it, for if it is accurate, we are in the presence not of a commonplace, but of a scientific truth. Since we are talking about a fact, it can be verified either historically or experimentally.

If we have some sense of the spiritual and do not feel that the religious impulse is the expression of an infantile

---

[1] When a theologian defends this doctrine, he is explicitly condemning Jesus Christ, who should have waited until all men had enough to eat before he came and preached, or should at least have proclaimed his Gospel to someone besides the poor people of Judaea!

stage of humanity, if we agree that the spiritual is intimately related to the phenomenon of conscience and that
the latter is the source of all civilization, it may be important to ask ourselves where and when spiritual life reaches
its peak, its force, its intensity, where and when the invention of spiritual expressions has truly synthesized every
aspect of human life. There seem to have been three great
centers—not religious centers, properly speaking, but centers of creation and invention or, according to your point of
view, of receptivity and understanding. These are India,
Judaea, and Arabia. There and there alone has the great
spiritual explosion taken place.

Of course, we cannot overlook what might be called the
minor quest, which is found among the Polynesians as well
as among the Indians or the Scandinavians. But among all
these peoples, among whom "spiritual" life takes only a
minor form, one could make the same observation regard-
ing our commonplace as in the three chosen cases. We are
not trying to judge the "truth" of a given form of spiritual
life, but only its intensity.

Now, were the Jewish people of the seventh century or
the first century B.C., the Hindu peoples of the sixth century
or the second century B.C., and the Arab tribes of the sixth
century after Christ rich, and did they have a high standard of living? It would be absolutely grotesque to pretend
that they were. These were poverty-stricken peoples. And
within these peoples, was it among the few powerful persons, the rich leaders and nobles that the spiritual movement developed? Absolutely not; on the contrary, it was
among the most disinherited. And if we turn to our Western culture, where and when have there been high expressions of spiritual life? Where did the growth of Christianity
occur? In the rich circles of the Hellenistic or Roman
world? Not at all, but among the slaves; this was one of the

main objections of Celsus! And the scholars of the early
church, those remarkable theologians, where were their
roots? Among the bourgeois? We know the answer to that!
The amazing spiritual exploration of the Middle Ages during its greatest period of poverty can be overlooked or
regarded as reactionary only by the most reactionary dog-
maticians of our age! And if there is a powerful spiritual
movement in our time, it is that of social-communism,
which appeared and developed within the industrial proletariat during its period of greatest poverty.

Conversely, it may be observed by following the history
of each society that spiritual life declines and tends to
disappear whenever comfort increases and the standard of
living rises. The prophets used to express the disappearance of the spiritual by saying, "Israel, you have grown
fat." When wealth begins to appear in the Middle Ages, we
know what becomes of spirituality; it certainly does not
reside among the merchants and the bourgeois! And when
the fortunes of the working class improve, we also know
what effect this has on its revolutionary vigor and the
intensity of its inner flame!

I know, of course, that the objection will be made, "You
are concentrating on ancient, traditional forms of spiritual
and religious life. The mere fact that *these* are disappearing is no reason why *something else* cannot appear." I say
to my honorable opponent that when I include revolutionary vigor and human aspiration in spiritual life, my view is
not that traditional! But even granting that all that is traditional, I am still waiting for someone to show me this
something else. I see no sign of the beginning of something
else. And it does not strike me as very serious behavior on
the part of our lofty and highly scientific intellectuals to
count on a *something else* that so far is not even an image
or a soap bubble. For you can't even say that, given the

right circumstances, this might happen; according to the wisdom of nations, this is known as giving up the substance for the shadow. Although the argument in question satisfies the most distinguished of our progressive social thinkers, it is on the level of pure nonsense.

Let's turn to culture. I am well aware that we are not concerned with the individual achievement of an exceptional artist or an intellectual, but with the culture of a society. But what are the societies of high culture, in the broadest sense of the term? Are they the rich societies? And within societies, is it the rich class that originates culture? Whether you consider Persian society, Japanese society, Byzantine society, Greek society, Roman society, or the Bantu groups at the point when they create culture, you see very clearly that it is always a question of poor societies. It is absolutely inaccurate, for example, to claim that Greek culture is the product of a rise in the standard of living. The alleged prosperity of Greek commerce, the alleged wealth of this society in the sixth and fifth centuries B.C., are exaggerations. Modern historians have tried to demonstrate this, but concrete evidence indicates a commerce that was actually ridiculously insignificant and a very modest industry that was sporadic and uncertain,[2] neither in any way comparable to what we know or to the role industry and commerce play in our society.

It is a misuse of language, a failure of perception (taking *our* society as criterion and point of reference!), that leads us to overestimate the commerce, industry, and wealth in those centuries. Greece is a poor country, the Greek people

---

[2] All the textbooks cite a *single* Greek industrial enterprise involving more than a hundred workers! What capitalism!

in the fifth century were a poor people, and the Greek
miracle was the product of a poor society. And it certainly
is not in the milieu of *nouveau riche* tradesmen that artists
and intellectuals have been recruited, or that they have
been accepted and supported.[3] A culture that is the expression of a whole people, a culture in which a whole people
participates, is not a phenomenon of rich peoples. In Medi-
terranean antiquity there was only one truly rich country,
Tyre and its colonies. Only there was a powerful wealth
concentrated and a high standard of living attained for
everyone except slaves. But what culture has Tyre left us?
What civilization? What spiritual discovery? Like Car-
thage, it fed on borrowed culture! [4]

If we consider modern peoples in countries where the
standard of living is high, do we see the emergence of a
culture? Up to now has the United States had a culture
that may properly be called original, new, indigenous?
Here again, almost everything comes from the outside:
people, ideas, forms. And if we consider peoples who have
a culture and who acquire a higher standard of living, we
can make the same observation as for spiritual life. Cultural
creativity declines in proportion as the general standard of
living rises; the society then begins to exploit the legacy of
previous ages, it devotes itself to antiquity and folklore,
and when it does not find enough sap in its own past to
maintain the appearance of a culture, it seeks transfusions
of new blood, which it draws from barbarians.

Thus Rome after the first century B.C., when it had

---

[3] At most they came from impoverished aristocratic families or modest
liberal circles.
[4] It is historically false to say that in the Middle Ages culture was the
prerogative of men who did not have to work—clerks, nobles, etc. The
nobles were certainly the most uncultured of all! And the clerks, for the
most part, came from the peasant class and a great many worked with
their hands.

become rich and the standard of living was rising, turned
to Virgilian or Ovidian folklore, to Greek culture, or to the
Oriental passion, and later would seek new blood from
Germanic "culture." Thus our European West since the
nineteenth century has turned more and more to the Bohe-
mian, the primitive, the Tahitian, and the Negro, in order
to rediscover in foreign music and forms a cultural vitality
it has lost. Exoticism is always the fruit of a high standard
of living as well as the mark of cultural sterility.

Can it be said, then, that within a given society it is in
the upper classes that cultural creation occurs? The cultural contribution to Rome was made by its slaves. And
must we take the example of the bourgeoisie in Europe?
This is the very class that has circulated all the false images
of culture that we live on, and that has emasculated all
profound collective creativity, reducing culture to a game,
the peacock feathers of individualist vanity or the fake
ermine mantle of academic *Kultur*.[5]

But then what, as far as culture is concerned, can be the
source of such a big mistake, such an obvious blunder? The
very idea that culture is a game, a luxury, a supplement to
the standard of living, a symbol of wealth like a fine dia-
mond, the prerogative of an elite. To connect culture with
standard of living is to be taken in by the most bourgeois
view of man and the world. It is the normal result of

---

[5] There is a very amusing book of statements made by various personalities called *Je vis en République allemande* (1962), in which there is agreement on the following ideas: "Prosperity, the economic miracle, and well-
being have killed all spiritual life in West Germany;" "In West Germany
people eat instead of thinking;" "Mental stagnation is the consequence of
the dynamism of production." I am quite aware of all that may be question-
able about these statements. This is why I call this book "amusing"; it
shows modern man in contradiction with himself.

patronage, which has been the bourgeois notion of the matter ever since the good Maecenas! The rich man, prince, banker, or industrialist, who embellishes his life by buying a collection of paintings, by supporting a poet or a sculptor. On the one hand, there is the producer of ideas or art, who becomes an individual completely cut off from his society and from real life, an isolated forger of unreal but very seductive illusions. On the other hand, there is the consumer of ideas or art who relaxes, distracts himself, passes the time between two love affairs. It is familiarity with this system, which is as negative and antihuman as possible, that causes us to associate culture with a high standard of living. The fact is that the hired painter and the official poet of the seventeenth and eighteenth century produced important works of art. The mistake is to believe that this was the *only* culture, or even that it was representative of the culture of this period. It is as victims of this narrow outlook that our opponents are judging—and rather hastily at that.

But the most remarkable part, as I am well aware, is that they are giving me back my own argument when they say, "You are clinging to a view of culture that is much too traditional, outmoded, and unilateral, in not accepting the contemporary form of mass culture! You are defending a cultural mandarinate! We are witnessing the emergence of an authentic new culture associated with a high standard of living. Why reject it?" Let us note in passing that the question has shifted slightly. It is no longer being said that culture is associated with a high standard of living, but that this situation makes a new culture possible. But what culture? What are we being offered? The great discovery is leisure, the gadget, the audiovisual! Man will improve himself when he has nothing better to do, to fill the void, and, of course, with no relation to his work—shut up in the living room and hypnotized by the little screen. Making the Eiffel Tower out of matchboxes, collecting miniatures, experimenting with space ships in the garden, inventing a lethal fountain pen—this is culture! Watching old movies, a documentary on Mount Athos, a production of Racine rebroadcast over television—this is culture! Reading *Paris-Match* and glancing casually at the reproductions of Van Gogh while an ear distracted by clinking dishes and playing children catches fragments of Mozart—this is culture!

Actually, we are surrounded by false culture! [6] By passivity, by the mass distribution of Good Humors, by the pseudo and the laminated, precisely because all this remains within the magic circle of culture drawn *by the bourgeoisie:* the game and the luxury. The only solution is to admit the people into the false culture that the bourgeoisie have carefully forced on the world. But in the last analysis this is not taking creativity seriously. It is remaining outside of the problem. Everything is falsified when you associate culture with the leisure of a technologized society, which is compensation, counterpoise, antidote, rather than the fulfillment of a complete personality, which *includes* rather than excludes work. It is marking culture a piece of a puzzle instead of a force for synthesis and unity. What is offered us has nothing to do with culture, it is not even an image or an avatar, it is not even a counterfeit; it is the cutting off at its source of any subsequent possibility of culture.

And if we turn from the observation of societies to the observation of man, let us merely question ourselves: At

---

[6] I am not adopting the whole argument in E. Morin's *La Culture industrielle,* but only one point that I find essential and that is not generally seen by analysts of the problems of culture. See especially B. Charbonneau's *Le Paradoxe de la culture* (1965).

what age is man seized by the spiritual problem in all its
acuteness? At what age is he a creator of ideas and forms?
At what age does he find a vocation? At what age is awareness of the self and of the world intense, lucid, exacting? At
what age does man raise the decisive and ultimate questions, and at what age does he want to grasp life in a
synthetic fashion? At the age of fifty? When he has reached
the summit of his career, made his fortune, satisfied his
appetites? When he is settled in an established and secure
situation, when he is independent and has collected the
ancestral inheritance he expected? You all know that this is
not true; that it is at the age of twenty, when the teeth of
the young wolf are sharpest, that the spiritual, the creative, and the intellectual have vitality, meaning, and
power. And you know very well that the mature man can
only rehash the discoveries of his youth, explain the ideas
of his youth, and perfect the syntheses of leaner times. No,
surely, it is not with the rise of his standard of living that
the spiritual or the cultural come to him; on the contrary, it
is then that they disappear.

And if we address ourselves to those who obviously
know something about it, do we find that they advocate
comfort and easy living to promote spiritual life or the creation of culture? What was the attitude of the great spiritual
leaders toward comfort and material conveniences? It is
well known. Isaiah and Buddha, St. Theresa and Ramak-
irshna, the preacher of Ecclesiastes and Confucius, all,
unanimously and without a single exception, say that only
poverty is favorable to the spiritual life; that all wealth,
even moderate, is sterilizing; that all security and all comfort are destructive of meditation and the search for truth.
They all reject the idea that it is with a full stomach and

when he has an hour to kill that man can turn toward eternity and has the leisure to do so! *They* know what they arc talking about, so I am forced to conclude that those who defend our brilliant commonplace are quite simply unaware of the meaning of spirituality.

Here, however, we encounter an obstacle: "The spiritual leaders are talking about *voluntary* poverty; so in our society let man live in comfort, hygiene, and a high level of consumption, and let whoever wants devote himself to the ascetic life, renounce everything and become spiritual." But if this is true for Buddha or Francis of Assisi, it is false that the others are talking about a choice. No, it is the human condition itself, and when Jesus anathematizes the rich man (that is, what modern society wants to make of each of us, to which end it invites us to employ our energies), he does not mean the man who could forsake his riches, but the one who *has directed his energies toward the acquisition of wealth,* that is, the very spirit of our society and our commonplace! For the fundamental question is much less that of Having (as opposed to Being) than that of "Wanting to Have," by which the will subordinates Being to Having even when one has nothing. The problem is to know whether it is legitimate to direct all our vital energies toward "Having More"!

Furthermore this agrument is pure hypocrisy in the light of the economic organization of our society. Can you choose the path of poverty? Ha! Short of joining organizations that specialize in the vocation of poverty, it is no longer possible to be a beggar or a pauper by vocation, because work is becoming compulsory for all (cf. the commonplace relating to work). Even someone who was content to accept the discipline of labor without accepting its fruit would be completely incapable of a spiritual life, because the schedule and the nature of work—any work, bu-

reaucratic, industrial, or otherwise—in our society excludes
all spiritual life. To deny this is to believe that a man's life
is made up of airtight compartments: from eight a.m. to
noon, drudgery; from noon to two p.m., relaxation and
culture; from two p.m. to six p.m., more drudgery; from six
p.m. to eight p.m., family life; from eight p.m. to ten p.m.,
spiritual life. But to imagine that eight or even six hours
work in the modern world do not alter the whole life, do
not sterilize all capacity for culture or spiritual life, precisely because it is work that is nonassimilable, impossible
to integrate into the whole life, is to have absolutely no
sense of what spiritual life or culture can be.

In spite of its stupidity, this commonplace is amazingly
widespread. But in order to understand it, we must ask
ourselves *who* and *why*—remembering the classic adage *Is
fecit cui prodest!* Plainly, it is the technologists, social
thinkers, economists, and to a lesser extent the technicians
who spread this obvious truth, more often than not at the
end of some paper on "The Civilization of the Year 2000"
or "The Great Hope of the Twenty-first Century." After
showing that the whole problem is to raise the standard of
living, that everything will be solved by economic growth,
they add *in cauda* (and that is certainly where the *vene-
num* resides!), "Naturally, we do not presume to make a
value judgment; naturally, as humble economists, we simply serve man; naturally, the important thing is spiritual
life, culture, human development; but everyone knows that
all these depend on raising the standard of living!" A casual
salute to values that is supposed to justify the rest of their
work. The economist or social thinker will tell you, "You
see, all the rest of our work is perfectly serious, useful,
'authentic,' and 'valid,' since we know the *true* values and

since, knowing them, we have based this research on them; so you, who are as concerned about man as we are, can trust it."

Of course, if by "culture" you mean a hodgepodge of miscellaneous and unrelated information, a game of double or nothing, the world of fantasy and leisure, specialized technical knowledge; if spiritual life is a vague religiosity, if morality is social conformity, if conscience is a literary phenomenon—then there is no contradiction between this nonsense and the raising of the standard of living, economic activity, the vocation of *homo faber*, automation, and *tutti quanti*. But these elementary notions, which certainly are the ones referred to by this commonplace, do not bear much relation to the truth. If we take human creativity seriously, we are forced to realize that it is intimately related to work and that it expresses the whole of a civilization [7] (and if there is no culture right now, this is because work is not cultivated, in spite of technical education!). If we take morality seriously, we must say that it is precisely when man is hungry that the moral problem is raised! Otherwise is it only an abominable sham! And if we take conscience seriously, we must say that it can be expressed and refined only in concrete debate. Conscience does not exist when it is sitting on foam-rubber pillows.

When these judgments are made by spiritual leaders, creators of moral or aesthetic values, I put my faith in them. When Mr. X, the brilliant economist, talks about the spiritual in terms that contradict Isaiah, I put my faith in Isaiah, and conclude that Mr. X doesn't know anything

---

[7] Among the thousand definitions of civilization, I offer mine: "The living and continuous creation of intellectual, aesthetic, spiritual, and institutional forms which express the capacity of a people as a whole to synthesize its experience of life and to integrate into a whole, subject to certain values, the various activities, ideas, intentions, aspirations, and organizations of man at a given moment."

about it. When Mr. Y, the brilliant sociologist, talks about
artistic creation in terms that contradict those of Stendhal
or Rimbaud, I put my faith in those gentlemen, and conclude that Mr. Y doesn't know anything about it. And I am
beginning to think that the very fact of associating standard of living with the spiritual, conscience, morality, and
culture is sufficient proof that those who believe in this
commonplace simply don't know what they are talking
about!

But after all, why bother with all this? Why not take the
clear, consistent, straightforward attitude of the rational
materialist (but how difficult it is to be one!), that the only
thing that matters is filling your belly. Culture! Unimportant. The spiritual? It doesn't exist. Conscience? Negligible.
Morality? Mere convention. Religious worship? A threat to
the economy! [8] In this case I would have no complaint. The
economist who would tell me this would impress me as
very honest, and would seem to me to put the problem correctly, in terms of a simple either-or choice. If you want to
be successful, you must sacrifice all the rest: that's how it is.

But alas! We live in a pseudo-Christian, post-Christian
society, we are the ineritors of a spiritual legacy, our pseudo-
philosophers believe in values, our novelists (even M.
Butor!) are forever raising moral problems, and the good
people no longer want *panem et circenses,* which was good
enough for the pagans, but bread and justice (or liberty, or
fraternity, etc.). After all, we are Westerners, aren't we?

---

[8] An excellent article in the Bulgarian newspaper *Otechestven Glas*
for July 10, 1961, explains that the frequent kneeling and genuflecting
during religious ceremonies constitutes a threat to economic progress because it physically weakens the congregation and sends them to work exhausted. Here is an honest position!

And in the eyes of history we have a heavy responsibility to bear, etc. Hindered by our long medieval robe, how do we expect to drill for oil in Hassi-Messaoud?

Fortunately, the social thinkers are here to reconcile everything. That is their business. The main thing is to be sure you win on all fronts and lose on none. We want to have our cake and eat it too. Of course, we want to have the refrigerator and the car, but we also want freedom, truth, culture, and all the rest of it. We want to win on the material front without losing anything on the spiritual. Money and the Holy Ghost, that's our motto, and we won't be happy until we have proved that this is how it should be. For immediately and instinctively you don't like to lose anything, even if you don't know exactly what it is, even if you don't care very much for it, even if it has been relegated to the attic or the closet shelf. You always look like a fool when you lose something. It means that you lost control of the situation, and it is just when you lose something that you realize you were very attached to it. No, no, no, we mustn't lose anything.

And besides, the revolution of '89 was not for nothing; we always need assurance that we still have these things. After all, we aren't base materialists, we have souls. And for this reason we cannot accept the impossible choice offered by Jesus Christ: your money or your soul. We have outgrown this childish wisdom, we know that one can have both. Our social thinkers have taught us that. And our commonplace seems eminently useful. For after all, the rise in the standard of living is obvious. Our whole civilization is oriented toward it, all our efforts converge in this direction, and it is true that even in the most underprivileged classes living conditions are rapidly improving. There is no more problem there.

When it comes to values, culture, and the spiritual, how-

ever, the problem has not been broached. Here it is difficult
to give statistics, to provide clear proof. Accustomed to
solid and mathematical certainties, we flounder in a bog
that would seem repugnant if we were not on such a lofty
plane! Especially when there are evil minds talking about
the culture crisis, the loss of values, the sterilization of the
conscience, and the people shout as one man: "Give us
reassurance!" So our commonplace seems an inspired find:
to relate the spiritual to the standard of living. It is obvious
that the standard of living is rising, therefore the spirtual
must be on the right track! An admirable solution, especially since by inverting the commonplace you also justify
the raising of the standard of living. For after all, we know
how difficult it is to ask of modern man all the sacrifices
that we demand purely for the sake of material results: a
little more comfort, a little better sanitation, a little more
food, a little more security. In the last analysis, all this is
rather meager and will not arouse wild enthusiasm.

But if in the same breath you guarantee values, the
justice of the society to come, and the whole song and
dance, then your efforts are justified, economic development acquires a spiritual meaning (on which subject the
augurs are winking behind the backs of the idealists), and
the good people, hungry for an absolute, find themselves
enlightened by this integration of the most absolute with
the most contingent, in a ridiculous parody of the Incarnation.

The extreme utility of the commonplace explains first of
all why this typically materialistic doctrine is prevalent
among idealists who are preoccupied with the spiritual and
with culture. But by this very fact, the more idealistic they
are the more they reveal themselves as ignorant of true

spirituality and culture. The conscious materialists don't talk about these things, they have nothing to do with the spiritual, and the subjects "art" or "morality" are for them carefully labeled and filed away. These things do not interest them. They do not try to justify themselves or to find spiritual justification for the pursuit of a higher standard of living: they are consistent with themselves. But, like all our modern "post-communists," they very quickly turn back into idealists. Then they cease to be consistent. Our good idealists, troubled by their consciences, worried about culture and religion, incapable of defending themselves before the economic onslaught, incapable of calling into question the triumph of technology, resort to the baroque consolation of flight into illusion.

The utility of our formula also explains why our economists and social thinkers are most particularly venomous when you attack this specific point. They are, generally speaking, nice liberal academics (there is truth everywhere), but they become enraged when, in treating spiritual decay, the dentist's drill hits the little nerve of this very trite commonplace.

NO MORE WORDS—
GIVE US ACTS!

How noble it is, this cry of ardent youth full of devotion and burning to serve! What difference does it make *whom* they serve or *whom* they burn? This is all stupid rationalization. Kill first and look afterwards! Weary of the pointless discussions of old men, youth has risen up at last! It wants to emerge from the confusion into which it has been led by professors and politicians. It is sick to death of a wordy, rhetorical, parliamentary democracy. After all this talk it wants results. It wants to come to grips with reality, beyond the deceptive images of orators. This youth is dissipating its vitality among the feather cushions of prudence and explanation. Eliminate the old windbags, poets,[1] explicators, imitators, the showers of slides and singers of political ballads. The fury of men long deceived is going to be

---

[1] Although it was a poet (Autran) who brilliantly stated this moral in the nineteenth century: *"Qui tient que l'action vaut mieux que les paroles"* (count carefully, it has twelve feet!).

unleashed, the contempt of men suspicious of speeches is
going to overwhelm your fragile ramparts.

Ah! How admirably fascism understood this hunger on
the part of youth and virile men! How well it knew how to
make this commonplace the pivotal point of its propaganda
and its doctrine! And all the activists, the realists, the go-
getters, the truth-lovers (since truth consists in actively
confronting doctrine with reality by praxis—but I'm getting
off the track) rushed into fascism. They acted. They eliminated thought and speech. And we know the famous remark, "When I hear the word philosophy, I reach for my
gun." They made the world reverberate with the exploits.
And then, fortunately, everything fell through. Fascism
was wiped out. The men of action got back in line. And our
commonplace has lost its place, hasn't it? It is old, outmoded, buried with these heroes. But then why is it still
invoked?

For, indeed, we find it cropping up all over. Young
people, eager to get into the swing of things and throw out
the old, are dinning it into our ears. The hatred of the word
and the desire for the act: not a speech is made that does
not allude to this idea. The good Dr. Schweitzer also lent
his support to this incontestable truth. When he gave up
the teaching of theology to go and take care of Negro
children, it was because he wanted to leave the realm of
words for that of deeds. He said so himself. It goes without
saying that all good Frenchmen give him their unanimous
approval! Indeed, what comparison can there be between
the grotesque occupation of teaching logical eschatology to
four theology students and the admirable vocation of
plunging into the bush and curing thousands of sick people? Is it not *self-evident* where the truth lies?

The fact that you approve of action and look down on words does not make you a fascist! Quite so. Just look at this tanned, virile, and serene young man with his confident air and his passion for mountainclimbing. He looks contemptuously at the round shoulders of the professor and the pale face of the barfly. He does not talk; why should he? The mountain speaks for him. Danger lends color to the pure act, the act for its own sake, simply to prove oneself. The clay pipe can remain tightly clamped in his closed mouth; here the man of few words does not hide a single thought, never fear, but only a great confidence in movement. This attractive face that we saw pictured ten thousand times in certain illustrated newspapers in the good old days (1933-45)—surely it is not the face of a fascist? And what is one to say about the great concern for efficiency in our society? Efficiency above all: is this not the watchword of technicians, politicians, soldiers, engineers, economists, communists, and other activists, thanks to whom the modern world is what it is? Put your forces to the best possible use, lose as little time as possible, reduce waste of all kinds, produce the most with the least. We know very well that *everything* is dominated by this concern, and that the greatest effect obtained with the minimum of means strikes us as the proof of truth.

No, our commonplace is not dead. It is more universal than ever. It is only a little camouflaged. It no longer has the cynicism and impudence of youth. It lurks in the dark corners of the modern soul; it has adopted masks. But it is still the same, it has the same meaning and expresses the same contempt.

No more words! We have been lulled by them long enough. No more dialogue: what good is it? No more explanations about intentions, plans, hopes, regrets: all hot air. Worse still, it confuses the issue, for there is nothing better than dialogue for obscuring action. You come face to face with the enemy. You kill the little bastards, because they are all fellaghas. All very clear and simple. But then you begin to talk it over with a friend, and it becomes less and less clear, and the more newspapers you read, the more lectures you listen to, the more you talk about it, the less simple it is!

You demonstrate, you march through the streets, you shout "Release Popaul!" Somebody stops you and asks you who Popaul is, and suddenly you realize that you haven't the slightest idea. It was so simple before you started talking! You go and sign a manifesto—everything is clear; you read it—it is less clear; you think about it—it is no longer clear at all.

The tiresome part is that you must act. You hear it said, you hear it shouted, on all sides. A thousand times a day I am requested to intervene—by the newspaper, the radio, friends, leaflets. But the more I find out about it, the more I talk about it, the less capable I am of acting or intervening. But my conscience forces me not to remain on the sidelines like a coward and an incompetent, and I realize that I must choose between action and words. My choice is obvious! No more conversation, no more deliberation, no more subtleties. No more words, which confuse everything, but acts, which make everything clear.

The moment you act, everything becomes simple. There is the man who marches beside me, I cooperate with him, he cooperates with me, he is a good man. We have the same background, the same economic level, the same habits, the same opinions, the same techniques. We don't need to talk to each other, our actions coincide. There is the man opposite me, who is an obstacle, who does not have the same background, who does not obey the same images, who impedes my action: he is a bad man. We don't need to talk to each other, our actions contradict each other. I need only eliminate him. I need only demand satisfaction from him, final satisfaction by means of fists or knives. No more words, give us acts! In either case, the act makes it possible to obliterate the personality of the other. That is an undeniable advantage of action, which simplifies life enormously.

The relation of the technician to society is the same as the relation of the fascist to politics. If you reflect about all aspects of your acts, you are lost. If you reflect about the significance of your acts, you are paralyzed. If you look for a reason, you won't find one. If you really look at the man opposite you, you will never move. Such is the profound wisdom expressed by this commonplace. The act has intrinsic value. The act is what gives meaning to the world and to life. How right good old Goethe—who may be the originator of this commonplace—was when he refused to accept *Am Anfang war das Wort* and replaced this statement with *Am Anfang war die Kraft.* The act is sufficient unto itself, it is complete, and it is in the act that man is tested and proved.

Despite all the indignant looks that are leveled at me, I maintain that this commonplace well expresses the truth of man today. The act and the word do not complement each other: this is the heart of the matter. The act does not prove the word, nor does the word explain the act. To see things this way is to remain in the Middle Ages, to practice scholastic philosophy. In our time, the act and the word are mutually exclusive, irreconcilable enemies. He who talks condemns himself to renouncing action. All the conditions of modern life make action impossible for him once he has engaged in explanation and the search for meaning. He who acts can no longer talk, first of all because he simply doesn't have time! He only has time to shout. For a society impatient for proof and achievement, it is only the act that counts. And because only the act counts, henceforth the clamor of the active idiot will fill the sky alone.

ANYWAY, IT'S
A FACT!

That shuts you up, doesn't it, my good man? What do you
have to say to that? That puts an end to the arguments, the
paradoxes, the nonsense, the fallacies, the whole endless
blather of intellectuals—for the most curious part is that it
is an intellectual who invokes the apophthegm "It's a fact."
There is no rebuttal. You can talk yourself blue in the face,
you can't argue away the fact. And it is the fact that
prevails. Naturally, having been raised on a strict historical
discipline in which I learned to respect the sanctity of the
fact, I am forced to give in. I can still hear my dear old
Professor F. criticizing one of my papers and telling me,
"Above all, no ideas; facts, only facts."

It is certain that here I have a sure value. I can hold
forth about the truth ad infinitum, but if the truth is reduced to fact, I am sure to get hold of it somehow or other.
I may make a mistake about the direction of my life, but
not about the direction of traffic. I may be deceived about
the content of justice, but all success is assured me if the

fact of government dictates the only possible content for justice. After the uncertainties of language and thought, the fact gives me every guarantee of existence, certainty, objectivity, permanence, etc. Recourse to the fact is an admirable solution—convenient, simple flexible.

It's like Fleischmann's Yeast. You could take a picture of the intellectual—before, pale, gaunt, shifty-eyed, his brow furrowed, his head drooping, his speech halting; and after, the same man, shoulders back, with a confident expression, his head high, his cheeks rosy, his eye serene, his conversation sparkling: after recourse to the fact. The same man, first as philosopher, then as technician in petroleum—excuse me, in the fact: the Fact as argument, the Fact as sufficient reason, the Fact as value, the Fact as symbol (yes, even that, it is good for everything), the Fact as king, the Fact as God. "You can say what you will about technological progress, my dear fellow; obviously there is no question of turning back or denying what it is. All your talk is utterly useless, the machines are here to stay. You don't want to destroy them, do you? Of course not! Well then, you must adjust to them and live in the present. Oh yes, I know about you intellectuals—*laudator temporis acti!* That's what you're there for. But after all, let's be reasonable, even if technology does entail all the dangers and disadvantages you like to describe (but which do not belong to the realm of pure fact!). You say you are powerless in the face of the technological fact? In that case, stop all the talk; it bothers serious people who are Working."

Another tone: "Yes, of course, culture may be in danger, but it is up to us to invent a new culture based on the instruments which exist around us. Let's stop theorizing about what a culture should or might be. We have some admirable media—cinema, television, microfilm, *Paris-Match*, etc.—at our disposal. Develop a culture out of these

things, for the choice is between your imaginary desires
and regrets and reality, and *What is* is vastly superior to
What is not!"

These arguments were so persuasive that I immediately
felt freed of a great weight, and began to apply this all-
purpose handle to everything. "In 1933 there was a man
who established a harsh and implacable regime, revived a
great nation, established institutions, and created an army
and a power where before there had been only inchoher-
ence, rhetoric, chaos, disorder, impotence: this is the incontestable, unalterable Fact. He put an end to debate, he
established the Fact on its throne. Nobody ever surpassed
him in glorification of the accomplished fact. He made
a whole policy out of it! He was the personification of
this doctrine! Long live Hitler, for he is the Fact par
excellence!" "In 1940 there was a vanquished army that re-
treated in disorder, a prostrate nation, and an enemy moving in. One regime collapses, another takes its place. The
king is dead, long live the king! It is a Fact, and the Fact is
its own Justification. Long live Pétain, Vichy, and the rest!"
"They practiced torture in Algeria? But what do you want,
it's a Fact, a pure Fact. All your talk won't change anything. And anyway, your talk won't help us get the necessary information. In the face of your sophisms, I possess an
instrument that is effective, reliable, practical. *What is* is
greatly superior to *What is not.* Long live the Fact!"

But across from me I see my opponents frown and shrug
their shoulders. No, I do not understand, I do not understand *anything.* There are Facts and Facts. I am only trying
to learn; but when I ask how one can distinguish among the
facts those that are sufficient reason and those that are
worthless, it becomes very complicated! There are some
values that must be mixed in, there are some points of
reference that must be established by means of a spiritual

surveying. Clearly I am over my head. I think I have grasped the simple idea that the more ineluctable, inexorable, inevitable the Fact is, the more true, just, and good it is, but I immediately get dismissed for my insolence.

Here is the only fact worth considering: Did man become man by bowing before the Fact? When prehistoric man was threatened by glaciation, when he was almost eliminated by the cave bear, did he simply bow, saying, "It's a Fact, I can't do anything about it, I might as well disappear"? Surely the very thing that distinguished man from all the animals, the thing that is implied by his vocation as *homo faber, homo ludens,* and even more so *homo sapiens* and *homo vocans,* was that he rejected the Fact as final justification, that he refused to surrender to *What is,* that he challenged what could have seemed inevitable, that he strained all his forces so that the Fact would cease to be the fact, so that it would be deflected, mastered, rejected, exorcised.

If he had taken another attitude, he would in fact have been eliminated, and would be extinct. For this is the logical conclusion of the declaration of superiority of *What is* over *What is not,* the supremacy of the real, the self-sufficiency of the Fact. The recognition of the sovereignty of the Fact means the elimination, sooner or later, of what accounts for the nobility, the uniqueness, the truth of man. There remains only one solution: adjust. The intangible Fact is man, submissive from head to foot, from his instincts to his thought, length and breadth, inside and out; and since the Fact is more and more expected, more and more pregnant in our methodical society, the margin for initiative is constantly shrinking, in anticipation of the ideal moment when we will see a perfect identification between man and the Fact (no matter *what* Fact—biological, social, scientific—we want all facts, known, established, tamed, and wild!), when man himself will be only another Fact. Then, at last, we will be rid of ourselves!

YOU CAN'T MAKE
ART OUT OF NOBLE
SENTIMENTS

One can argue, of course, about the meaning Gide really intended in the famous passage that is the source of our axiom—but we are not here to engage in literary exegesis! We shall consider this commonplace as it appears in all literary or cinematographic criticism. One immediately notices that it is invoked by authors to justify the introduction of obscenity into their films and novels. Does obscenity have something to do with art? What a farce! Who is going to make us believe that the thighs of Brigitte Bardot have anything whatever to do with art? Art? Our producers and writers don't give a damn about art. Art is nothing but a pretext, a window dressing, a front; the goal is commerce and money. The more pornography there is (emphatically characterized as eroticism, with a whole philosophy behind it!), the better it sells. That's the long and short of it. And as soon as you utter a word of criticism, they scream like

Buffalo Bill being scalped: "Those awful moralists, those
bourgeois hypocrites, they are attacking artistic freedom,
the creative faculty, the source of inspiration!" Unanimous
protest in the name of the supremacy of Art, Human Dignity, the Responsibility of the Creator. It reminds me of an
admirable drawing by Brüller which shows bitterly that
when it comes to holding people's attention, no real poet
can compete with a woman's buttocks.

The source of inspiration is on approximately the same
level as those art photos that unsavory little old men offer
you on the *grands boulevards*. Except for the esoteric deco-
ration, those who invoke our commonplace have the same
conception of Art as these worthy tradesmen. With perfect
reciprocity and correspondence, the commonplace in question is also invoked by the consumer of books and films to
justify, also in the name of Art, his personal taste for porno-
graphic representations. You see, the poor fellow has so
little real opportunity to devote himself to his artistic
tastes! Between the family and the office, it is so difficult to
find artistic freedom! Vicariously, at least, thanks to the
film and the novel, he can immerse himself in a sea of
obscenity that will give him "ideas." (He has so few ideas
that we have to give them to him! Appropriately enough,
the word "idea" has acquired the same lewd connotations
as the word "art.") And very gravely and pompously the
merchandise will be covered with the aesthetic canopy.
Tsk, tsk! Naturally, what interests us is not Henry Miller's
detailed descriptions of—well, you know what; but what
profundity, what style, what aesthetic vitality, what a reap-
praisal of "man, society, morality, and ideas," etc.! But to
get the real story, simply leaf through secondhand copies of
the aforementioned books by Henry Miller, and you will
notice that 95 per cent of the pages are not cut, only the

interesting ones—otherwise you never would have noticed them, dear disinterested reader!

Now the term "noble sentiments" is very broad, but when it comes to applying the commonplace, it is quite clear that the principal target is sexual morality, and that the freedom from noble sentiments of the work of art in question is simply a matter of pornography. It is rather remarkable to observe that if Christians have been much criticized for having made sex a taboo, the domain *par excellence* of evil and of moral questions, the immoralists of our time have fallen into precisely the same trap. When they talk about Art *vs.* Morality, it is only sexual morality that is at issue. And when they talk about noble sentiments, they mean only purity in love, marital fidelity, respect for the beloved, family life, modesty, etc.; as long as you make fun of these values, you are liberated from noble sentiments. It strikes me that if we are going to attack the noble sentiments, then we ought to kill a few others: the brotherhood of man, for example, social justice, compassion for the workers, the glorification of the nation, antiracism, freedom, progress, etc. But no, all these things leave our great artists perfectly cold. They do not regard them as noble sentiments, they do not even consider them; in their eyes the noble sentiments have been catalogued once and for all. Especially if this "sexual morality" has a Christian appearance.

And yet the problem is more complex, for there are contradictions that on first sight seem amazing. For example, the same critic will make a face over *Le Curé de*

campagne, saying, "Really, noble sentiments in the work of
art . . ." but will rave about *The Ballad of the Soldier.* In
this dreadful decoction, the universal goodness and purity
will not shock him at all. The soldier is brave, the sergeant
is good, the lieutenant is good, the general is good, the girl
is chaste, the neighbors are sympathetic, the parents adore
their children and vice versa, and in this torrent of noble
sentiments the critics do not hesitate to find a work of art
that is infinitely poetic, reminiscent of François Coppée. If
a French screenwriter had produced this kind of poetry,
everyone would have remembered our commonplace; but
no, this is a Soviet screenwriter, and consequently these are
not noble sentiments, but evidence of the new proletarian
morality, the virtues of the people, and the sovereign freedom of the distinguished artist of the USSR. For naturally,
it is in the name of artistic freedom and creativity that our
commonplace is invoked, and it is for the same reason that
it is ignored when it is a question of the communist
world.

Art is above everything, as was very well said by the
Polish director Kovalerowitz (*Le Monde,* June 1, 1961) in
connection with his film *Mother Joan of the Angels,* in a
fine string of commonplaces that all followed from ours. "I
did not want to make a film of antireligious propaganda, or
an ideological film, but a work of art; it goes far beyond the
religious problem. (?) [1] It is a very superficial approach to
judge it from this point of view. (!) . . . It was my intention to speak out against lies, conformity, and dogmatism
(so much for the struggle against noble sentiments, and the
independence of Art!) . . . My materialistic personal position is clear . . . the lives of the nuns, the act of the priest

---

[1] These parenthetical remarks are mine and not, obviously, Mr. Kovalerowitz's.

. . . end in total failure; it is the failure of the idealistic position." (Which proves that this is neither an ideological film nor a thesis film!!!) How clear it is from such statements who is guilty of the noble sentiments that must be combated, the noble sentiments from which Art must be liberated! How clear it is that all this aesthetic creation occurs in complete independence, free of all conformism! And if this marvelous film coincides with the great antireligious campaign of Gomulka, that is pure accident! If it defends the very doctrines of the government, that is pure accident! And if Mr. Kovalerowitz is a conscious and organized materialist, it is likewise pure accident that he finds himself in the communist Poland of 1960! For it is obvious, is it not, that if he had lived in the Poland of 1450, he would *also* have been a conscious and organized materialist, in complete personal independence! And he would have asserted, in the same way, the same artistic freedom from the same noble sentiments!

After all, it may also be an accident that the remark that gave rise to our commonplace was made by a man who spent his life justifying himself for being what he was, and who devoted his art to that end.

For what characterizes our commonplace is its remarkable philosophical superstructure. We are in the presence of the process of justification in its pure state, but in all its fullness as well. On the one hand we encounter men afflicted with an abnormal sexual orientation, like Gide and Bataille, and who, cut off from any spiritual solution, can be relieved of their bad moral consciences only by collective approval, by reintegration into a group that will reinstate and justify them. This is why these men cannot be silent or keep to themselves: they talk, they shout in order to be admitted to the group (although the motive is completely unconscious!). And they construct a system that is intellectually superior, solidly built, apparently objective. They present a new view of man (the intellectual validity of the structure will provoke, among other things, anger and the refusal to analyze on the part of the reader!) based on the sexual singularity of the author and intended to show that the man whose life is worth living, the antibourgeois, revolutionary man, the man who helps to advance human destiny, is the very man who, as a pederast or a masochist, opposes society *on that point*. This system will be the better received in a decadent society like ours when it is more extreme, more total, and when at the same time it carries a weight of testimony, a density of experience and vocation that give it considerable force of impact in the human heart. On the other side of the barricade there is the social body—that is, each of us—no longer obeying any morality, eluding all social control and abandoned to itself.

Each of us would be quite tempted to follow his inclinations and instincts, but does not dare because there are some old dusty remnants of morality hanging around in the corners, flimsy scales of conscience that are flaking off but are still bothersome. And along comes this System, offering us liberation, authorization, justification. Of course you can do It! And in doing It you become the daring, revolutionary man, you challenge God, Society, and all the rest. Not only that, but you are Man! On with the music!

The social body—that is, each of us caught in the whole. And the social body follows the movement. That panting old body, overtaken by paralysis, less and less suceptible to suggestion or excitement, must be stimulated by stronger and stronger drugs in order to keep on feeling something, in order to keep on feeling that it is alive.[2] Finished the reserve and modesty of the classics when people knew enough to appreciate the subtle shades, when a single nuance was enough to raise a tempest and a single harp note enough to evoke all the harmonies of passion. Our frayed nerves, our exhausted senses, our surfeited minds have been of more violent assaults. No, indeed, works of art are not made of noble sentiments! Because the purpose of art is to move us—to anger or to pity, what difference does it make?—to force us to look at ourselves, to force me to transcend myself, to wake me up and force me to become a man. But suppose I don't give a damn for noble sentiments—and nobody else does either. What then? Well, I must have ignoble sentiments, or "pseudo-ignoble sentiments." But in this very process the work of art ceases to be itself.

For it becomes a justification of the social body, and ceases thereby to have any but a social meaning. There is no need to wait for the classless society for the universal reconciliation. The reconciliation between the outcast artist and society? But it is happening here, much more than in the USSR. How much do you pay for a Picasso? How much do you pay for a book by Sade? Our commonplace is an admirable force for international understanding, and we have changed national anthems.

The social body must have ever stronger stimulation in the form of the indispensable and justified work of art. But our writers have almost reached the end of their rope. We have seen real love-making on the public screen. We have

---

[2] This is why in the Soviet social body, which is not yet completely deadened, noble sentiments are still used to make works of art.

seen real hysteria on stage. One thing more remains, however: we have not yet seen a man really die on stage or on
the screen; we have not yet seen anyone really being tortured. This strikes me as an embarrassing gap that should be
filled in as soon as possible if we are to reach the summit of
artistic creation. After all, it would not represent an enormous expenditure in actors. I turn the Idea over to you, O
Producers!

ANYONE WHO SAYS HE IS NEITHER A RIGHTIST NOR A LEFTIST IS A RIGHTIST

The mere fact of having discussed the commonplace "Politics first" will no doubt lay me open to another commonplace: "Anyone who claims that politics is not everything is a rightist, a reactionary, an aristocrat, etc.," which is the twin of the famous "Anyone who claims that the left-right dichotomy is outmoded, who refuses to identify himself with the right or the left, is a rightist." Of course, the person who appropriates Alain's idea, which has become a commonplace, is always a leftist who thus expresses the profundity of his political judgment.

What does it matter that this division into right and left has been purely accidental in history, that it has been a

peculiarly French phenomenon and has not had much
meaning outside of France, and that the boundaries between the blocs have been more than confused? It is still
the *summa divisio* among men! It is useless to try to define
the content of these notions. What is the left? What is the
right? What are their criteria and their distinguishing features? Their ideological and sociological content? Consult
twenty individuals and they will give you twenty conflicting answers. Twenty general investigations will lead you to
twenty different conclusions. Ask a man whether he classi-
fies himself with the right or the left: this may be simple.
Ask his friends, colleagues, and opponents the same thing,
and you will evoke as many different opinions.

Here again, what's the difference? We are in the domain
of acceptance and belief; all the rest is literature. Besides,
there is an Action Française, there is a Communist Party,
isn't there? Well, then? Everything is clear. Of course, it is
quite clear! Given the fact that everything is political, the
fact of "Politics first," it follows that men must be classified
politically, just as everything used to be classified in terms
of religion. There were the atheists and the Christians; it's
the same today, nobody can escape! Whether they like it or
not, men cannot escape a political bias, and those who
claim to be indifferent are classified in spite of themselves
by political believers.[1] Now I have searched vainly and
desperately for a reasonable interpretation of this statement. For after all, it is political, it expresses a division of

---

[1] As is usual in these matters, we must nevertheless point out some
inconsistencies. I have said this commonplace is used by the leftist, but he
does not apply it at all times or in all places! For example, at the time of
the elections there is always a group of abstentionists (from 15 to 40 per
cent) who clearly demonstrate their decision not to participate and not to
identify themselves with either the right or the left. But at such times the
leftist generally forgets his commonplace, and would be most reluctant to
classify the mass of abstentionists with the right!

political opinion, of political attitudes. A man votes leftist; he is a leftist; agreed. A man votes rightist; he is a rightist; agreed. But what about a man who refuses to vote?

I understand perfectly well the alleged meaning of the statement, namely, that it is a question of deeper judgment. The man who affirms the right-left dichotomy is a man who knows what is meant by division of opinion, who knows the values he defends and those he opposes. He is a man who is fighting for a better world that he will attain through politics, therefore he is a leftist. . . . But I don't see the necessity of this conclusion! Actually, the fascist fits this definition perfectly. Besides, let's not forget that the same thing occurred during the Nazi era, when the regime did not tolerate abstention, the refusal to participate, political neutrality: it was necessary to belong to the regime. And with the same merciless logic they told you, "You refuse to be a Nazi, *therefore* you are a communist."

But the supporter of the commonplace, rejecting such a comparison, will explain that it rests on a psychological criterion. Psychologically speaking, the man who attaches no importance to politics is a man of the old regime, a man of the right. A man who regards the division between right and left as secondary does not understand that it is the left and the values of the left that have brought about this division and that these values contain the seeds of Progress. Therefore he proves that he is not devoted to these values; therefore he is a rightist. A man who thinks he can go beyond this division shows that he has not grasped the seriousness of the struggle of the left; therefore he is a rightist.

Here again, alas, I admit my imperviousness to these subtleties. For then according to the first argument, would not the militant of Action Française, who attaches the utmost value to politics, be considered a leftist? In effect, if

you reject the idea that the right-left dichotomy is an intra-
political division and attribute a universal value to it by
likening it to "political and apolitical," then the right and
left internal distribution of politics is located completely on
the left! As for the second argument, the rightist, also
convinced of his values, will claim with equal good faith
that it is the preexistence of these values that has provoked
the division in question, and consequently that to deny this
division is to be—a leftist! And the third argument mani-
fests a desperate concern with questions which may be
slightly out of date! For the famous struggle of the left
consists today in violently berating the shadow of the institutions, ideologies, and structures of yesterday and the day
before yesterday, a shadow that grows longer as the declin-
ing sun of bourgeois capitalism sinks lower on the horizon.
It is a war against shadows, and "the left," which in the
nineteenth century had the genius to expose pretense,
now has the genius to avoid the real problems. Obviously,
to say this is to challenge the organizations, slogans, and
taboos that the left of 1900 bequeathed to the left of 1960,
and therefore, in the eyes of the leftist, to reveal oneself as
an enemy, and therefore as a rightist! Whereas it may in
fact be simply to remain on the level of the real human
battle, or to prepare for that of tomorrow.

However this may be, the fact is that this commonplace
is employed by the man who calls himself a leftist, and
despite the stupidity of the statement, its use is revealing.
It tells us that this man of the left is the most politicized. In
using it he rejects all possibility of avoiding politics; he
thus makes politics an ultimate, religious value. This man
of the left does not believe in religion; indeed, he has
replaced it with politics, and he brings to politics the same

fervor, the same intransigeance, the same concern for the defense of the church and its dogmas (that is, the party and its doctrine). The leftist is a believer, and for this reason he brings to the political struggle a toughness and vigor that are unavailable to the man for whom politics has an altogether relative value, does not necessarily lead to glorious tomorrows, and is simply one activity among others. To the leftist, politics is the highest form of action; indeed, the use of our commonplace demonstrates that in this area the leftist is a totalitarian. Politics is All. The left-right dichotomy is in truth the *summa divisio* among men: all must be included in it. He who claims to be independent of it and denies this truth is an enemy. And he who is not with me, who does not declare himself for me (and who therefore does not accept this division), is against me: he is an enemy. Obviously, the nonfascist who calls himself a rightist could just as well use the same argument and apply the same commonplace, but *in fact,* this is not the case. In fact, it is the leftist who utilizes it. In so doing he indicates that he is more intolerant than the other, since the nonfascist right allows for exceptions and does not excommunicate the person who rejects the labels. The leftist indicates thereby that he is the most susceptible to a Manichean division of the world into good and bad people, and that when all is said and done his celebrated humanism amounts to very little.

IT'S SACRED

The advantage of this commonplace is that you can change the subject to suit yourself. Thus it is popularly said in our good society, "The nation is sacred"; or again, "Work is sacred." On a loftier plane, as we have seen, "The right of peoples to self-determination is sacred." This commonplace can be tacked onto the majority of those we have thus far vivisected, bringing to them value judgment, the guarantee of eternal sanctions, and the glamour of mystery. It would be unfortunate, however, to assume that any subject at all would be appropriate. The proper use of this commonplace is extraordinarily indicative of one's good adjustment to society. I am even surprised that the devisers of personality tests have not yet made use of this formula for their little games.

Thus, we do not say, "Love is sacred," or "Truth is sacred," or even "Science is sacred." There are also sacred values that avoid exposure. It would be in very bad taste to observe, "Property is sacred"! But others, after a period of decline, recover their former rank. Thus in 1936 it would have been as grotesque to say, "The fatherland is sacred,"

as it was in 1900, but now, ever so faintly, this commonplace is beginning to reappear, and in unexpected quarters.
The proper usage of this commonplace also requires audacity, and we sometimes hear declarations that are all the
more significant because they are surprising. For example,
"Communism is sacred." Up to now, it has been the adversaries of communism who have insisted on the religious
character it has acquired—the sanctity of the party, the
irrationality of the slogans and beliefs, the mystique of the
worship of the leader, the exegesis of the sacred works of
Karl Marx, etc. But now our commonplace is making its
entrance through the front door! For it was Mr. Khrushchev himself who announced, "Communism is sacred." [1]
On May 3, 1961, Mr. Khrushchev, addressing himself to Mr.
Nasser, declared, "In all good faith I tell you that communism is sacred."

It was a dazzling confirmation of analyses of the phenomenon that until then had been violently contested by
the communists. And since Mr. Khrushchev knew what he
was saying, since he possessed great shrewdness and did
not use words loosely, it is probable that when he said that
communism was sacred, it was not a figure of speech meaning, for example, that it was a very fine thing. It was not
even exactly, "Don't touch it or it will explode!" No, indeed. There is much more to it than that! Communism has
entered the domain, at once invisible and intangible, formi-
dable and mysterious, where the lightning and the rainbow
ripen according to the ambivalence of the sacred; and the
Great Master has come to bear witness to this change, as
well as to the appropriation of the sacred by materialism

---

[1] It is true that Mr. Khrushchev seemed given to this vocabulary. Thus
in September 1960 he had announced that the independence of the Congo
was "sacred," and in January 1961 that the war in Algeria was a "sacred"
war.

and the left, whereas up to now we found ourselves in the presence of an essentially rightist word.

Now, it was certainly no accident that Mr. Khrushchev said this, or that he made use of his full powers! He was sanctioning custom, fact, opinion; he was in agreement with the masses, with the untold believers, and he was therefore completely within the tradition of the proper usage of the commonplace. No doubt you will tell me that these statements of Mr. Khrushchev's are quite outmoded. Since he himself has been eliminated, what he said no longer has much importance. But it is not true that his successors are doing the opposite of what Mr. Khrushchev inaugurated. Indeed, it can be said that except on one or two points, they are following him to the letter. And à propos of our subject, they are adopting the same vocabulary. In August 1965, Mr. Pavlov, head of the Komsomol, severely criticized Mr. Khrushchev for depriving young people of the communist ideal, but concluded with this peroration: "Young people must be imbued with a *sacred* feeling for the flag, the national emblem, and the heroes of the socialist fatherland." Well! But the Chinese are also joining in and proclaiming the person and government of Mao to be sacred. They are reacting, moreover, with a seriousness worthy of this sanctity, and will not tolerate levity: the sacred is a fiery principle, and never suffers humor.[2]

Contrary to what one might think, modern man takes the

---

[2] I am alluding to an excellent takeoff that appeared in the English liberal weekly *The Tribune* in December 1963, according to which Mao was developing a secret plan to liberate Europe, whereby he proposed to give Calais back to the English and to free Goa from Indian dictatorship and restore it to the magnificent chief Salazar. This humor was taken very seriously by Chinese politicians, and almost provoked a grave diplomatic incident. When it was explained to the Chinese *chargé d'affaires* that it was a joke, he replied, "It is a crime against the People's Republic of China."

idea of the sacred very seriously. The greatest liberals are terribly shocked when two fanatics start frying eggs over the flame of the Unknown. Even if you don't believe in patriotism, or ceremonies, or flags, this still isn't done! And deep down, your sense of the sacred stirs a little. So this word is not used lightly, and to be able to say of a given phenomenon that it is sacred, we must have the support of collective belief. We are truly in the presence of the commonplace in its purest form, because it does not exist without the adhesion of all, communing in a single sentiment. The exact definition of the sacred! If in France I were to say, "Christianity is sacred," since virtually nobody believes it, my statement would fall flat. I would have attributed the essential quality to an inappropriate subject. Therefore the sentence does not mean anything. On the other hand, the statement "The Nation is sacred" may be quite meaningful, because the majority believe in *this* sacred, so that the statement is and must necessarily be a commonplace.

Whatever its subject, I find the resurgence of this statement in mid-twentieth-century France enormously significant. Here we are in a secular country, where religion is gradually disappearing, where an energetic educational campaign has been waged against obscurantism, where schooling has been developed among the people, where, more than anywhere else except the USSR, science has been presented as the light dissipating darkness, credulity, and magic and has incessantly been set in radical, irreconcilable opposition to faith, where free thought has gained steadily, where rationalists abound—and it is in this very country that the commonplace thrives! This should give us food for thought. But let us waste no time on justifications. The response is not "You see, religion is rooted in the heart

of man, so come to church!" The reality is somewhat different. We are rediscovering, not too surprisingly, that man
cannot live in pure rationality, that life is not logic, that
science does not explain everything, that constant and merciless light is torture, that night is a repose and a blessing
for the soul as well as for the body. Man is so constituted
psychically that he needs a background of mystery in order
to live and become rooted in something.

But let us draw no conclusions from this about Christianity. All the commonplace reveals is a need and a search for
the sacred; but a sacred created by man, or rather by
society, secreted, as it were, by the social body, which
provides man with this too, responding to all his needs.
And since there is no question of returning to bygone religions, reviving old rites, or investing outmoded beliefs with
sanctity, it can be said that we are witnessing the invention
of a new sacred. For what has been once divested of its
sacred quality cannot become sacred again. But the need,
the inclination, the call of the sacred are at this moment
seeking a new vessel—the institution, the phenomenon,
that, with the full consent of all, can be invested with the
fullness of the sacred.

And the fact that this event has not yet occurred explains the variety of subjects at our disposal. We are still
searching for the One that will triumph, that will embrace
all that is sacred and banish the others into the profane
world. The most obvious tendency today is to designate as
sacred what once played a desanctifying role with regard
to the old values. Thus, democracy and education are sacred. But there is still no way of foreseeing which will
prevail, especially since certain fundamental elements cannot play this role, at least not yet. People will not say,
"Technology is sacred" or "The state is sacred," even if
everything about man's behavior forcibly demonstrates

that, unconsciously and deep in his heart, he believes that they are.

The transition to explicitness, the step that Mr. Khrushchev took in the case of communism, has not been made, and this step is crucial, for it is this step that implies the agreement of a society. But as long as it has not been taken in the case of forces as decisive as those named above, no other value can monopolize the sacred to the exclusion of all others, for it would constantly come into conflict with the vigor, the efficiency, and the indomitable ambition of these other forces, which are not ready to abandon their authority based on the secret belief that dwells within us. And this is why we have not yet gone beyond the level of the commonplace. It is the plurality of possible subjects that keeps us on this elementary level in the use of the phrase. When it can be applied to only one of these subjects, the total victor, when we recoil with horror at the idea of any competition for this divinity, then we will leave the realm of the commonplace for that of horror, silence, and faith in mysteries in comparison with which those of Eleusis or Quetzalcoatl were mere child's play.

THE MACHINE IS A NEUTRAL OBJECT AND MAN IS ITS MASTER

It is a fearful thing to attack this commonplace, for it represents the base, the foundation, the cornerstone of the whole edifice within which the average man, taking his clue from the social thinkers (an optimistic group), likes to include technology, its glories, and its achievements, humanize it, and, in so doing, reassure himself. If we weaken this stone in any way, the entire structure threatens to fall on our heads, and since it is made up of arguments as heavy as the Arc de Triomphe, we won't get away unharmed. Of course, we can maintain our poise by deciding that this commonplace is unassailable, solid as granite. For after all, what could be more certain? I am in a car; it does not move without me; only I can make it turn right or left; only I can stop it or gun the motor to top speed; and, according to the happy and satisfying (and above all, original) analogy of the well-known writer who elucidated this problem, "Man is to the machine as the soul is to the body." The idea of machines declaring their independence from man, of robots that become capable of consciousness, is pure science fiction, and there is no chance of its being realized.

Let's remember that species of superstitious fear that seized the good people when the idea of a thinking machine was introduced. Man saw himself stripped of what he regarded as his highest prerogative, the superior function that distinguished him from the animal. What? To be robbed of one's function by a machine? But this was only a nightmare of excitable primitives. For we know now that the machine does not think. It solves problems, processes data, and computes probabilities, but only on the basis of the terms presented to it by man, the program established by man. But the intelligent, decisive part of the operation is precisely to *see* the problem and state it correctly, to program the job properly. Everything else is merely a mechanical operation, and the machine comes into play only after the thinking has been done, and at the service of man, who is the king. This is even more obvious, of course, if we consider moral neutrality! For how could the machine, of itself, be oriented toward good or toward evil? How could the machine decide between good and evil? It is a mere tool, and the man who uses it does so for good or for ill according to what he is himself! Is it necessary to enlarge upon what seems to be a convincing argument, a satisfactory explanation? But this argument is merely a superficial truism, which takes no account of *another* reality.

. . .

This other reality is first of all the fact that there is not *one* machine but hundreds of machines that surround man and create a new environment. If man can claim to be the master of a machine, and even of every machine considered successively, can he claim to be the master of the technological whole of which each machine is a part? The driver of a car has an accelerator, a clutch, a brake, a steering wheel, etc., at his disposal. He can tell himself that he is the master of each of these instruments. But this is not the problem; he must be the master of the *combination* of these elements; it is only be manipulating one in relation to the other that he can drive the car. The same is true of the technological society; it is not a question of single machines taken individually, but of their combination. But who possesses this combination, this mechanical and technical complex? When a worker is obliged to maintain a given rhythm of work and a given output because of the machine, can he be said to be its master? Maybe not, but what about the employer? If he has adopted this machine, it is because it represents the last word in technical progress. He is no freer than the worker is to choose it or to modify its use. This use is dictated by the internal structure of his society, the raw materials provided by other machines, and the requirements of the machine next in line.

The network of all the machines—those in the factories, those used for transport, those used in offices, those used for entertainment, those having to do with food, sanitation, and communication—causes the whole society to be modified—scale of values, processes of judgment, customs, and manners—and creates a situation in which there is no exact center where man can pretend to lay his hand on the machine (which machine?) in complete independence and utilize it as he sees fit! If man does utilize the machine, it is within a society that has already been modified, nay transformed, by the machine without reference to the will or decision of man.

Furthermore, let us at least acknowledge the fact that man himself has already been changed by the machine. I do not mean his social forms and institutions and social relations: man, in his affective life, his intentions and ambitions, his judgments and prejudices, his habits and manners, his needs and thoughts, has been changed, whether he likes it or not, whether he knows it or not, by the simple fact that he lives in a mechanical environment, in obedience to the logic of machines. It is absolutely superficial to say that on the one hand there is man, a dauntless and blameless knight, independent, autonomous and sovereign, and on the other the machine, an object, a lifeless tool. What exists in reality is a constant and stable interrelation between man and the machine: constant because man spends his life going from one machine to another, stable because the same relation is always established between man and each machine. It is this man living in this society (constructed in terms of the machine) and himself modified by the machine who uses the machine. But how could he claim to master it and force it to do his will when before even becoming conscious of the problem he has already been transformed, adapted to the machine, and structured by it? If the machine remains a tool in the hands of man, the man we are talking about is a man conditioned by this tool. This is even more true now that psychological techniques have undertaken this very conditioning of man as their object!

"Perhaps; but even so, when it comes to good and evil, it is man alone who makes the decision!" This is not certain at all! For the criteria of good and evil fluctuate according to time and place. Indeed, it is becoming increasingly apparent that the technological milieu is producing a new moral-

ity,[1] with a conception of good that is absolutely different
from that of the Greeks, the Middle Ages, or the eighteenth
century. And it is the influence of the machine that is
leading man to this new vision of good and evil. Besides, to
say that the machine is neutral and consequently incapable
of making decisions does not mean anything. For there are
perfectly neutral things that are harmful to man, that do
not evil, but harm, apart from any deliberate abuse. Carbon
dioxide is morally neutral, but if it fills a room, the results
are not very fortunate for the occupants! The morally neutral machine may therefore have vital (but also moral)
effects that are not neutral at all. I know that this is a
matter subject to heated debate, that there are some psychologists and sociologists who believe in the beneficial
effects of the machine and other psychologists neither less
courageous nor less numerous who believe in its harmful
effects. I do not intend to say which are right, but only to
point out that however neutral it may be, the machine
inevitably produces psychic and moral effects that—
whether good or bad—are definitely not neutral!

Let us take the question by the other end. "Man": when
I pronounce this word I am always filled with uneasiness,
uncertainty, and anxiety. What is meant by "man"? After
all, the first man I know is myself. Am I the subject of this
statement? But who am I, what can I do, and how could I
master the machine, or rather the machines, all of them?
And the technological complex? What effect can I have on
the growth of technology? Or on the use of atomic energy?
Or on the results of industrial development? I hear the

---

[1] On technological morality, see J. Ellul: *Le Vouloir et le faire*, Part II,
Chap. vi.

answer: "You personally have only to act upon the machines at your disposal, your car and your television set. And if every man does the same, we have nothing to fear."

Is that so? Well, I say that whoever offers this argument is a hypocrite and a fool. A hypocrite, because any thinking man knows the extraordinary expenditure of effort, awareness, will power, and judgment that is necessary if he is to remain truly the master of the machines that ordinarily invade us and not give in to them and become a slave to their convenience. It is impossible to demand this effort of every man; it is unthinkable that every man could succeed in making it. Never has the whole human race been capable of submitting to a real discipline. Today less than ever! A fool, because even if every man really became the master of his own machines, nothing would be solved, for there would still be the problem of the mastery of technical progress as a whole, of the massive structures of technological society, and that is out of anyone's hands. Indeed, a great many installations do not belong to a single man, and they are the most important; who can call himself the master of atomic energy?

No! Man, in this commonplace, must be someone other than the private individual! But who? The politicians, the heads of state, those who exercise authority? Alas! We know how little control, in all the countries of the world, the political man has over technology, how little effect he has on it, to what an extent he (along with the state and the administration itself!) is conditioned by it.[2] We know very well that the politician has no control in these matters: first, because no one person decides, but ten or a hundred persons scheme together; next, because their determining motives are defined by competition, and for this reason

---

[2] Cf. J. Ellul: *The Political Illusion*, Chaps. ii and iii.

they are forced to obey technology, which assures them
more power and effectiveness; and finally, because not one
has the intellectual and spiritual breadth to try to master
the phenomenon, which, for that matter, most of them have
not begun to understand.

What about the technicians, then? But the technician
cannot master technology, because he is ultraspecialized,
perceives only one small corner of the whole, and never
sets foot in his neighbor's territory. Besides, the technician
is less capable than anyone else of mastering technology
because he is completely dominated by it.

Who then? The intellectuals? The religious? Some of the
most perceptive people belong to these groups; they see,
understand, and possess certain necessary qualities, but
they have no power. Contemporary society as a whole
leaves them on the sidelines, places them in the position of
spectators, and denies them all jurisdiction, *unless* they
accept the technological civilization and, renouncing their
rank, their independence, place themselves at its service
and become statisticians and great "intellectual and spiritual justifiers" of the status quo.

Decidedly, no man is qualified to perform the function
that our commonplace assigns to *man*. Fortunately, the
question is easily settled, thanks to idealism. It is quite
obvious that the man in question is neither you nor I
(Whew! that was a narrow escape!), but Man. Of course!
That excellent prototype, archetype, monotype, antitype
(but not just plain type); that excellent Abstraction; that
Universal, Absolute, All-Powerful, but elusive and unknow-
able essence who really exists (perhaps only in conceptual
form, but even so!), as soon as we are told that he does.
Where is he? I have no idea. Who is he? I don't know that
either, and have yet to encounter anyone who can en-
lighten me. What does he look like? Oh, an average nose, a

low forehead, an ordinary chin, nondescript eyes . . . What else? Nothing. It doesn't matter, the point is that it is he who is responsible for the most difficult, the most superhuman (this must be why he has been honored with a capital letter!), and the most crucial operation that has ever been proposed since the dawn of history.

Now that I know who is in charge, I can put my mind at rest and turn by attention to other matters. You know how it is . . . life isn't easy—work, money, children—God knows! If, on top of everything else, you had to complicate your life with this sort of thing . . . But since there is someone in charge, let him worry about it. It is Man, not I, who will be summoned to appear before the tribunal of History if he makes a mess of it. I take my hat off to him, since thanks to him I can go about my business in peace.

For this is the purpose of the commonplace! Above all, let's not worry too much. That would be psychologically unhealthy and would threaten our efficiency. "Don't you see that that poor man beside you has enough troubles as it is! It's really mean to bring up more difficulties and questions, especially when they are as insoluble as those you insist on raising! What this man needs is to be calmed and reassured. To refuse him what he so profoundly needs is mental cruelty, and not at all Christian. Besides, let's be serious, don't forget that the good man works for the post office and has to sort six thousand letters an hour. This is a fact; you can't deny it. And you know very well that if you fill his head with these ideas about machines, he will no longer do his work wholeheartedly, responsibly, and efficiently. And that will be bad for him (he'll end up getting fired), bad for the addressees (a lot of good it will do you to get your letters two or three days late, you'll be

the first to complain to the government!), and bad for
society. If, on the contrary, you reassure him on the subject
of the machine and technology, everything will go
smoothly. And it is only in this way that some day, no
doubt, we will be able to solve the problem that you raise,
and that, rest assured, we do not overlook!

But even so, don't forget what man has done up to now!
His great and noble achievements! Time and again he has
found himself in situations just as critical, just as difficult,
and he has always found a solution, hasn't he? He has
always managed to get the best of his adversary. If it is true
that the machine is an adversary—which we by no means
believe—why could he not also control the machine? Un-
questionably, we are the masters of the situation. The
greatness of man cannot be called into question for so little.
On the contrary, this mastery of the machine gives man an
opportunity for the full development of abilities that were
thwarted by lack of means and by a whole group of unimportant preoccupations that will henceforth be set aside.
Besides, it would be too sad to think that man did not use
his greatest inventions for the good; it would be too sad,
and it would be unthinkable, for you know very well that
man chooses the good. The very fact that we can discuss
these matters proves this, does it not? Man chooses virtue
and freedom, and it is precisely because you are free, in
spite of all the machines, that you can undertake the criticism of technology. In proceeding this way, you yourself
bear witness to the contrary of what you wish to demonstrate!"

This little speech, which I have heard a hundred and one
times, artlessly reveals the real reason for our commonplace. The commonplace has no foundation in observation
or reflection, no intelligible content, especially when it is
uttered by our great pseudo-philosophers, but it does have

a very important psychological and moral function, a mind-healing function. It is there to satisfy man's vanity, which cannot allow his supremacy to be challenged by the object, and which assumes the honor and credit for being its master as well as the master of the universe (including machines). It is there to protect man from all uneasiness, to assure him a good conscience, and to prove to him that he really has nothing to worry about. It is there to assure the proper functioning of technology and to prevent either the crystalline clarity of the soul or the luminous purity of mechanical designs from being tarnished by bad feelings, suspicions, or negations.

IT IS FASHIONABLE
TO CRITICIZE
TECHNOLOGY

This commonplace is really very common among technicians, technologists, technolasters, technophagi, technophiles, technocrats, technopans. They complain of being unappreciated. They complain of being criticized. They complain of the ingratitude of these people for whom they work and whose welfare they desire. It is not enough for them to have all the jobs in the administration and the state, and all the prestige. It is not enough for them to have the blissful and universal admiration of the frenzied crowds when they receive word of the sputnik. It is not enough for them to embody all the hope of the masses when they are told about penicillin or automation. It is not enough for them to make the crowd tremble with fear at the advances in rockets, fusion, fission, and other mysterious secrets. It is not enough for them to have all the glamour, so that everybody calls himself a technician, no matter what he does. It is not enough for them to win boosters and flatterers even among the least technical of men, among the pseudo-philosophers and theologians. It is not enough for them to have the future all to themselves; it is not enough that the game has been won and that the only foreseeable future is "more technology, always more technology; more powers for the technicians, always more powers for the technicians." It is not enough for them to be surrounded with honors, not enough that we look to their ranks for the celebrated "sages" of whom we have such need. It is not enough for them that in all places and among all kinds of people their word is law because they are the ones who both know and act at the same time. It is not enough for them to be beyond good and evil, because the necessity of progress is not subject to meaningless contingencies. Finally, it is not enough for them to have clean consciences, to know that they are on the right side of the barricade, the side of Justice and Fortune, to have a perfectly clear and definite path before them, with no doubts, retreats, misgivings, hesitations, or feelings of remorse. No, all this is not enough for them.

They need one more thing: the martyr's palm and the sanction of Virtue triumphing over the venomous and all-powerful dragon. Oh, didn't you know? Yes, indeed, we are still in the age of Pilâtre de Rozier and Fulton. There are still vile reactionary capitalist artisans who smash the looms of science and progress. There are still dreadful peasants, scarcely emerged from their earthy animality, who mercilessly mow down the poor, virtuous technicians who are working for their good. Haven't you read about it in the papers? But you see it every day, don't you? There are still idiotic philosophers who want to impede the advance of progress with sophistical oratory and arguments as vicious as they are false, based on a radically outdated conception

of man. Didn't you know? No doubt you also did not know
that it is these evil philosophers who make up government
councils, who succeed in the university, and who have the
respect of *l'Express, Paris-Match, Réalités,* and other opin-
ion-makers.

You didn't know this, and you were right, for none of it is
true. But the technicians, technologists, etc., need this supplement of honor and virtue. They also need to be pitied
and loved. They invent this mythology in order to present
themselves as persons forced to make an enormous effort to
overcome hostile forces. Furthermore, they are extremely
sensitive, and their sense of honor is highly refined. The
mere shadow of a doubt as to the *absolute* value of what
they are doing, the most circumspect examination of a
given result, the most cautious inquiry into the ultimate
value of their activities, immediately brings forth cries of
despair, harsh judgments, or an avenging finger pointed at
the wretch who has dared to challenge the majesty of
progress. If the government refuses them the smallest grant
for their most pointless and senseless enterprises, they
immediately cry injustice and persecution, and the press is
alerted and comes to the aid of the miserable victims.
"What kind of a government do we have? Now they are
refusing us money for laboratories!" Everything else can
wait. They must be not only the heroes of knowledge and
power, but the victims of incomprehension and reaction as
well. They need not 98 per cent of public opinion behind
them, but total unanimity, for any reservation is a grudge
against them. Technology is totalitarian.

But at the bottom of this peevish attitude I think I
detect the twinge of an anxiety, the gleam of a suspicion,
whereupon they collect sandbags and fire extinguishers to
keep it from burning. "After all, what if somehow we made
a mistake? What if somehow we were leading humanity to

its end?" I am not thinking so much about the atomic end as the end of consciousness, the end of freedom, the end of the individual, the end of creativity, the end of the humanity of man. What if somehow they were really leading us to the anonymity of that anthill so often falsely predicted? It is most essential that they take their precautions; it is essential, in the final flash of lucidity, to be able to say that we have all been in this together. All together, in full agreement. And that the avant-garde was the least responsible and the most exposed to danger: "Pity us, pity us, good people. We have had our share of trouble and we did not want *this* . . ."

ALL SCIENCE IS NUMERICAL

No sooner is this statement made than I hear indignant protestations: "But that isn't a commonplace! You don't find it in *Paris-Match* or *l'Express* (I am not so sure about that) or on the lips of the great initiators and authors of commonplaces! It is a problem of scientific method, it is the most fundamental doctrine of progress. There is nothing unreasonable here; you can make a perfect case for the veracity and excellence of the mathematization of all disciplines of human thought!"

I could reply, of course, that if this statement is not a commonplace, it deserves to be. But rather than make such a value judgment, I prefer to stick to the facts. To be sure, here we have not yet reached the stage of the crystallized commonplace, formulated, engraved, and immortalized in literary marble; on the contrary, we are catching the commonplace in its gaseous state. It is not yet a commonplace but it has all the earmarks of one; it is about to become explicit, to be formulated, to find its face. It is quite true that it has not yet received definitive popular expression. It is not yet a coin that, by dint of being passed from hand to hand, has gradually become worn and acquired its definitive shape.

Already, however, we find it in the writings of many authoritative authors—econometers, sociometers, psychometers. "To deny a mathematical approach to psychology is to rule out all hope of scientific progress in this field." It was not I who wrote this! It was an eminent man. It is obvious that a statement of this kind is destined for a great future; but as yet only professors, scientific investigators, statisticians, people connected with the National Council for Scientific Research, academics, and para-intellectuals understand its profound meaning and are dedicated to it. It has not yet arrived at popular usage, although the beliefs of the people are completely disposed in its favor. Already, even without adequate formulation, the public believes it. The prestige of the number is known, and in innumerable hearts the prestige of the scientist has replaced that of the soldier. But this prestige necessarily includes a portion of mystery and magic, and this is one of the prerequisites for the commonplace. The attachment that is formed for the truth expressed by the commonplace is emotional, even if that truth pretends to be rational. No opposing argument can destroy it because it corresponds to a magical profundity, a *carmen* that can be contested, but whose resonances in the human heart nothing can still. However rational our doctrine of scientific method may be, it is already invested, among scientists themselves, with this potential for belief and illumined with an aura of magic. Even among these professional critics, it has become untouchable.

All the sciences are mathematical, the social sciences as well as the others, and psychologists, sociologists, political

scientists, and economists look contemptuously at those
who claim to know man without reducing him to figures
and who claim to describe society without using the
method *par excellence*, mathematics. "They are not serious: these are only ideas." "As long as you do not use
figures, as long as you do not reduce the problem to statistics, as long as you do not plot curves or establish percent-
ages, you can say anything you like about society, its
trends, its structures. Any idea, no matter how absurd or
fantastic, can be advanced and defended. How are you
going to distinguish truth from error? We have had enough
of those false theories that, after a brief success, fall into
ridicule twenty years later! Numbers, on the other hand,
don't let you down."

This really is the problem. The first step toward this
belief is the resignation of the intellectual. There are so
many ideas, so many theories, that you don't know where
you are! It gets so complicated that you can no longer tell
right from wrong. The intellectual abandons the attempt to
exercise his intelligence, to come to grips with ideas, to
understand the facts, to confront with his mind a reality
that is, no doubt, increasingly complex and elusive, to practice analysis in depth, to pass judgment, to commit his
whole life to his function of intelligence. He runs away. So
often have intellectuals been deceived, so often has one
theory eliminated the one that preceded it, that now not
one of them dares to take responsibilities. They have
looked for irreproachable matter and unequivocal method,
and only number is irreproachable, only the new mathematics is unequivocal. The results are guaranteed at the
price of invention and the integrity of the individual and
his thought. We ignore everything that does not result from
the application of this method, for in this way we are
assured of risking nothing. We are assured of avoiding the

disagreement of imbeciles. Until now every thought, every truth was open to the judgment and inspection of imbeciles. One man was equal to the next. One "thought" was equal to the next. Who could decide between the two? But today mathematics provides us with an impregnable fortification! Especially as we also find ourselves influenced by the prestige of scientific investigators and because the "scientist" (that is, the physicist, the chemist) enjoys this prestige, every intellectual must be able to take advantage of it by applying the same method. The rigorous application of this method provides us with incontestable results and at the same time forces people to accept our findings. How could we resist?

To tell the truth, investigators in the exact sciences are none too happy about this assimilation. In September 1965, a conference of these researchers protested the abuse of the word "science." They particularly stressed the undesirability of transposing from one science to another methods that do not belong there. And the experts vigorously rejected the designation "mathematical" for men who should be referred to as experimenters, observers, analysts. "For them the greatest danger is premature formalization" (by the mathematical method). They even went so far as to talk about a "scientific façade." Fortunately, the very next day these boors were put in their place by an eminent professor of literature who showed them clearly that they had understood nothing.

For this path provides a solution to the impossible dilemma of our subjectivity. Everything that has been written in psychology, sociology, history, and politics has born the stamp of subjectivity. Everything has depended on education, environment, digestion, religion, and matrimonial quarrels. How could science be so dependent on the contingent! But the great, the supreme discovery was that only number, only algebra is truly objective. Only that which is capable of being stated numerically is objective; only numerical science produces objective results. Indeed, the plotting of a parabola in no way depends on my moods or opinions. At last we are going to be able to shed that terrible guilty conscience familiar to every historian struggling against himself to express a reality disclosed by texts that are read by *his* eyes and understood by *his* intelligence, and not by the Eye of God and the Pure Intelligence!

The conquest of objectivity: so be it. But we must not forget what this means! It means that the moment the mathematical method is put into operation, everything becomes *object*. This must be, if we are to achieve *objectivity*. I no longer participate. I cease to be myself, I dissociate myself from this instrument that is applied, beyond my joys and sorrows, to something that is alien to me and that must remain alien if it is to be known. There was a time when it was possible to say that there was no true knowledge except in and through love. We are no longer interested in achieving true knowledge, all we want is accurate knowledge. And the latter requires that the subject become pure object, under the cosmic indifference of the observer, for whom this object is nothing but an object of cognition.

This much I understand and accept! But when it is a question of man and his society, his state, his law, and his history, can I treat them simply as objects? Can I objectify them so completely that they are no longer anything to me and I am no longer in them? We must pay attention: these are not rhetorical questions or oratorical sophisms. How can I, more aristocratically than the haughtiest lords, claim to be so isolated from the rest of men that I can apply these methods of analysis and these techniques of cognition to them as if they were nothing to me, and as if I no longer belonged to the same species as they? Is there not, from the outset, some element of illusion in believing this to be possible? Am I such a stranger to my nation and my class that I can study them with a serenity and objectivity that not only disassociate me from them, but reduce them, but reduce them to a dismal state in which everything is possible now that nothing is real?

And if, aware of this illusion—that is, of the links and dependencies that bind me emotionally, intellectually, mystically to the object of my study—I try to break them, to detach myself from this condition in the interest of a more scientific understanding, I can do it only by making my method more rigorous, more exclusive of the human element, so that this object will be an object and nothing more. So it is with the man whose psychology is analyzed by the mathematical method, the groups subjected to the methods of group dynamics, or public opinion subjected to the method of the poll. But we must be logical and rigorous. The moment this decision is made—the moment this impulse is followed, the moment the numerical becomes the law of all knowledge, the moment everything becomes an object—from this moment on, the way is open for everything to be *treated* as an object.

Are we ready to assume this responsibility? We applaud when psychology becomes mathematical, but we recoil in horror from the doctors of Struthof. And yet there is a close, logical, and inexorable connection between the two phenomena. If you treat man as an object with respect to his psychic life and his social relations, why not do it with respect to his body? No doubt you are too materialistic and believe that only the body counts, and consequently that only what happens to the body is important. But then why pay so much attention to the psyche and human relations? The truth is that the road, although opened and paved, has not been followed to the very end, but we are moving down it little by little. The obstacle is the superficial sensibility and the animal sentimentality that are still part of us; but these do not amount to much. Science has overcome bigger obstacles than these. It has conquered the sense of God and the sense of Love; the rest will follow. For we must face the facts: if in the name of knowledge you treat the object of cognition with pure objectivity—that is, without love—you will, in the action that follows knowledge, also treat without love this object that you have robbed of its individuality by reducing it to a number.

In spite of all efforts, in spite of the subtlety of the methods, in spite of intellectual contortions, the mathematical method cannot be applied absolutely everywhere. You can try to equate a "psychological field" with a magnetic field and you can attempt parallel and comparable calculations in the two areas, but it seems rather ridiculous, and mathematicians will shrug their shoulders at what only nonmathematicians could mistake for a mathematical method. Moreover, there exist areas that are totally irreducible: all those that are dependent on the qualitative. Let us only mention as a reminder spiritual life, individual and collective emotions, authority, and noneconomic motivation. When you try to reduce these to numbers, you grasp only the outward forms, the behavior.

Do you want to create a sociology of religion? Since it is understood that any sociology worthy of the name has a numerical foundation, you must reduce everything to numbers. But then you can include only religious practices, horizontal intrahuman relations, ecclesiastical structures, and customs; in other words, everything except religion, everything that is merely the distortion, the awkward and misleading expression of the religious impulse. The impulse itself cannot be reduced to numbers, for it dwells in the pure realm of the qualitative.

We encounter the same difficulty when we try to make a serious study of public opinion. There are, of course, admirable mathematical methods of research, but no matter how carefully the questionnaire is planned, the qualitative aspect of opinion remains elusive; understanding of intensity and motivation is of the crudest and most schematic sort. One must have a very profound contempt for and a thoroughgoing ignorance of man in order to lump abstentionists in the elections in a single bloc, or to reduce the qualitative aspect of opinions to a simple yes-no dichotomy. The easiest thing is not to worry about this aspect.

And indeed, this point is very quickly reached. The moment you agree that the only sure knowledge of an object is mathematical knowledge, then where this method cannot be applied, no knowledge is possible. No objection so far—but you go on, *mezza voce*, hesitating, not admitting it to yourself, because you are not a cynic, "Therefore, there is no object." Such is the conclusion at which, without saying so, all supporters of the mathematical methods arrive. Even if what they say is always very spiritualistic and very formally respectful of the Soul, Religion, the Individual, etc., their conclusions can be observed in their behavior. They will readily explain that you must proceed "as if"! As if the relation to God did not exist, as if religious formalism corresponded to the essence of religion, as if the individual expressed himself accurately in his opinions and his words; otherwise their task would become impossible. You must proceed as if the nonnumerical did not exist so that the numerical can. For if you admit that there is a constant and intimate relationship between the two, what appears to be reducible to numbers ceases in reality to be so. In other words, to apply the mathematical method to man and everything that has to do with man, you must begin by dividing this material into numerical and nonnumerical. Then you must eliminate the second part—otherwise you would get nowhere.

Thus we obtain this very impressive result, which consists in denying the object or a part of the object because the Method *par excellence* could not be applied to it. But all you need to do is raise the question (I go no farther, but as long as a negative answer is not proved, I have the right to ask it, and any scientist is obliged to grant me this right!): "*What if* the relation to God existed? *What if* Justice were the key to social relations? *What if* the sense of the beautiful were determining (rather than determined by human relations) in the work of art? *What if* the quantitative could be explained only in relation to the qualitative?" At this point *everything* that has been arrived at by the application of the mathematical method becomes false. I could raise a thousand other questions of the same sort in economics or sociology. And I can state positively that in these fields the greatest reliability depends on preliminary choices, exclusions, nonscientific decisions that radically invalidate the conclusions obtained by the use of this absolute method.

And yet what is well on its way to becoming a commonplace is unanimously believed and accepted. I have no illusions that my arguments will convince anyone. Someone will reply that the division between subject and object is passé, someone else that since Engels the opposition between quantitative and qualitative is a false distinction, etc. Everyone will remain very sure of the result, and only I will be forced to wonder about the basis for this belief.

Obviously, we can pass very quickly over the reasons known to all: the effectiveness of the mathematical method in the natural sciences, our dazzled admiration in the face of the technical "miracle," which rests on this method. The deepest, most serious reason is also revealed to us by this budding commonplace. In our time as in the past, man, every man, has need of absolute certainty; there is no more metaphysical absolute, there is no more revealed knowledge. *Therefore* it is necessary, *absolutely* necessary, that man find elsewhere what is refused him at this source. He must have a substitute for revelation, a surrogate for the absolute, a final cause, a perfect knowledge. But everything around him is moving, flowing, without reason or root; everything follows the direction of history. Everything except mathematics! Here is the timeless, the certain, the knowable. The craving for an absolute may be satisfied by a certainty that is completely dependent on man and that is nevertheless invested with immutability. Under the circumstances, how could one fail to believe that the application of this abstract discipline to the concrete world would also provide the absolute and the perfect, would transform the contingent into the ultimate, and would at last satisfy man's desire for eternity by the glorification of the very thing that denied it?

ONE MUST TAKE A POSITIVE ATTITUDE

Rarely expressed in the form of an adage, this common-place clings stickily to all judgments about people dissemi-nated by *Marie-Claire, Paris-Match,* and *The Reader's Digest,* as well as to the injunctions of public relations, personality tests, theological writings (notably the good Father Teilhard!), literary criticism, and the thinking (as it were) of our most visible and authoritative moralists and sociologists. But it is time to stop and get our bearings before we lose our way completely. For forty years ago a commonplace was prevalent whose wording was almost the same but whose meaning was altogether different. In 1920 a person had to "be positive." This forceful expression had a very simple meaning: "The main thing is to make money." Anything that did not "produce" was not positive. The positive man was the businessman, the colonialist, the man who was "making his way." I won't dwell on these lofty ideas; Léon Bloy had already done justice to this commonplace before the fact.

In our time we have gone into the idea more thoroughly and have extended it to the level of "values." The point is to look upon everything with a favorable eye, to have your heart and mind wide open to what is happening, to take an optimistic view of man and events, to adopt an active attitude (here we see the connection with the necessity to be "positive" of 1920), and to participate in everything around you. Man, men, our neighbors—how good they are! Technology—how wonderful! Politics—the noblest profession! Etc. Of course, we are not content with these Anglo-Saxon niceties: we demonstrate, we prove. Conversely, we put to shame the monster who is not satisfied. Everybody knows today that every proposition must be formulated in a positive way (and never in a negative way), that the critical mind is a small mind, that the pessimist is simply a man with liver trouble, that negativeness is merely a sign that the man has never gone beyond adolescence, that he is not an adult. In our world, if you're not a good guy, the "keep smiling," extroverted, rah-rah type (though not necessarily a parachutist) who welcomes progress and is satisfied with contemporary thought, you are immediately suspected of profound villainy. It is not society that is open to criticism, or your disagreeable neighbor, but yourself: you, the Denier (and everyone knows that the Devil is the archdenier—but we will get back to the theologians later!); you, who contaminate things and people with your critical attitude.

And this attitude goes back to those dreadful complexes you have not been able to shed. "Are you sure you're not a little incestuous around the edges? Eh? Surely that explains your resistance to progress." It's clear as day: resistance to progress equals attachment to the past equals the desire to return to infancy equals longing for the womb equals incest. Q.E.D. All the psychologists today urge you to have a

positive attitude toward life. It appears that this is the
virile attitude. All the sociologists today show you that
there is only one solution: participation. It is only through
positive participation in the group, its accomplishments
and its unanimity, that man finds and fulfills himself. There
is no salvation outside the group! He who takes a negative
attitude toward the group not only will never find either
happiness or peace of mind, but also shirks his destiny,
which is to help others find themselves, which they can do
only in that harmonious group life in which good relations
are the psychosocial panacea.

Thus we arrive at the domain of morality. Virtue today
consists in being open to the positive realities of this time,
in exorcising the demons of negativism, denial, and passivity. Virtue consists in agreeing on the positive tasks to be
accomplished collectively. Virtue consists in providing positive, active, and optimistic solutions in the face of obstacles and problems. As they are carried along by such a
powerful current, it is inevitable that the theologians exploit it, as is their wont. So, in the name of Christian
Revolution, they ask us to have a positive attitude toward
the state, man, and technology. It is no longer necessary to
make old-fashioned judgments based on outmoded theolo-
gies: all you need do is proclaim the Great Yes of God,
pronounce the Great Benediction upon all human achievements. We must remember that the Creation is good; that
the Fall does not exist; that the world evolves according to
a continuous creation, or else that it evolves spontaneously
toward its fulfillment, which is automatically the Kingdom
of God; or else that the lordship of Jesus Christ means that
from now on everything is saved, redeemed, conducted by
Goodness and Truth. Away with monks, ascetics, and cen-
obites! Away with puritans, all those nay-sayers and wet
blankets! They were very bad theologians, since they re-

tained nothing but the Fall, the judgment, and damnation, and forgot all the rest. (Not being a theologian, I am tempted to remark that our modern theologians, for their part, retain *only* the rest, forgetting the Fall, sin, the judgment, damnation. And at the risk of a generalization, I might say that it seems as though theologians *always* forget half of the Revelation . . .)

It is very curious to observe, however, that it is only now, when the existential philosophies are revealing the baseness of man and the absurdity of the world, and when the psychoanalysts, in rolling away the sacred slabs of consciousness, are bringing to light the beasts and phantoms that dwell in the heart of man and constitute his profound reality—it is only now that they tell us that we must take an optimistic and positive attitude, because everything is really going very well. And even here, no doubt, to feel that there is some contradiction is to fall into that damnable habit of criticism and pessimism.

But perhaps, on the contrary, this brings us to one of the profound meanings of the commonplace, not just this one, but all of them. In their grotesque absurdity, their general contradiction of the real, and the fanatical attachment of those who believe in these commonplaces, there is clearly to be found a process of magic and exorcism. It is precisely because reality *is not* what we would like it to be that we must publish its contrary: in order to destroy its power over us, to evoke the appearance of the desirable opposite, to invoke by word and belief the contrary of the real. The commonplace is the incantatory formula of our time, based on false evidence, but calculated to help us avoid what worries, troubles, and threatens us. It is incantatory, because it has no meaning, because the person who repeats it does not assign it any actual content—for although based on evidence, the commonplace is part of a collective code, and receives its force and meaning from infinite and universal repetition. It is magical, because its purpose is to act upon and in some mysterious way to alter the reality it claims to express. The commonplace always contains an imperative to action, an indication of attitude; and consequently it really does alter something—a simple thing called man.

THERE ARE
ONE BILLION
ILLITERATES

The question no longer arises. It is perfectly obvious, and the answer is established: not to know how to read is a sign of disgrace, the mark of lack of culture and barbarism. To know how to read is an intrinsic good. It is the door to culture, the guarantee of intellectual freedom, the entrée into civilization, the opportunity for a human life that is finally complete. The whole nineteenth century based its hope for the improvement of man and society on the alphabet. How could this improvement fail to result from the communication of all the best that humanity has produced? So true is it that literacy is regarded as an intrinsic good that UNESCO statistics bluntly offer the number of "illiterates" in each country as an index of its level of civilization. And no doubt the outstanding proof of the excellence of a government is the fact that it has struggled against illiteracy. This is our guarantee that this government was honest and serious, that it was concerned about man and his soul, and that it was not immersed in sordid materialism, since it was spreading culture.

In a similar vein the good Victor Hugo declared that when illiteracy disappeared, tyrannical and dictatorial governments would cease to exist: the alphabet is the foundation of liberal democracy. Under the circumstances it is understandable that the most serious grievance African peoples can address to their colonizers is: "They have not taught us to read." The scandal of Algeria is that after a century of French occupation 75 per cent of the children have not received a primary education. And *l'Express* rides this subject to death in order to demonstrate the hypocrisy of colonization. It is quite true that it is better for a newspaper if people know how to read. Let us never forget that a reader is a customer. The more batches of little instant scholars the school produces, the more copies the newspaper can print.

A good recent book on the subject,[1] full of noble sentiments, tells us that illiterate people are "totally deprived of knowledge." For of course the man whose mind is untutored has no knowledge! The author tells us that these illiterates are hungry to learn in order to give a concrete meaning to their existence in a world in transformation. For of course man, creator of the great orally transmitted myths, was unable to give a concrete meaning to his existence! And a pious ecclesiastical notice in a church vestibule brings tears to our eyes at the thought of these poor illiterates who "do not participate in any culture, who are forgotten by history," and who are "depriving humanity of their potential for strength and intelligence." Now, that is really nasty and ungiving of them. If you think about all that

---

[1] Montvalon: *Un Milliard d'analphabètes* (1965).

wasted time—in fifty thousand years, think how many men have deprived humanity of their potential! Talk about selfish!

As for the relation between literacy and human dignity, one of the finest statements on that subject was undoubtedly made by a very distinguished man who is perfectly competent in his field, but who made the mistake, like many others (myself included), of going beyond his field and attempting general ideas. M. Rivet wrote in *Le Monde* on February 1, 1959: "Everywhere material poverty is associated with intellectual poverty. Eighty-eight per cent of the population of India are illiterates." (Thus illiteracy equals intellectual poverty; when you have known a few illiterate Arabs, natives of Cevennes, or Indians, you discover a great deal about their intellectual poverty!) "A person who cannot even read a newspaper is not free." (Once again we meet that blessed freedom, this time wrapped in newsprint!) Because of illiteracy, "peoples who arrive at independence are in danger of sinking into disorder and anarchy . . . people must find out that the road to freedom passes by way of culture," the latter being defined by the ability to read, culture obviously being dependent on the printed word. When we observe the disintegration of culture, the sterilization brought about by the diffusion of this printed word to what used to be centers of culture and cultivated peoples, we can bow to the inevitable, but at least let's not embellish it with the very values it destroys!

Finally, M. Rivet proposes that international assemblies adopt "a balanced voting system that would give each nation a number of votes inversely proportional to the number of its illiterates, which would restore cultural equilibrium and create a stimulating competition among backward peoples . . ." This idea is truly staggering. To

identify the ability to read with political maturity and capacity to reflect soundly about political problems is rather
amazing. Obviously ancient Greece would not have been
entitled to many votes at the UN. On the other hand, Nazi
Germany would have triumphed all along the line; and the
bourgeoisie is much more mature than the proletariat, since
the latter is full of illiterates!

The most obvious way in which literacy is useful in our
society has to do with the government. If the citizen cannot
read, he becomes impossible to govern. I am perfectly serious, and I do not say "difficult to govern," I say radically
impossible. Given the present administrative complexity,
the multiplicity and variability of decisions and given also
that nowadays nothing works without the active participation of the citizen and his informed good will, it follows
that the citizen must be kept up to date on new regulations,
provisions relating to traffic and the police, time schedules
and working hours, statistics and notices of elections; he
must know that he is to present himself at a certain office,
that he must fill out a certain form, that his rights expire at
a certain date, and all this can only be learned from the
newspaper. Every day the man at the bottom of the bureaucracy must, if he wants to be in harmony with the
government, receive the little dose of administrative information necessary to his existence.

On a higher level, literacy is the cornerstone of propaganda. Of course the educated liberal will protest loudly,
and accuse me of partiality and evil-mindedness. "Propaganda is only an accident. It is regrettable that such a fine
invention as reading should be spoiled by being put to such
bad use. But there is no necessary connection between the
two phenomena. And anyway, propaganda existed before

people knew how to read, didn't it?" I will restrict myself to the level of actual situations. I know nothing about the intrinsic nature of literacy, whether it is a good thing or a bad thing. I know nothing about what might be; I try to consider only what is, and I observe that the governments that have acted most energetically to promote literacy have always had an idea about propaganda in the back of their minds. Our worthy Third Republic, which did so much for elementary education, was neither so ingenuous nor so liberal as people like to believe. Literacy has succeeded in permanently implanting the republican passion, in turning all Frenchmen into republicans in two generations, and in developing a group of propagandistic myths the most successful of which have been the myths of the Great Revolution, the Bastille, the imperiled fatherland, liberty and equality, Valmy and the Avenger—so many dubious historical truths whose mythification forms the foundation for the political competence of the French citizen.

In our day the phenomenon is even more obvious. It is a question of teaching people to read *so that* the citizen can read the propagandistic writings of the authoritarian state, and nothing else. The most typical example, no doubt, is that of the Viet Minh and North Korea, where the campaign against illiteracy is the pride of the communist governments. These governments teach people to read from the works of Marx and Lenin, and the only reading matter furnished to the people is government propaganda. No work of literature, no book by a foreign author or a dead author is issued to the people. Thus literacy places man much more in the hands of the state than ever. "But come now, you have only mentioned two countries out of a hundred, and one moment in time: let's not forget that literacy is a permanent acquisition. Some day the people are bound to come across something else. They will read other books,

and at that moment they will turn violently against the
state. The reader will long passionately for freedom and
will force the state to become liberal."

It appears that we must restate our basic premise. The
fact of knowing how to read is nothing, the whole point is
knowing *what* to read. Must people learn to read so they
can read the serialized novels in *Paris-Presse* or the propaganda of Ho Chi Minh? In that case it is infinitely prefera-
ble not to know how to read. So much wasted time, so
much lost effort that could have been saved. "I tell you
again that it is a false problem! For what one reads depends on the choice of the reader. By teaching him to read
you give him the means to educate himself, enrich himself,
improve himself. If he does not do it, that's his own fault,
not the fault of reading! You know very well all the excellent things there are to read." Yes, of course. But what *does*
he read? He reads primarily what is provided for him.

In the so-called free, capitalist countries, he reads the
tabloids, the comics, "true romance" magazines, and *Paris-
Match*. To tell the truth, if this is primarily what is provided for him, that is because this is what sells. And if it
sells, that is because literate man wants and desires this
kind of reading matter. And this is quite understandable!
For where and when does this man who is "cultivated
because he knows how to read" have the opportunity to
read? In the subway, on the bus, and in the evening after
work. It is obvious that under the circumstances he will not
look for difficulty, but for distraction. It is more exciting to
read a detailed report of the latest murder than the latest
speech by De Gaulle. It requires a large share of energy
and virtue and a highly developed civic conscience to come
home and analyze economic statistics rather than to turn

immediately to the cartoons. The reader looks for something that is easy and will take him away from the daily grind. He will read love stories to satisfy his need for the emotional life he does not have, murder stories to make up for the banality of his daily routine, and pornography to release his inhibitions. But with rare exceptions, he will not look for something that will "improve his mind," demand an effort of him, or give rise to reflection, awareness, or sustained thought.

Primary responsibility for this rests not with man himself, but with the very condition of his life at all economic levels and for all professions. It is childish to believe that the lawyer or doctor can do any real reading outside of his work, for this work overwhelms him. Here again, it requires an exceptional effort, an outstanding virtue, a sacrifice of family life to read books for any reason other than amusement. And since this is what the reader desires, why shouldn't he be provided with the titillator and the tranquilizer? After all, publishers don't have to be martyrs and heroes: they are making money. That's what they're there for. And in the process they make the good reader a little duller than he was.

The "liberalized" communist countries, on the other hand, are a feather in the cap of the defenders of literacy. Look at what the Soviet people read. Here, at least, is culture: Balzac, Aragon, *Madame Bovary*, Garaudy—the classics! Gogol and Pushkin. No nonsense, no fluff. And look at Soviet newspapers: serious, solid stuff, the real thing; no pictures, no romantic anecdotes. Nothing but political economics, ideas, science. Now, here is a cultivated people; you'll look in vain for "true romances," for Clement Vautel or Paul Guth! With a good government, then, it is possible to use the ability to read to create a true culture; all you have to do is be firm and the people will be

well trained. I quite agree, and the key word is *trained*. For
what is placed at the disposal of the Russian people for
their edification is no more innocent than what is provided
for the French people or the American people. The reader
has no more choice than they do. He reads what is provided him—and what is provided him, in *all* books, all
newspapers, is in the interests of a propaganda that simply
happens to be subtler than that of Ho. Why Balzac and
Flaubert? Because they are eloquent witnesses to the moral
and economic corruption of the bourgeoisie. But will he be
given Pascal? Certainly not, nor Dostoevsky, nor Nietzsche,
nor Steiner, nor Racine, nor Berdyaev! Reading is intended
to destroy the personal ideas of the individual, to incorpo-
rate him into the social mainstream, to make him a good,
orthodox socialist, to prove the correctness of the ideas of
Marx and Lenin. The newspaper must not amuse (for
amusement is a dangerous manifestation of bourgeois individualism), but "educate" in the truth of Marxism and
Leninism. A train accident or a murder is not a miscellaneous fact, but a doctrinal illustration of the perversity of
capitalists, the gravity of negligence when you are a socialist worker, or the monstrousness of cosmopolitanism. To
hound a man with the truth of the doctrine in everything
he reads, to besiege him in every line, thus eliminating all
possibility of criticism or comparison: yes, surely literacy is
the most powerful force in the modern world for the enslavement of man. And in the last analysis, the literature of
the heart strikes me as less damaging to the individual,
because less systematic, than the so-called literature of the
mind!

I am familiar with my opponent's line of retreat. "None
of this has to do with the ability to read *per se*, but only

with the use man makes of it. Raise the morals of the newspaper editors, liberalize the Soviet regime, educate the reader, show him that it is in his true interest to read the lofty thoughts and profound feelings expressed by universal literature, and reading will be what it should be." Undoubtedly. But I cannot satisfy myself with hypotheses or console myself with a future of which I see no promise. To say that everything depends on the use man makes of it is to say nothing at all. I see man as he is, and it is on this basis that I can state that the ability to read makes no positive contribution; quite the contrary. Now, I too can play the little game of wishful thinking. If the reader (the ideal reader, that is, all readers!) were virtuous, if the reader were intellectually and aesthetically sophisticated, if the reader had a taste for effort, if the reader worked only three or four hours a day, if all newspaper publishers and editors were indifferent to money, agreed to lead lives of saintly self-denial, and had a sense of their high mission, if all governments were honest and scrupulous and respected the complete freedom of their citizens, then we would be living in the kingdom of God, and there would be no need to learn to read because we would know everything by means of intuitive and immanent knowledge.

YOU ARE WHAT
YOU ARE

When the nineteenth-century bourgeois hypocrite so perfectly exposed by Léon Bloy made this statement, he
would assume a sanctimonious expression and add with an
inane smile, "You can't change your nature." But what he
was really doing was excusing himself. And this is where
the famous homage that vice paid to virtue came in: We
really should . . . but we can't. We really should . . . but
already the justification was showing through the excuse.
For where did he get this idea? After centuries in which
man had been fired and tempered by the ecclesiastical
imperative "You must be made new," could it be that he
was being given a sudden freedom? Impossible! But what
was as yet only a loophole was already being offered by
science: There is no absolute, there is no morality, there is
no revealed truth. The only thing that counts is the real.
Don't give up the substance for the shadow. And the
shadow of what the moralists propose is surely not worth
that solid substance which the sciences reveal to be the

outside world. You belong to that world. You are what you are. Don't try to change. A very convenient course for man, for whom it is never pleasant to be measured against an absolute.

Now, this refusal to confront a spiritual and moral absolute was a fundamentally bourgeois attitude. So we see that this rather self-pitying excuse originated with the bourgeoisie. But now the armored cars of science have rushed forward with a great clatter. Psychology, psychoanalysis, sociology, and biology have come to confirm the idea "You are what you are," which has now assumed a triumphant stance. Supported by the sciences and accepted by everyone, it is the blunt expression of a sound, straightforward realism. Man, a little flushed and in good health, handling the instruments of power and shouldering heavy responsibilities, closes the door on all discussion: "You are what you are." Enough of all this nonsense. Remake human nature? What an illusion!

Besides, everybody knows very well that the point is to remake society, that that is the end from which to attack the problem. And it is only when society has been remade, organized, perfected, when institutions are running like well-oiled machinery, when the economy is distributing a superabundance of goods uninterruptedly and in equal shares, when higher education is the lot of 99.9 per cent of the population (the 0.1% being the insane), where everybody is well housed, homogenized, washed, and ironed, then and only then will man become—automatically and effortlessly, of course, like everything else—different from what he is now. Until then we must go on being the way we are.

And let us note that man uses this commonplace only in one circumstance: when he has just done something vile. Its precise meaning is: "I'm acting like a bastard, but how

can I help it?" So we are always in the presence of a refusal
to face a challenge, a refusal to consider an opposing point
of view, a justification in its most animal form; but this
attitude, once shameful, has become glorious. We are very
far from the sublime justifications of the intellectuals or the
devious justificatory machinery that society as a whole offers its members. No, this is justification in its crude, ele-
mental state, exactly right for the man of action who keeps
his eye on the ball, the scientific investigator who knows
that all this talk about moral qualms and spiritual imperatives went out of style long ago—let's talk about something
else—and the politician who knows that if you start won-
dering about things and trying to reform men, you'll never
get anywhere. At least these are men of experience, and
what is more they are, as we were saying, supported by the
findings of science. How could that man fail to be magnificent and sure of himself who tells you right to your face:
"You are what you are"?

Of course he's turning his back on himself. But after all,
is that so important? Of course he refuses to exercise his
conscience. "My 'moral' conscience?" he will ask me sarcas-
tically. Not at all. His psychological conscience, his sense of
himself. For that's where the shoe pinches, in spite of everything. The person who says "You can't change your
nature" is pretending that he accepts himself as he is, in full
awareness and understanding. But this is simply a lie. The
reason he says it is that he does not accept himself. And the
reason he says it in that aggressive way is because he is
expecting you to put a dagger between his shoulder blades,
where he knows he has a weak spot, and he is making the
first move. He does not accept himself, so he resorts to the
time-honored wisdom of the junior officer: "I don't want to
know about it."

I do not want to know who I am or what I am, I just

want to be it. What's the good of looking beyond that? I do not want to know either my capacity, or my responsibility, or my vocation. I walk, I act, I react (and since I behave like a complete extrovert, science assures me that I am perfectly normal); what's the use of examining myself, questioning myself, analyzing myself? What's the use of measuring myself? Against what? The great movement that carries me along submerges me in that glorious collective current which can only be progress, which assures me of both my own existence and the subsequent improvement of man. I don't have to try to be better than I am, for this will be the necessary result of progress. Here, then, is the logical conclusion of this proud affirmation: it is a case of resignation to the collective anonymity that I expect somehow to relieve me of myself.

So perhaps we should amend the statement slightly. When you say "You are what you are," what you really mean is "I am nothingness."

CULTIVATE YOUR PERSONALITY: BE A PERSON!

The scene is a beauty salon. The cosmetician advises, "Madame, your make-up should bring out your personality" or "Learn to personalize your make-up"; and after that she sells you a personalized make-up. An admirable example of the way things return to their source: it is by making oneself a mask of ruse and artifice that one becomes a person.

A large and pious Dutch firm features an inscription: "Each of our employes is a person." Think about that: a whole glorious and almost transcendent ethic is based on it. Management regards you as a person. No matter what your salary or your living conditions, you are a person. Among yourselves, you must regard your fellow workers as people. Your department head is a person. (And even if you are a page or errand boy, you are on an equal footing with your employer.) Your subordinates are people. Whatever your complexes or the dismal grind of your daily life, you can draw yourself up with pride: you belong to the vast enterprise and glorious firm of P. Brothers, therefore you are a Person. You are Somebody!

Another large company, this one American, and I suppose no less pious, announces earnestly, "All we ask is that you think for yourself." If I am not mistaken, it is a manufacturer of electronic machines. Here again, the glorification of everyone participating in the company is of major importance. Nothing can be done without your thinking. You are dehumanized by your work, you must make automatic gestures or be bored to death in a room that is scrupulously clean, in front of panels of switches and flickering lights—so: "Think."

Above all, "Think for yourself." Don't be afraid. Don't follow the ordinary and everyday pattern, don't think you have to conform. No, on the contrary, you must fulfill yourself. And to fulfill yourself, you must Think. This is the only aim, the only purpose of the whole company. Did you think it was there to manufacture machines? To make a profit? How wrong you were! It is there for you—so that you, who work there, may think for yourself. Still, let's understand each other, the company is talking about Thinking with a capital T, that is something edifying, no daydreams. That is the worst thing you could do. You who are daydreaming about your girl friend, you must Think.

You who withdraw into yourself to nurse your rebellion—very bad, my friend, it will give you complexes. You who turn to God with gravity and pray—just as bad, it will give you other complexes. You must be realistic.

You who are thinking about your "salary cut"—come now, you must rise above such thoughts! Your dignity as a person demands it. Think.

But what about, then? Well, about useful things—things

that will be a Service to your Neighbor—for example, how
to improve your work or the machine you use, how to
achieve a better output. Think about the interest of everyone, think, therefore, about how to do your job well . . .

The least mass-produced item now invokes your personality. Somebody makes you a suit in a commercial size. This
is not so it will be your size, not at all: it is to bring out your
personality. And we can consider ourselves lucky when it is
not the product itself that is endowed with a personality.
On a splendid midnight-blue billboard gleams a perfectly
ordinary   watch,   but   with   the   enormous   legend:
"PERSONALITY: dependable and accurate." After all, everybody has one, and the great preoccupation of modern psychological techniques, groups dynamics, role-playing, and
other psychodramas is precisely to allow you to discover, or
rediscover, or express, or balance your personality. Did you
think these were merely the abuses of advertising? But
advertising provides the most reliable expression of the
underlying beliefs of a society. Surely you don't imagine
that those excellent gentlemen we refer to as hucksters
have made this up all by themselves! Nowadays people
wear their personalities the way they used to wear garde-
nias in their buttonholes; advertising has merely made the
ideas of the Great Prophets available to all. And specialists
in psychological techniques are not comedians. Nobody is
more serious or more dedicated than one of those objective
observers of a group ordered to be dynamic, who will
eventually reveal to everyone his hidden self: his Personality.

But already this is merely a secondary, a derived product. It all began with the philosophers. While the chemists
were closing in on the origins of life, the philosophers were
closing in on the heart of man and discovering that unnam-
able, that mystery, that fundamental though invisible real-

ity, that heart of existence, that source of our drives and of our yearning toward a "further beyond," that enigma which cannot be explained by either social psychology or psychoanalysis and which remains more essential than anything that comes to the surface in your dreams. That immeasurable which is your common measure with your fellow man. That universal which is your most individual aspect. That All which both sets you apart and unites you with the rest, which is you and more than you . . . I could go on indefinitely, merely by copying over the homework of the personalists of every stripe. But let's face it, those who are not personalists suffered such a shock when the Person fell on their heads, that they have never quite recovered from it.

After all, Beckett looks for the person in garbage cans, and Gabriel Marcel looks for it in heaven, which amounts to the same thing.

I would not pay any attention to this battle of words (anxiety, tragedy, and organ swell) if it had not reached the level of the man in the street. If he had not been provided with these titles of nobility, if you didn't come across a person at every street corner and in every bundle of laundry. For today the whole society, as maternal as the native land used to be, leans over every newborn's cradle to make a person out of the wailing infant.

The person ascended to heaven when people became fully aware of the vileness of the individual. Everything is the fault of this Individual. If democracy has never been able to function, the citizens being only abstractions, the right to vote a joke, and parliamentarianism a lawyer's device, it is the fault of the individual, as we have already seen.

If science has not given man happiness, if it has deviated from its original purpose, if the truth has disappeared behind the smokescreen of the cult of science, it is the fault of the individual. If the state has become totalitarian, if bureaucracy has become all-consuming, if the affirmation of freedom has never taken any tangible form, it is the fault of the individual. If capitalism has become established, if the exploitation of man by man is, alas, the rule, if profit has set the capitalist and the proletarian at odds, it is the fault of the individual. If the arts have declined, if literature has congealed into crude forms, if painting has become fragmented and at the same time is destined to adorn the walls of bourgeois homes, if culture has deteriorated until it is merely "bourgeois" culture, it is the fault of the individual. And if in the end morality has only been the triumph of hypocrisy, it is still he and he alone who is to blame.

For the Individual is the Villain. First of all, he is the equivalent of the bourgeois. It was in the age of the bourgeoisie that the individual was held up as an example of man. Man without any ties or restraints, man who was to fulfill his destiny by himself, man alone in the face of a hostile society. The "either—or" that expresses a radical conflict between the group and the individual, man in conflict with the others, competitive man, man of "May the best man win." The man of introspection and individual piety. The paternalist who is concerned about the lot of the poor, the citizen who needs neither enlightenment nor leadership to figure out what policy should be followed. The man of sacred egoism and well-protected interests. The man of love as a passion but also of love as an object. This individual, at once terribly concrete, because he represents a society that is disintegrating and thus remains his own sole witness as to what man is, and pure abstraction, because he is composed of ideal traits that make him the measure of all things. Whichever he may be, let us examine this foetus in its bottle of formaldehyde with compassion, for his era is over.

There is no more individual—what is more, from now on there must not be an individual, for we have pronounced judgment on him. Now we see the truth. It was a great error to believe in the individual. He was a hateful type of man, and those who tried to live up to this ideal were in reality nothing but the great swindlers of finance, politics, or the army, what are called Great Men. But once the individual was weighed, measured, dissected, dismembered, hung from meat hooks, and thrown into the garbage can, we still had a problem on our hands. It seemed difficult to combine everything in a sufficiently mixed collectivity. Outright collectivization was distasteful to the squeamish, especially since at the time extremists were talking about a collectivization of women—really! The most relentless foes of individualism—artists, men of letters, orators, political theorists—were, alas, themselves rather fine specimens of individuals, and their curses never went beyond the carefully aligned margins of their various writings. The nuisance, the great nuisance, was that collectivization was agreeable only to those proletarians most overwhelmed by their class, that is, the very ones who had never been able to come forward or exert themselves as individuals; for the others it was very painful to take the great plunge into the murky pond of a collectivity that resembled anonymity. No more individuality, of course!—but still, equality at the bottom . . . Then the Philosopher came along and created the Person.

Saved! For in this paragon of all the virtues, the most singular and the most collective were harmoniously joined.

In reality, there was no conflict between man and his society: this conflict had been invented by the Villains. The
reality is that man exists only by the grace of society—and
society only by the grace of man. And the same goes for
God, and culture, and morality, and Everything Else. What
could be more convenient!

It was no accident that at this precise moment there
appeared that estimable entity known as the Person. And it
is still less an accident that, after a few initial hesitations,
its appearance brought on the stampede that led us to this
society in which everything is dominated by the person.

The situation had been vaguely experienced as disturb-
ing. The surest values had been tottering since the crash of
1929. It is true that the First World War had already
somewhat shaken people's confidence in civilization and
Western man, but still everybody knew that right and justice had triumphed. This, at least, could not be called into
question. Whereas with the collapse of 1929, the ground
gave way under their feet. There really was no more justice
if the good little saver, the honest speculator, the great
captain of industry, and the inspired inventor saw themselves deprived of the fruits of their labors. The crisis in the
stock market was a crisis of conscience, and seeing his
actions brought to nothing, the individual began to lose
faith in man.

And then came the rest: large-scale industry and the
inhuman lot of the workers, the proletarian revolt and the
inadmissible demands of those without whom no progress
is possible, the Russian Revolution and the inhuman lot of
generals driving cabs, urbanization and the inhuman lot of
urbanites going back and forth between the tenement and
the rabbit cage. People began speaking in frightened whis-
pers and trembling voices about the Masses, the Mass age,
and Mass man, and it was as if everyone felt threatened

with castration. It became clear that the bourgeoisie had
been a huge mistake. But there it was, all the values had
been taken over, swallowed up, masticated, and digested
by the bourgeoisie—including morality, art, virtue, culture;
where was one to turn? Surely we couldn't take Freud and
the surrealists seriously. But still, the barbarians were at
our gates, and those gates seemed very worm-eaten.

All of a sudden, in the stormy sky, appeared the liberating gleam. The illumination of the masses followed that of
the Philosopher, and the Person appeared to all. What did
the workers want, those communists, those labor unionists?
Why, to be a Person. Whew! That was close. And Freud?
With the Person, we don't need him; he can still take
everything apart, but there remains the imperishable center that is located neither in the Self nor in the Ego nor in
the Superego, but somewhere else, and that eludes him.
They can say all they want about me, I am an inaccessible
Person.

I may be a part of the Mass, I may even be swallowed up
in the army or the concentration camp; what does it matter,
as long as the Person is intact? There have been some very
nice demonstrations on the subject of Soviet propaganda,
in which three levels were distinguished. Naturally, in the
realm of sociological, political, economic behavior (superficial, all this!), propaganda was all-powerful. But on a
deeper level (the level of private life, personal opinions),
propaganda was much less influential; and then—ah! freedom!—on the deepest level there is the Person, over whom
propaganda is powerless. How sweet and good is this reassurance! And this solution is good for everything. In the
subway, you feel like one sheep in a flock; in the bureaucracy, you feel like a number; in the street, you feel lost in
the crowd; in the factory or the office, you feel like a
cog . . .

All this is your imagination: what you are is a Person.
Advertising tells you so if you are not up to reading the
philosophers. The personalist or existentialist philosophers
tell you so if you are an intellectual and look down on
advertising. Then there are the novels, which multiply ad
infinitum for the express purpose of guaranteeing the
uniqueness of the adventure they relate to you, and consequently of your adventure. And the movies . . . how can I
doubt that I am a Person when the star offers me an image
so obvious, a face so seductive, almost an absolute of the
Person? Let's not kid ourselves; the philosopher holding
forth about the Person is doing exactly the same thing as
the copy writer who invites you to become a Person by
drinking Pepsi-Cola. And the Baron de Charlus is simply
Guy l'Éclair for another category of minds. The point is that
we have a common fate and that we cannot make up our
minds to live it.

Essentially, you are becoming a consumer of innumerable objects that arc forced on you and that you must con-
sume; but by consuming more, you see, you become a
Person. Manufactured articles are mass-produced, all identical, but in reality they are extraordinarily personalized.
You have the impression of being horribly passive, and of
being stuffed with culture, information, and politics, as if
they were so much spaghetti; but don't forget that you are
a Person. The more you are trapped by the mass, the more
you must *believe* that you are a Person. The more standardized the object is, the more you must *believe* that it is
unique. The more helpless you are, the more noble and
awe-inspiring the Person *must* become.

Nor is it an accident if the regimes of totalitarian massifi-
cation have led all others in exalting the Person. The totalitarian regime was dominated by the absolute Person, the

Führer; the collectivist police state implied the cult of
Personality. It cannot be otherwise. And we have all
reached this point. If Soviet Russia seems to be repudiating
the cult of Personality, that is because the liberalization
(?) of the regime is beginning to allow each citizen to play
the same little game we play and to have his own personal
little cult of personality, as we see from the new literary
trend in the USSR. It is precisely because everyone finds
himself caught in a denser network of pressures, obliga-
tions, surveillances, and influences in which his freedom
disappears that the absolute freedom of the Person must be
affirmed more loudly and clearly than ever.

It is precisely because in all the countries of the world
the individual is treated like a molecule, tortured, despised,
devaluated—by colonialists and anticolonialists; by fascists
and communists; by white racists, black racists, and yellow
racists; by liberals who use napalm to liberate peoples and
by technicians who use the evidence of the results to in-
corporate them; by men of good will who often despise
them in spite of themselves—it is precisely because of this
that the person must be more elevated, that it must distill
all human dignity, all human nobility, and the mystery and
enigma of man. We know now that each of these smaller
units contains everything that is human, because it is a
Person, and of course we all know how truly each of us can
be a Person.

Nor is it an accident if the great watchwords today are
Encounter and Communication. Here again, a matter of
Persons. When the other person becomes elusive and incomprehensible—because we have not in fact the time to
consider him, because we are being stirred in a giant blender
that is preparing glorious tomorrows, because we speak
languages that, as we are becoming increasingly aware, are

now drained of meaning—the ineffable happens, Communication: communion, Myth and Symbol, a more profound
language, final and personalizing, the quasi-mystical encounter, as by God the Father alone, which belief in the
Person absolutely guarantees. For after all, if this did not
happen, life would be unbearable. The commonplace always rests on a profound human necessity.

But it also reveals the nature of this famous intangible
Person: the little compensatory device that enables us to
bear the unbearable. The consolation that the philosopher
invents and the merchant uses—the one because he has to
think and the other because he has to move his stock—one
is the same as the other. The Person: a little lovelock of
living hair on a death mask, a perfect illustration of culture
in the most bourgeois sense. It is the little supplement we
need, and this supplement of soul, purely virtual, is nothing
more than the wrought-iron flourishes that an aesthetically
conscious industry added to the McCormick reaper and the
Singer sewing machine in 1880—the useful and the decora-
tive—and the 1 per cent allotment for aesthetic purposes
that French law stipulates today in all budgets for the construction of public buildings.

The reason the murky notion of Person has had such a
success that it has become a commonplace is that man in
modern society could not consider himself as he is, in the
real condition that is imposed on him by technology and
the state. The Person is the dirty mask that spirituality
(and Marxism is as much a part of this spirituality as
Christianity) hangs over the open sores that our society
inflicts on the average man, every man, so it won't have to
see them. Ironically, the Roman *persona* was only a
mask—but at that time there could be no doubt; the fact

was known. We have advanced; now we ourselves are caught in the trap of innocence. The symbol that exhausts the whole subject is that we have succeeded in turning the theatrical mask into the most intimate, the most profound, the noblest, and the most spiritual aspect of man.

MAKE WAY FOR
YOUTH!

Another of those polymorphous commonplaces, this idea appears as "The rise of youth" or frequently today as "The future belongs to the young." Biologically speaking, the matter is indisputable. But is becomes a bit comical when an old duffer observes: "Youth performs a biological function of renewal"; but being idealists, we immediately add, and this is where the imposture sets in, "In the advance of the people, youth fulfills a prophetic mission." Prophetic of what? Of the fact that they will grow old? "No, don't you see? Of the fact that they will make the Future."

It is the tautology that accounts for the success of certain political thinkers. For one wonders anxiously to whom the future *could* belong. From the human point of view, not to nonagenarians! And since the young were born thirty years after we were, it is indeed they—still from the human point of view—who will have to manage during the period to come. The only thing people forget is that by the time the young are in a position to make this future, they will have become the same old wrecks that we are now, and will make just about the same present as the one that served us as future.

Am I a pessimist? Not at all! If this statement is a commonplace, it is because for almost fifty years people have been proclaiming this truth, and for at least thirty years they have been busy making a policy of "youth"! Figure it out. If we agree that "youth" covers the period from eighteen to twenty-five, say seven years, this makes seven generations of young people who have had the responsibility for the future placed on their shoulders by old fauns playing at optimism! In 1919 the territorials declared, "We have missed our vocation: we were unable to avoid war. It is up to you, the young, to create a world in which we will never see it again!" At that moment youth was valiantly preparing for the future by learning to fly, participating in strikes, and discovering jazz. In 1929 the veterans (those who were twenty years old in 1917!) declared, "Alas! We won the war, but we have not won the peace. Our peace is a failure; the world we were going to rebuild is falling to pieces. . . . Fortunately there are the young. . . . We pass you the torch that . . ." There were some rather fine displays of eloquence on this theme.

The year 1936 saw the victory of youth, that is, the creation of a Department of Youth. Long live leisure, youth groups, and unwed mothers (for it is obvious that the rise of youth implies the emancipation of woman!). Alas! This youth, brought to power and made aware of its rights and responsibilities, did not last the space of a morning, and in six months its purple robe had lost its vivid hue and become a washed-out pink. In 1942 everyone knows that the dyspeptic old man put all his hope in the young who were going to make a new France, and indeed there were many who marched, and the youth camps had their day. Those who took part in them redeemed themselves afterward by explaining that in these Vichy camps they were developing the Spirit of Resistance—but enough of that. In 1945 the young people, like the Republic, were called upon to be pure and strong. But at this point youth was M. Bidault. Why go on? And today . . . !

The absurdity of population experts: We must have young people, and more young people! France is an old country. The birth rate profile, etc. But suppose we increase the number of young people considerably? Won't this mean that in fifty years the number of old people will be even greater, this excessive number of young people having become old themselves? We will be caught in a vicious circle: there will have to be more and more young people, in geometric proportion. Meanwhile, on all sides people warn us of the great dangers of overpopulation! If you do not push today for the drastic increase of young people, it will mean that in thirty years France will be a country younger than the countries that are now overrun with young people, young people who will by then be a crushing weight of old people!

But when the populationists tell us that *today* we must at all costs by a young people, then carefully repress the thought: *"Après nous, le déluge!"*

A policy of youth: but who makes this policy? Who prepares this youth? Why the old, of course. Those who today hold the jobs, pull the strings, and have the authority proclaim the importance of the young, the necessity for a policy of youth. There follows a very difficult transfer of authority. Let's not say that this commonplace is proclaimed for political reasons (by the politician) or for the sake of popularity (by the professor). Its roots are at once nobler and deeper than that! These old people were young once. At the age of twenty, they thought (most of them have since stopped, but nevertheless, at the age of twenty, they thought); they felt and understood the evils of their age. They had a vision of what had to be done (generally a true vision), and they had the revolutionary ardor and the courage to risk everything (having nothing to lose but their lives). So the best among them went to work. In the labor unions, the parties, the universities, the serious magazines, and the businesses, they gradually climbed the ladder, fought for their ideas, pushed through legislation, influenced thinking, and won followers, and by the age of fifty they finally had sufficient authority to take the lead. But suddenly they realized that they had very little time left to put the ideas of their youth into effect, that they had very little revolutionary fervor any more, and that the machinery they had become a part of and over which they had some control was terribly clumsy and complicated. So they were inevitably inclined to turn to the young and say, "Look, everything is ready: we've broken the back of the job. It's up to you young people to take over!" And the sexagenarian placed himself on an equal footing with the student.

But, alas, the latter had no interest in these achievements, which he saw as worthy of historical interest, at best. For what had happened in the meantime, what the old man had been completely unaware of, was that things had changed. When the former youth arrives at power, he applies his ideas, his doctrines, his vision of things, which were acquired, developed, and formulated thirty years ago, to a situation that is altogether different. By the time he is in a position to act, he has spent his whole life climbing the ladder, and he does not know that his baggage is now made up of motheaten blankets and rusty cans. He does not know that his revolutionary schemes are only scratches on a bank of clouds, and that his ideas have prevailed and are accepted by many only insofar as they no longer have anything to do with the reality of today. And the former youth congratulates himself on the fact that personalism, or socialism, or syndicalism has triumphed. But this no longer has any importance.

Sometimes the former youth wonders why things don't seem to be going right; he is seized by a vague uneasiness and calls in the young to put the pieces back together. More often still, he deplores the fact that the youth of today seem to be incapable of this and take no interest in that . . . but in what, exactly? In the ideas and theories of thirty years ago? If the young do not enter into this game, it is because quite unconsciously and without any particular value, they are operating on the level of today. I am not going to berate beatniks and hooligans, any more than the adults who have made them a world to which, according to another commonplace, they cannot adjust. Neither group had any choice. The old always try to make a policy of youth: that is, to make the young people enter into their game. Thus you get various youth groups—communist, socialist, Catholic, Protestant, UNR, patriotic, etc. Simple mechanisms of adjustment to the adult world.

And, alas, it is quite true that when you consider the serious young people who are trying to accept the role that the old are offering them (Make way for youth!), you notice that they are magically transformed into old people, that they think and talk like the old. A sad example of this is offered by the present student associations (all of them!), which only reveal the way in which certain young people have been invaded by senile obsessions. The problem cannot be erased simply by making laborious distinctions between the Values of Youth and the Myth of Youth. Youth has value only because it has become a Myth. And Mr. X would take no interest in this youth if the myth had not been there to begin with.

Alas! We must ask ourselves who has put the slogan into actual effect. As Perrault [1] has perfectly demonstrated, only fascism and Nazism have glorified youth. Where have we found important dignitaries of twenty-five? Among the Nazis. Where did youth have its heyday? In the Third Reich. And it is true that only a society of that type can fully satisfy the ardor, the vitality, the taste for risk, the sense of crossing old frontiers, the "Everything today and to hell with tomorrow," the creation of true equality in a communal style of life, the recognition of leaders who are leaders and not established authorities. These are characteristics of the young. But to ask the young to increase their technical knowledge in order to have good careers or serve the nation, to assure them a rise in the standard of living, to show them a reasonable course that will lead to the perfect society of tomorrow, to promise them comfort, plenty, institutional equality, and freedom of opportunity—all this is in the style of the old. The people today who relish the expression "Make way for youth!" must realize that if we take them seriously, they are saying: "Long live Nazism!"

But we must not take them seriously. This is only a slogan like any other. The young will have their day when they are no longer young. And the commonplace spread by

---

[1] *Les Parachutistes.*

our elites is only an alibi of old men to attest to their liberalism, to show how ready they are to admit their mistakes and to administer the tranquilizer that every society distributes to its youth.

But the established old have their little ideas; don't think them innocent, O youth! *In petto,* the adult today thinks the same way he did a hundred years ago: "Youth will have its fling," "A young man must sow his wild oats," very innocent admissions of senile impotence.

Clemenceau pitied men who had not been revolutionaries at the age of twenty—taking it for granted, of course, that when one has become serious and reasonable, one gives up these foolish notions.

It never occurs to anyone that if the young are calling something into question, if they are beating desperately against our walls, it is they who may be right, and that what they are attacking may really deserve to be attacked. No reasonable person can conceive of the idea that the asocial teddy boy may be in the right, that what must be questioned is not he, but the society he opposes, and that the more we restrain the young, the more we cry, "Give youth some room!" But what we mean, of course, is room on *our* councils, on *our* committees, in *our* administrations. You don't understand? But it is so simple, paternal, and sensible. This vast body of young people is a living, sometimes explosive force that must be channeled. A torrent left to itself is good for nothing, whereas confined in a high-pressure pipe, it furnishes light. This apologue actually illuminates the whole problem. The old man provides the machinery, the young man provides the power, and you're in business. Here's to you, young man, good little soldier for culture, the university, the church, the nation, the party, science, and technology. Without you all these honorable façades are only lifeless dust; it is you who assure their continuation. The cunning old man who detests you wins your support by offering you the back seat in a ready-made world that only needs to be developed in the direction he has established. But above all you must not look for another seat, another direction, another world, for then you would discover the implacability of the technical organization maintained by the serious people to whom you constitute a threat.

O old men, of whom I am one—psychologists, sociologists, politicians, journalists, men of letters, all you who praise and charm the young—if you had the least semblance of honesty, you would have to shout: "Death to the young. Throw them all in jail!" For that, in the end, is exactly what you will do.

WE DON'T WANT CHARITY—WE WANT JUSTICE

The great cry of the oppressed has become a commonplace. Such is the tragic decline of all things human. The supreme virtue, the gift of God himself, that which never fails and is fully accomplished only in the Eternal—Charity, perfect love, without fault and without end—had, in the hands of the bourgeois, been reduced to charity. Your conscience was at peace when you had done charity. You did it so you wouldn't have to feel it. It was a screen for injustice and a compensation for the oppression that the necessities of work, money, and progress forced us to inflict on others. The oppressor is always ready to offer charity to the oppressed. In this way he demonstrates his noble sentiments toward him.

But business and sentiment are two different things, are they not? It is quite obvious that society can live only in terms of efficiency. And when you talk about efficiency, it means that somebody is going to be run over and left by the wayside because he can't keep up the pace. If we start worrying about sentiment when what matters is output, where will we be? How do you expect the employer to make a profit, production to increase, and the state to endure if you enlist the help of the disabled, the blind, and the psychotic? But apart from this, and when the serious work has been done, we realize with the greatest liberalism that these poor souls have to live, and we set up institutions for them, we dole them out a bowl of soup. We are not like those Nazi barbarians who eliminated useless mouths. We have received a Christian education and we know what we owe to our neighbor—it being understood that he is our neighbor only when he does not stand in our way, and above all when he does his duty to society and to us. Then, from the height of our success, from the height of our knowledge or wealth, we let fall a few crumbs to this wretch, but we refuse to consider the possibility that he may be this way because we have led him to it.

We are moved to tears at the thought of our good heart and our profound understanding of man, and when we consider ourselves, we arrive at the conviction that man is inherently good. Naturally, having arrived at this lofty thought, we require the confirmation of the poor man who has just received his alms. This poor man must be a good poor man, since I am so good: full agreement and harmony of the goodness of man. If this poor man does not fall all over himself in gratitude and respect, then he is the one who is spoiling the idyll. For this is the point. We must rise to the heights: away with petty financial considerations when what matters is the Soul and Humanity. Charity, that is the proof. So don't look any farther, don't try to find out where the money I give comes from or if the poor man can live on what I give him. Remember that here we are in the

realm of the Spiritual, the realm of Symbols. This piece of
money is and can only be a symbol. How vulgar it would be
to look beyond that! The poor man has his role to play in
the matter. And he must play it properly, for otherwise my
spirituality makes a hasty exit.

It is truly the cry of human pride to proclaim, "We want
no more charity. I spit in the face of the man who gives it to
me!" If Baudelaire picked fights with beggars, after all, he
ran the risk of not winning. But the bourgeois does not
understand any more. He was so full of good will and noble
sentiments; the countess of humble origins is still brimming
over with them. Man rises up against this lie, this farce, and
tears away the curtain, revealing what was behind: the real
relation of man to man. He does not want to owe anything
any more. He is sick of owing gratitude or thanks for the
dole and the lie. He is sick of providing an excuse for a
good conscience in return for the smile and the hypocrisy,
sick of owing the unfathomable debt of love in return for
the pity and the counterfeit coin. Austere and proud, he
prefers his hunger—that is, he prefers it until he decides to
reverse the situation. Once he reached out his hand to
receive. He has stopped doing that, out of dignity; but now
he reaches out his hand to take. He no longer expects
anything from anyone, and decides to seize, to conquer.
For neither does he want justice to be accorded him. He
wants to become master of the situation, to establish his
own idea of justice and accord it to others, should the
occasion arise. The cry of man's pride has become his Gospel.

And lo, the thing is done: he has taken only one step,
and he has crossed the Rubicon. He is now on the side of
the great wild beasts and conquerors, the side of the fight-

ers who become the powerful, the side of the efficient who become the oppressors. On the side of the bourgeois (even if he is antibourgeois), with the single difference that he will not offer charity and will have pity on nobody—at least, not for a while. And the great cry of the oppressed, the great cry of human pride, has now become the commonplace of the good conscience. Of *our* good conscience, our collective good conscience—for we others, bourgeois and intellectuals, having learned the lesson perfectly, have become ardent believers in the slogan. Let us despise charity and unanimously demand justice. We must side with the best man, must we not? And the best man today is the poor man of yesterday. We no longer want to owe anything to anybody! This means purely and simply that today we no longer want any human relation, we no longer want the interplay of glances, the communion of speech, the give and take of assistance, the brotherhood in a common weakness, this outstretched hand of mine that might hold all the love in the world . . . No, we have become Adults, we do not want to depend on any man or receive anything from anyone. We want to deal with a pure Abstraction. The Abstraction respects my Dignity (thus man's legitimate pride very quickly turns into the most ridiculous vanity). It is with the essence of government (without either minister or representative, of course!), the most theoretical state, the most impersonal administration that I want to deal. Then I will be free from all duty, and I will in turn be able to despise every man to whom, in fact, I shall owe nothing.

We want justice . . . that is, *now*, no longer what is due, but the power to dispossess the possessors, to appropriate their wealth and become wealthy ourselves, to bump off the Other—that is our justice. The justice of the commonplace is the justice of the killer, a justice to which we are quite accustomed. When the victor judges the vanquished,

naturally he condemns him to death to assure himself that
he is right, that justice is on his side, that the sentence of
the Law and the Tribunal confirm his own excellence.

We no longer want charity: we want justice. And flour-
ishing this flaming sword, you feel like an archangel of
justice. But you must pay close attention, for after all it is
not so reassuring to demand justice. Dear angel, are you
sure you really want justice? Are you sure you owe nothing
to anyone? Are you sure that you have never oppressed
your neighbor even a little, if only by playing your radio
too loud? Are you sure that you never deceived your wife?
Are you sure that you have scrupulously respected justice
in your relations with all? With your friends and your
inferiors, but also with your superiors? Are you sure that
you have always paid your taxes scrupulously? Are you
sure that you have never done any wrong to anybody? That
you never stabbed a friend in the back to get his job? Are
you sure that you always gave to the hungry man (without
offering charity)? Are you sure—
    What's that? You find all this irrelevant? Excuse me, but
you are asking for justice, aren't you? How can you limit
justice to what is coming to you? Must you not also consider what you owe to others? The beam of the scale of
justice is a rigid thing (though we are always complaining
that it is not rigid enough!). There are no two measures, no
two standards (though we are always complaining that
there are!). And you will pass under this beam, and you
will be weighed against this standard. Are you so certain,
then, dear angel, that you are able to pay your debt? You
did not want to owe anything to anyone. But simply by
virtue of being a man, you are constantly and deeply in-
debted to someone, you always owe something to someone,

even if it is only bread to your children! And if you do not give it, you remain in debt, whether you like it or not. You do not want to owe anything to anybody, but every single time you do a wrong to your neighbor, even an involuntary one, you owe him reparation. Are you sure, dear angel, that you can make amends? Suppose you killed somebody by accident?

And justice, the only justice—for there are not thirty kinds (social justice, legal justice, moral justice, divine justice, bourgeois justice, communist justice, retributive justice, distributive justice, etc.), there is only One—the justice you demand implies that you have scrupulously paid every debt contracted in the course of your life, everything that, while reading me, you contest with indignation and disbelief. Have you, then, become just as much of a hypocrite as the bourgeois whom you rightly condemned? Is your demand for justice simply a way of avoiding punishment? You say you want justice, dear angel? Perhaps in the final analysis you may need a little dose of charity, the real kind. And perhaps it will not be wasted.

THE END JUSTIFIES
THE MEANS

I was really hoping not to have to deal with this common-place. It seemed that we had finally seen the last of this nasty Jesuit, ever since moralists of all persuasions widened their eyes and explained that it was bad, and that of course one did not have the right to make use of absolutely any means, although . . . There followed a pretty casuistic development that flourished in the seventeenth and eighteenth centuries and that I will spare you. But our age, alas, is a field particularly rich in applications of this excellent precept, and we have given it a new lease on life. Among all our intellectuals it flaunts its self-righteous cynicism before our eyes.

For after all, when a soldier ventures to advance this proposition, what can I say? He is in the order of things. His purpose as a soldier is to win. He has no other end. He can therefore make use of all means likely to give him victory. We are in the presence of a simple test of strength (until the contrary is proved, war is nothing else!), and consequently the means of force cannot be challenged. Whoever wants the end, wants the means: the correspondence is perfect. If the soldier says that in order to win the war we must use torture, napalm, and other refinements, since it is necessary to win, what can I say? Similarly, when a Nazi proclaimed the legitimacy of the Gestapo, the extermination camps, etc., I might conceivably take exception to the use of the term legitimacy, but that is all. For with Nazism there is no longer any end, any objective, there is only a frenzy of means gone wild, a continuous explosion of formidably precise techniques converging toward Nothing. It is not until the moralist, the orator, and the ideologist appear and attribute ends to war that everything begins to get confused.

If the purpose of war is said to be glory—the glory of the king or of the nation, it makes no difference—the harm is limited. Besides, that objective has lost currency and is rarely invoked in our time. The harm is more serious if you associate war with the nation's Greatness or its Civilizing Mission. It reaches the dangerous stage when people talk about a war of Justice or Right. But it is absolutely fatal when the purpose of the war is said to be the defense of Christian civilization or the liberation of oppressed peoples, for to obtain such desirable ends, what means would we not employ! In the presence of so perfect an end, our desire to reach it steadily increases, our frustration at not having it is always more cruel, and as a result I gradually reach the point where I am ready to do anything for this good. The loftier the good, the more dearly I will be forced to pay, the more different means I will be forced to employ, and if this good is truly very difficult to obtain, why should I not use *all* means?

Thus, the more ideal, fine, good, just, and grandiose the objective, the more likely we are to make use of all the means, for we *must* realize, we must achieve, this fine, good, just end. What are means, after all? Vile instruments, destined to disappear once the end has been realized. Who is going to remember these distressing means when we are enjoying perfect felicity? Hence the more just and noble the objectives we assign to the war, the more harsh, cruel, unlimited, total, and inexpiable it will be. For victory will no longer be merely victory, but the assumption of all Values! Once this point has been reached, it is the orator who invites the soldier to resort to all means to accomplish such an end—even if he has to repudiate the soldier when these means nauseate him, for the intellectual has a rather weak stomach! And this brings us to a fundamental axiom about our commonplace: the nobler, loftier, and more just the ends that man assigns himself, the more monstrous and inhuman the means he will employ. So let us begin by profoundly mistrusting all these too sublime objectives in which our civilization abounds, on the right, on the left, on earth and in heaven.

SOME RECENT USES OF THE COMMONPLACE

In March 1962 an eminent professor of political science wrote two contradictory propositions. At the beginning of his article he vigorously attacked "those who believe that the end justifies the means"—what luck! But there followed an attempt to prove that the terrorism of the FLN was absolutely different from the terrorism of the OAS. The purpose of the first group was to give birth to a nation, to give the Moslems a state. Therefore it was justified, for we all know that the nation is an excellent value and that the very existence of a state represents progress. The purpose of the second organization was to destroy democracy and to enable one faction to seize the power; therefore it was not justified. Thus our thinker was led to apply the very principle that he had rejected with horror thirty lines above.

This little anecdote is intended only to show how hardy our commonplace is, and how alive it is today. Everybody is taken in by its insidious flagrancy. It is not tragic when the mistake is so obvious; but there are far worse examples. At the time of the activities of the OAS, we all saw how the pacifist becomes a warmonger in the presence of an enemy who uses violence. He calls upon the citizens to use force against other citizens because the latter are using violence. In other words, he calls them to civil war, because *someone* is preparing for civil war. Of course, he executes this spectacular shift in policy (generally ignored in the collective passion) only because this adversary is really *very* bad. Those horrible fascists who are preparing the overthrow of the Republic and starting us on the road to dictatorship absolutely must be eliminated, must be defeated at all costs, and to attain this eminently just, liberal, republican, and democratic goal, all means are valid. Thus we have arrived at the conclusion that this end justifies these means. This is all you need to catch a philosopher in the emotional and sentimental trap. This is all you need to transform a nonviolent man into a military leader.

The phenomenon should not astonish us inordinately, for we saw the same transformation of pacifists in 1914 and 1940. It is the end result of an irrational love of politics and the absence of a critical spirit toward our visceral commonplaces. An eminent professor of theology who testified at the trial of Father Davezies in January 1962 declared, "There are violences that liberate and violences that enslave." This Dantonesque profundity filled the hearts of many young people with enthusiasm and light. For the author, being on the extreme left and in favor of the FLN, this obviously meant that the violences of the FLN are in the interest of freedom, therefore they are acceptable; the violences of the army are in the interest of colonialism, therefore they enslave, therefore they are worthless. It is clear as day that here we are in the presence of an application of our beloved commonplace.

But we still need a few more flourishes before we can feel the full profundity of this idea. Let us note first that it is always a matter of point of view. I have heard many generals and colonels serving in Algeria maintain that the FLN was a tiny Mafia of terrorists that obtained the support of the native populations only by murdering the pro-French (which may have been the case before 1956) and that dreamed only of establishing a crushing dictatorship over the Algerians, a system of exploitation far worse than that of the French, and that the French army came to defend the freedom of the Arabs against their pillagers, extortionists, and exploiters. In other words, in all good faith and in all good conscience, we found ourselves in the presence of a violence that liberates. Let us not forget, either, that when the French armies of 1794 and afterward conquered and exploited Italy, Switzerland, Holland, etc., it was also to liberate these peoples from the tyrants and monarchs who were preventing them from arriving at the Republic. Unfortunately, the peoples thus liberated did not seem to appreciate this freedom (see the massacre of Verona!). When the colonizers invaded Negro Africa, all readers of *L'Illustration* knew very well that it was to liberate those poor African peoples plunged in barbarism and under the thumb of abominable tyrants like Mahmadou, Behanzin, and the like. When the Nazis entered France, how many speeches did we hear explaining that the Germans were coming to liberate the French from a corrupt government and a degrading capitalism?

One can make a general rule that a person who uses violence always claims, and usually believes, that he is using it for the freedom of his adversary, for his own good. Unfortunately, there are always two sides. The one against whom the violence is employed usually does not understand that it is in his interest. Thus the violence of the FLN does not seem in any way liberating for the people of the MNA or for the French in Algeria. Everything depends on your point of view, and on this level ends are invoked only to wear down the adversary. It is understandable that a theologian accustomed to the absolute has a difficult time accepting such relativity. I am quite aware that I will be told, "Even so, objectively speaking, there are some political movements that lead to freedom and others that lead to the enslavement of peoples." But let's not allow ourselves to get sidetracked into fascinating dead ends like "What do you mean by freedom?" or again "What is the nature of your objectivity?" These are difficult questions, and I would be accused of changing the subject. Let us simply consider what, in very objective history, has become of these impulses toward freedom.

The bourgeois freedom of 1791 led very rapidly to the bloodiest dictatorship and the oppression of the vast majority of the people. The liberating explosion of 1917 led a little less rapidly, but by 1921, to a very severe dictatorship, and not just against the Kulaks and the Whites. Let us not forget the suppression of the sailors of Kronstadt and the massacres in the Ukraine. We know that the weight of the dictatorship grew steadily heavier for thirty years. And if we turn to movements of liberation in our time, what do we find? In those African republics in which order prevails, the impulse to independence has led to dictatorships that are completely repressive, propagandistic, antiliberal, and antidemocratic, like those of Nkrumah and Sékou Touré. In

Cuba the great impulse to freedom brought forth in six
months a terrorist dictatorship that has inherited all the
methods of the preceding dictator. The mere fact that the
previous dictatorship served the interests of the bourgeoisie and the capitalists against the peasants, while the
present one serves the interests of a party of peasants
against the academics, the working-class syndicalists, and
the Catholics, does not mean that the phenomenon has
profoundly changed. We could multiply "objective" examples *ad infinitum.* One thing becomes clear: *The use of
violence leads inevitably to the establishment of a dictatorship and to the denial of freedom.* All our commonplace
indicates is a desire to cloud the issue.

Thus we see that this harmful commonplace continues to
wreak havoc. I know the argument: The purpose of the
dictatorship (at least in the case of the dictatorship of the
proletariat) is only to prepare the way for freedom; just as
summary executions are preparing for the reign of justice.
(Since justice can be established only in a pure social body,
this body has first to be purified. When it has really been
well purified and when there is nothing left of the social
body, absolute justice can indeed reign with platonic purity!) One can go on indefinitely: the only purpose of war is
to prepare for peace (that is, a peace that will finally be
worthy of the name: true, good, just, lasting, etc.); just as
in the Middle Ages, the only purpose of the Inquisition was
to assure the salvation of souls (by means of the purging of
bodies).

Thus Bad Means are *always* guaranteed by Excellent
Ends and it is always for your own good. Like the bird-
catcher blinding nightingales and saying, "You don't realize it, my dears, but it is for your own good. You will sing so

much better afterward!" No, there is no question of accepting Ends. First of all, because one never reaches them; it is the perpetual bluff of Justice Tomorrow, the postponement of responsibilities to an inexpressible future. By accident, in exceptional cases, this future is realized—the day of judgment. Thus the Nazis arrived at responsibility at Nuremberg, or Eichmann in Israel. But they did so only to learn that their ends had in no way justified their means.[1] Alas! It is only the vanquished who ever live to see the future of their responsibility. The vanquished? That is, those whose means were not sufficiently effective! Have sufficiently effective means, and nobody will be able to question your Ends. If your Ends are not questioned, that will prove that they are in accord with history—and since they are in accord with history, they justify your means. After this, the postponement of responsibility into the most improbable of futures can give rise only to the perfectly useless protest of the moralist—like this just and eloquent protest of Péguy's over the betrayal of the rights of man:

"The politicians spend all the todays telling us that in all the tomorrows we shall be free to engage in morality. They even threaten to allow us to engage in morality in all the

---

[1] I think of the tragic testimony of Captain Estoup at the Godot trial in August 1962. The French officers were not torturers, because they had a sense of man's dignity and honor. If they did torture people, for many it was because they were convinced that there was no other way to win a *just* victory and to serve their country. These procedures, which they did not like, were justified by a valid end. They were not torturers because they were knights in a just cause, like the Crusaders. But now the end had failed, the ideal had died. Retroactively, there was no more justification. There was no more virtue. Nothing had been accomplished, and the evil that had been done endured: it was once again a stain and an injustice. The knight without a cause was once again a torturer. Under the circumstances, it was necessary to justify oneself at all costs. There was only one way to do this: find the lost ends, "go as far as possible in order to find this end that justified the means." And one became an OAS so as not to have been a torturer.

tomorrows only if in exchange we allow them to engage in politics in all the todays. We formally refuse to submit to this perpetual blackmail. We must save all the minutes without exception, one after the other, if, as we must, we want to save all of time, which pragmatically makes up our whole life. The politicians want to stop us at every instant of the action on the pretext that this instant is a turning point in history. We know all about their history that turns all the time: it is a merry-go-round."

No, there is no question of accepting the Ends to justify the practices of today, because in actuality these ends themselves are never anything but justifications. One accepts the shameful methods of one's friends for reasons that have nothing to do with a legitimate end. One criticizes the same methods in one's enemies, refusing to consider what might be legitimate about their objectives. No, dear moralists, we no longer believe in your values, which serve to demonstrate that the methods of your friends are excellent! The truth to which we must hold rigorously and relentlessly is the contrary of the commonplace: Means corrupt Ends. This is the precise meaning of the slogan of those admirably lucid Polish socialists who announced in 1961: "Yes, we are *for* socialism, but we are *against* all the paths that lead to it." This is the most profound wisdom and the most precise truth. There is no violence that liberates: all violence enslaves. The growth of the state does not result in freedom, but in greater dictatorship. Any method today that destroys a *single* man in his body or in his soul, though it liberate a million others, will never do anything but reinforce the slavery of the million men you are trying to help.

Ends are infinitely seductive and infinitely fragile soap bubbles that can shift direction at the slightest breeze and burst at the slightest pressure. Ends are incapable of justifying anything because they do not exist: at the most they are intentions, ideologies, programs. But when a man who has such good intentions resorts to the means of evil, he finds himself corrupted by the evil he does, and his good intentions become a farce. When ideologies come into contact with hard realities necessitating unjust means, they melt and are molded at the mercy of the moment. Even the most liberal platforms include shaded areas which are carefully hidden to take in the innocent, but that are crudely revealed when it is time to go into action. The noblest ends attributed to war are corrupted by war. A people that has become independent through war will always remain in some sense a people enslaved. A law established by violence will always be injustice. A good established by guile or force will always be evil. A faith obtained by proselytism will always be hypocrisy. A truth spread by propaganda will always be a lie. A perfect Society organized by shedding blood, even that of guilty men, will always be a forced labor camp. This is the truth; but such is the degree of man's mediocrity, inertia, vanity, and complacency, that he prefers all lies to the humble and everyday recognition of the importance of the means of today.

A NOTE ABOUT THE AUTHOR

Jacques Ellul was born in Bordeaux, France, in 1912. He studied at the University of Bordeaux and the University of Paris; from the latter he holds a doctorate in law. He has been professor of the history of law and of social history at Bordeaux since 1946. His European reputation is immense, and his reputation in America has been firmly established by the publication here by Alfred A. Knopf of *The Technological Society* (1964), *Propaganda* (1965), and *The Political Illusion* (1967). Professor Ellul is married and has seven children.

A NOTE ON THE TYPE

The text of this book is set in Caledonia, a typeface designed by W(illiam) A(ddison) Dwiggins for the Mergenthaler Linotype Company in 1939. Dwiggins chose to call his new typeface Caledonia, the Roman name for Scotland, because it was inspired by the Scotch types cast about 1833 by Alexander Wilson & Son, Glasgow type founders. However, there is a calligraphic quality about this face that is totally lacking in the Wilson types. Dwiggins referred to an even earlier typeface for this "liveliness of action"—one cut around 1790 by William Martin for the printer William Bulmer. Caledonia has more weight than the Martin letters, and the bottom finishing strokes (serifs) of the letters are cut straight across, without brackets, to make sharp angles with the upright stems, thus giving a "modern face" appearance.

Composed, printed, and bound by

KINGSPORT PRESS, INC., KINGSPORT, TENNESSEE